Knowledge of the External World

The Problems of Philosophy
Their Past and Present

General Editor: Ted Honderich
Grote Professor of the Philosophy of Mind and Logic University College, London

Each book in this series is written to bring into view and to deal with a great or significant problem of philosophy. The books are intended to be accessible to undergraduates in philosophy, and to other readers, and to advance the subject, making a contribution to it.

The first part of each book presents the history of the problem in question, in some cases its recent past. The second part, of a contemporary and analytic kind, defends and elaborates the author's preferred solution.

Private Ownership	James O. Grunebaum
Religious Belief and the Will	Louis P. Pojman
*Rationality	Harold J. Brown
*The Rational Foundations of Ethics	T.L.S. Sprigge
*Moral Knowledge	Alan Goldman
Mind–Body Identity Theories	Cynthia Macdonald
*Practical Reasoning	Robert Audi
*Personal Identity	Harold W. Noonan
If P Then Q	David H. Sanford
*The Infinite	A.W. Moore
Thought and Language	Julius Moravcsik
Human Consciousness	Alastair Hannay
Explaining Explanation	David-Hillel Ruben
The Nature of Art	A.L. Cothey
The Implications of Determinism	Roy Weatherford
Weakness of the Will	Justin Gosling
Knowledge of the External World	Bruce Aune
Political Freedom	George G. Brenkert

*Also available in paperback

Knowledge of the External World

Bruce Aune

London and New York

First published 1991
by Routledge
11 New Fetter Lane, London EC4P 4EE

Simultaneously published in the USA and Canada
by Routledge
a division of Routledge, Chapman and Hall, Inc.
29 West 35th Street, New York, NY 10001

© *1991 Bruce Aune*

Typeset by Witwell Ltd, Southport Merseyside
Printed in Great Britain by TJ Press (Padstow) Ltd, Padstow, Cornwall

British Library Cataloguing in Publication Data
Aune, Bruce
Knowledge of the external world. – (The problems of
philosophy).
1. Knowledge – Philosophical perspectives
I. Title II. Series
121

Library of Congress Cataloging in Publication Data
Aune, Bruce
Knowledge of the external world/Bruce Aune.
p. cm. – (Problems of philosophy)
Includes bibliographical references and index.
1. Knowledge, Theory of. 2. Other minds (Theory of knowledge)
3. Ontology. I. Title. II. Series: Problems of philosophy
(Routledge (Firm))
BD161.A82 1991   *90–48550*
121–dc20

ISBN 0–415–04747–1

22450827

To my daughters:
Alison, Patty, and Kirsten

On every subject on which difference of opinion is possible, the truth depends on a balance to be struck between two sets of conflicting reasons. Even in natural philosophy there is always some other explanation possible of the same facts . . . and it has to be shown why that other theory cannot be the true one. . . . When we turn to subjects infinitely more complicated, to morals, religion, politics, social relations, and the business of life, three-fourths of the arguments for every disputed opinion consist in dispelling the appearances which favor some opinion different from it. . . . He who knows only his own side of the case knows little of that. His reasons may be good, and no one may have been able to refute them. But if he is equally unable to refute the reasons on the opposite side, if he does not so much as know what they are, he has no grounds for preferring either opinion. The rational position for him would be suspension of judgment, and unless he contents himself with that, he is either led by authority or adopts, like the generality of the world, the side to which he *feels* the most inclination.

John Stuart Mill, On Liberty

Contents

Preface and Acknowledgements   xii

I Descartes

1   *Descartes and the Method of Doubt*   1
2   *Critical Remarks on the Method of Doubt*   6
3   *Descartes'* Cogito   7
4   *Descartes' Fundamental Principles*   11
5   *The Development of Descartes' System*   16
6   *Descartes' Approach to the External World*   18
7   *Criticisms and Prospects*   22

II Locke and Berkeley

1   *Locke on Knowledge*   27
2   *Locke on Judgment and Opinion*   31
3   *Locke on the Nature of External Objects*   36
4   *Berkeley on Secondary Qualities*   41
5   *Berkeley on Primary Qualities*   45
6   *Berkeley's Idealism*   51

III Hume and Solipsism

1   *Hume's Epistemic Principles*   57
2   *Hume on Experimental Inference*   63
3   *Hume and the Road to Solipsism*   71
4   *Hume's Attitude to Skepticism*   81

IV Kant and Phenomenalism

1 *Kant's Classification of Knowledge* 86
2 *Kant's Copernican Revolution* 90
3 *More on Objects of Experience* 93
4 *Kant's Transcendental Deduction* 97
5 *Some Categories and Principles* 101
6 *Kant's Transcendental Idealism* 103
7 *Remarks on Kant's Epistemology* 106
8 *Phenomenalism* 108

V A New Start

1 *Prelude to the "Private Language" Argument* 115
2 *Wittgenstein's Argument* 119
3 *On the Common-sense Basis of Wittgenstein's Argument* 124
4 *Reinventing the Problem* 127
5 *A Problem About the Self* 130
6 *Is Reference to a Self Inevitable?* 136
7 *On Basic Epistemic Principles* 140

VI Reforming Empiricism

1 *Problems with an Analytic–Synthetic Distinction* 144
2 *A Pragmatic Approach to Analyticity* 149
3 *Observation* 156
4 *Experimental Inference: Some Problems* 161
5 *Some Suggested Strategies* 164
6 *Bayesian Induction* 167
7 *Applying Bayes' Theorem* 170
8 *Inductive Probability: An Interpretation* 171
9 *Prospect* 175

VII The External World

1 *Hume's Problem and its Successors* 177
2 *Chisholm's "Critical Commonsensism"* 182
3 *Justification by "Coherence"* 185

Contents

4   *Standards, Ends, and Justification*   188
5   *Uninferred Premisses and Intellectual Bootstrapping*   191
6   *Inferring the Existence of the External World*   195
7   *On Scientific Realism*   201

    Appendix   208
    Notes   213
    Bibliography   235
    Index   240

Preface and Acknowledgments

As many readers will recognize, the title of this book is taken from Bertrand Russell, who finished the lectures published as *Our Knowledge of the External World* in the spring of 1914 – just a few months before the Great War began. I finished this book just after (as it appears right now) a great cold war is beginning to end. It is obvious that the philosophical scene has changed as much since that time as the political one.

When Russell published *Our Knowledge of the External World*, the problem that concerned him was considered a key topic (possibly the most important one) in English and American philosophy; fifty years later it was generally considered dissolved, the "confusions" responsible for its earlier currency definitively exposed by the later work of Wittgenstein. Although the problem has not yet regained a prominent position on the philosophical stage, most people now working in epistemology seem generally dubious about the success of Wittgenstein's alleged exposé. The time is ripe, therefore, to discuss the problem again. An added stimulus for doing so is the emergence of a new conception of experimental inference. Russell's book was written in a spirit of enthusiasm about the new "mathematical" deductive logic, his second chapter bearing the title "Logic as the Essence of Philosophy." I am suspicious of enthusiasm (even in the original sense of the word), but my book was certainly stimulated by what can be called the new mathematical inductive logic. As I see it now, the traditional problem about our knowledge of the external world was not owing to conceptual confusion, the misuse of language, or errors in deductive inference. It was owing mainly to an inadequate conception of legitimate experimental inference – something we understand better today than ever before.

In accordance with the aim of this series, the chapters to follow fall into two principal groups. Those in the first group are devoted to the history of the problem that I have identified. Instead of discussing the contributions of a wide range of writers, I have concentrated on the ideas of five major figures: Descartes, Locke, Berkeley, Hume, and Kant. To disclose the seriousness of the issues that concerned these philosophers and also to profit from their ingenuity in dealing with those issues, I discussed their ideas in significant detail. The chapters in the second group are devoted to more recent developments and to my own ideas on the problem. The reader will see that the solution I offer relies heavily on the probability calculus. I urge those who are daunted by mathematics to push on when they encounter some mathematical symbolism. Not only have I taken special pains to make my remarks on probability user-friendly (as one says nowadays), but the reader must recognize that it is no longer possible to discuss *a posteriori* inferences responsibly without adverting to probability theory. The reader attracted to the traditional problem about our knowledge of the external world is therefore faced with a choice: either learn some probability theory or take up a different subject. I can assure such a reader that the probability theory I introduce here is easy to understand and presupposes no mathematics beyond high school algebra.

Some years ago, an old friend expressed some perplexity about my tendency to criticize others in the course of presenting my own ideas. "Why," he asked, "don't you forget about others and simply give your reasons for the views you hold?" I can't remember how I answered his question, but this book should resolve the sort of perplexity he felt. The key point is that, since I reject the Cartesian presumption that axioms can be found from which interesting philosophical theses can be deduced, I cannot hope to support my ideas by impersonal deductive proofs. The best strategy available to me (as I try to show here) is to argue that my view is preferable to other views, actual and possible, bearing upon the issue at hand. The general character of this strategy is nicely illustrated by the quotation from Mill that I have taken as an epigraph to this book, but its rationale is best understood by reference to the probability calculus. In attacking alternative opinions and "dispelling the appearances" favoring them, I in effect lower the probability of those opinions; and since, as alternatives to mine, they can be considered true just in case my opinion is false, my success in lowering their probability has the effect of raising the probability of my opinion: this is evident (virtually) from the simple theorem that $P(p) = 1 - P(-p)$. Although I constantly criticize other philosophers in employing this strategy, I invariably do so in a friendly spirit, and I imply no disrespect toward my opponents.

I want to thank Steven Voss, Linda Wetzel, and Ernie LePore for reading parts of my first draft and offering comments. Although Wesley Salmon and Roger Rosenkrantz will no doubt disagree with what I say about experimental inference, I have learned a lot from the writings of both and I want to record my appreciation. My deepest debt is to Rosenkrantz, an old friend (once a student!) who has urged me since the late 1960s to adopt a Bayesian point of view in epistemology. Most of the work on this book took place at my home in Amherst, Massachusetts, where I spent a sabbatical leave from the University of Massachusetts. I thank the officials who granted me the leave, and I also thank my wife, Ilene, for her support and understanding during the past year.

The material quoted from *The Philosophical Writings of Descartes*, volumes I and II, translated by René Descartes, John Cottingham, Robert Stoothof and Dugald Murdoch, is reprinted with the permission of Cambridge University Press, 1985, 1984. The material quoted from my essay "Espistemically Justified Opinion" in John Bender (ed.) *The Current State of the Coherence Theory*, is reprinted by permission of Kluwer Academic Publishers, 1989.

CHAPTER I

Descartes

When questions are raised about our knowledge of the external world, two things are generally presupposed: a conception of knowledge and a conception (however vague and schematic) of "the" external world. Philosophers who have debated the questions have been in general agreement about the latter conception: the external world is the system of objects external to human consciousness that is thought to be responsible for (among other things) the sensory experiences human beings commonly have. But similar agreement does not exist about the relevant conception of knowledge. When Descartes spoke of knowledge, he meant rational certainty of a special kind. His conception differs, as we shall see, from the conceptions current today, but his approach to our knowledge of the external world set a precedent that is still admired and even emulated. It also created a nest of problems that are very difficult to resolve.

1. Descartes and the method of doubt

Descartes, born in 1596, was one of the earliest philosophers belonging to what we consider the modern period. He was educated in a Jesuit college, *La Flèche*, where he studied mathematics and classics, absorbing a good deal of scholastic philosophy in the process. As he developed as a mathematician, scientist, and philosopher, he became increasingly dissatisfied with scholastic philosophy and attempted to work out an alternative system of philosophy in a new way, starting from scratch. To obtain philosophical and scientific certainty, he thought we must employ what is now known as the axiomatic method – the method used in mathematical sciences such as arithmetic and geometry.

1

The axiomatic method, in which substantive principles (theorems) are deduced from axioms and definitions, offers a very plausible, tempting procedure for anyone seeking certainty in a subject. We all know that errors are easy to make and that we unwittingly form many of our beliefs uncritically, without careful thought. When we are asked how we know something, we may attempt to recall our source and to identify our reasons for believing it; but we are justified in thinking we really know only if our source is highly reliable or our reasons very compelling. In fact, if we are convinced that true knowledge requires rational certainty, our source must be utterly reliable and our reasons utterly conclusive.

When is a source utterly reliable or a reason utterly conclusive? The obvious answer is: when the source gives only certain information, the reason is certainly true, and the certainty of either guarantees the certainty of what we believe on the basis of them. Yet how can we know that our source or our reason has this character? The answer seems inescapable: if our source or reason is not intrinsically certain, its certainty must be guaranteed by some further source or reason that is no less certain. This further source or reason can provide the needed guarantee if, and only if, it has comparable credentials – that is, if it is either intrinsically certain or guaranteed by a still further source or reason of the same epistemic character. Since we cannot assess the credentials of an infinite series of sources, each one supposedly guaranteed by preceding sources, and since no source or reason that is not intrinsically certain can be guaranteed to be certain by a circular series in which something A is guaranteed by a B that is guaranteed, ultimately, only by A, it follows that we can be rationally certain and thus know something only if it is intrinsically certain or guaranteed by a manageably short series of reasons or sources of information whose first members are intrinsically certain and sufficient to justify the later members.

If any single item of knowledge requires that some item (it or something else) be intrinsically certain, the totality of anyone's knowledge must involve a totality of intrinsically certain items whose truth can be considered axiomatic. Descartes, in attempting to work out a system of genuine knowledge that encompassed such subjects as mathematics, physics, theology, and what we would call psychology, felt that he had to discover a suitable set of axiomatic truths. The strategy he adopted is known as the method of systematic doubt.

The idea behind the method is that a proposition (a thought, belief, or opinion) is intrinsically certain just when it is indubitable: if it can be doubted, it is not intrinsically certain; and if it cannot be doubted, it is intrinsically certain. Though plausible (at least initially) this idea could not be applied to every opinion a normal person possesses, for the stock of those opinions is not only extremely great but constantly augmented even by casual glances and off-hand conversations. To avoid this sort of difficulty, Descartes directed his doubts to the principles or foundational beliefs on which large classes of his beliefs are based; he did so systematically, identifying key foundational principles and attending to them one after the other. His official aim, as he described it in his *Meditations on First Philosophy*, was to rid himself of all dubious opinions and to reconstruct his knowledge on certain foundations. To facilitate his search for axiomatic certainty, he will reject or withhold belief from anything that he can find the "slightest reason" for doubting.

As this reference to a reason for doubting indicates, the sort of doubt involved in Descartes' method appears to be a rational one. This impression is reinforced by the first steps Descartes proceeds to take:

> Whatever I have up to now accepted as most true I have
> acquired either from the sense or through the senses. But from
> time to time I have found that the senses deceive, and it is
> prudent never to trust completely those who have deceived us
> even once.[1]

The idea that Descartes is concerned with rational doubts is very important, for some doubts are neurotic or even insane and their occurrence has no bearing on scientific certainty. Descartes seems to recognize this last point when he continues:

> Yet although the senses occasionally deceive us with respect to
> objects which are very small or in the distance, there are many
> other beliefs about which doubt is quite impossible, even
> though they are derived from the senses – for example, that I
> am here, sitting by the fire, wearing a winter dressing gown,
> holding this piece of paper in my hands, and so on. Again,

how could it be denied that these hands or this whole body are mine? Unless perhaps I were to liken myself to madmen, whose brains are so damaged by the persistent vapours of melancholia that they firmly maintain they are kings when they are paupers, or say they are dressed in purple when they are naked, or that their heads are made of earthenware, or that they are pumpkins, or made of glass. But such people are insane, and I would be thought equally mad if I took anything from them as a model for myself.[2]

If my doubt that I have hands or a body is as baseless as the madman's belief that he is a pumpkin or made of glass, it hardly shows that there is anything doubtful or uncertain about the proposition that I have hands or a body. What it does show, perhaps, is that I am too deranged to appreciate the obvious.

Descartes finds a reason, however, for doubting that he is actually dressed and sitting by the fire. The reason he offers seems to show that the doubt, or at least the lack of certainty, is rationally justified. The reason is that he has, in the past, been deceived by his dreams and that "there are never any sure signs by means of which being awake can be distinguished from being asleep."[3] If this is a good reason – if the assertion that there are no sure signs by which one can determine *with certainty* whether one is asleep or awake is actually true or actually accords with one's experience – then one is entitled to doubt whether one is actually awake. An attitude of certainty on this matter is rationally unjustified.

If our senses could deceive us in this large-scale way, they cannot be trusted, at least by themselves, as providing the kinds of certainty Descartes is looking for. Descartes then proceeds to consider another principle on which many of his beliefs have been based: the "demonstrations" of mathematics and mathematical principles that have formerly seemed quite self-evident.[4] Again, he finds it possible to doubt the principle and to offer reasons in support of its rational dubitability. One of his reasons is formulated best in his *Principles of Philosophy*; it is that many people who have fallen into error in mathematical reasoning "accept as most certain and self-evident things which seemed false" to him.[5] Another reason, which Descartes thinks is more important than the first one, is that he has been told God can do anything He desires and he is ignorant whether God may not have desired to create him in such a way that he will always be deceived even in those matters which seem to him "supremely evident," for this does not seem less possible than his being occasionally deceived, which experience tells him does actually occur.[6]

To make the possibility of such deception vivid and to keep himself on guard against dubitable opinions, he supposes that a malicious demon, one as powerful as he is cunning and deceitful, is using all his powers to deceive him. This supposition is very extravagant, but Descartes has no basis at this point for ruling it out as definitely false. At the basis of his thinking here there is a modal argument, which happens to be valid. The argument is:

1. If the malicious demon hypothesis were true, Descartes would be deceived in almost everything he believes.
2. It is possible, for all he knows, that it is true.
3. Therefore, it is possible, for all he knows, that he is deceived in almost everything he believes.

As if explicitly entertaining the conclusion here, Descartes asks himself "What is there, then, that can be regarded as true?" and then answers, "Perhaps only this, that nothing is certain."

This last answer is not certain, of course; and Descartes acknowledges that there might be many certainties that he has simply failed to consider. One possibility is that his current thoughts have a particular cause – God, the malicious demon, or even his own self. If he were the cause of them, he would certainly have to exist. But he would have to exist if his thoughts were caused by some other being! If he did not exist, he could not have any thoughts. Thus, his own existence is, at the moment, an utter certainty, which could not be destroyed by the hypothesis of the malicious demon. To be deceived by the malicious demon, he would have to exist even if he lacked a body. "Let him deceive me as much as he can," Descartes says, "he will never bring it about that I am nothing so long as I think that I am something." Having considered everything "very thoroughly," Descartes thus concludes that "this proposition, *I am, I exist*, is necessarily true whenever it is put forward by me or conceived in my mind." [7]

In his *Principles of Philosophy* Descartes summarized this stage of his meditations by saying that "the first thing we come to know when we philosophize in an orderly way" is that "it is not possible for us to doubt that we exist while we are doubting." He added that "it is a contradiction to suppose that what thinks does not, at the very time when it is thinking, exist" and then, a bit carelessly, asserted that "this piece of knowledge – *I am thinking, therefore I exist* – is the first and most certain of all to occur to anyone who philosophizes in an orderly way." The assertion is a bit careless because he had just identified something else as the first thing we come to know when we philosophize in an orderly way: knowing that it is not possible for us to doubt something is not the same as knowing that we exist because we are thinking. His considered opinion, clearly, is that the latter is what he first knows: he knows it (he believes) because he cannot doubt that it is true.

2. Critical remarks on the method of doubt

I have emphasized Descartes' claim that the *cogito* proposition "I think, therefore I am" is the first knowledge he obtains by his method of doubt because it raises a serious problem about the interpretation of that method. I have noted that the doubting appropriate to the method is rational doubting – doubting issuing from, or based on, reasons for thinking something doubtful. But what is the status of these reasons and their relation to what is doubted? Descartes advanced them as if they represented items of knowledge, things he did not doubt at all: "we have caught out the senses when they were in error"; "we have sometimes seen people make mistakes in [mathematical demonstrations] . . . and accept as most certain and self-evident things which seemed false to us"; "we have been told that there is an omnipotent God who created us." [8] If these reasons are indeed items of knowledge that render Descartes' doubts worthy of serious epistemological interest, then the *cogito* proposition will not be the first item of knowledge that he *has* or *uses* when he philosophizes in an orderly manner. It may, of course, be the first item of knowledge he obtains from his reasons for doubt, but it will not provide an axiomatic basis from which those reasons can be inferred without circularity.

If the method of systematic doubt is to be a plausible method for discovering primitive certainties, this difficulty must somehow be avoided. What can Descartes say about his reasons for doubting a proposition or principle? Perhaps the modal argument given earlier (on page 5) provides a useful model. In that case Descartes' doubt was based on a mere supposition – one that, for all he knew, might

6

be true. As I reconstructed Descartes' thinking, he was advancing the malicious demon hypothesis as an epistemic rather than a genuine possibility, as something not ruled out by anything he knew or, better, was certain about. At the time, he was certain about nothing! His other reasons might be interpreted similarly. Nothing he knew ruled out the possibility that his senses sometimes deceived him and were deceiving him now; he was aware of, or certain about, no indications that could distinguish sleeping from waking experience; he was aware of nothing that ruled out the possibility of making mistakes even in simple mathematical reasoning. This way of viewing Descartes' reasons for doubt would not require them to be substantive elements of knowledge.

Unfortunately, the strategy does not save Descartes' method. The reasons may formulate only relative epistemic possibilities (things not ruled out by anything he is certain of) but they are doubt-exciting only because Descartes can identify their relevant consequences – that is, only because he is aware of what (relevant to his epistemic situation) *would be true if they were true*. He must, in other words, be aware that premisses such the first one in the modal argument are true.

If *any* premiss is required for rational doubting, the method of systematic doubt will be powerless to identify the sort of basic premiss Descartes is officially concerned to discover. Thus, if Descartes were ever in a state of utter uncertainty and had no premisses on which he could confidently rely, his doubts would be as baseless, as irrational, as those of a madman, and the fact that he doubted (or could doubt) a particular proposition *P* would not imply or even faintly suggest that *P* is doubtful (that is, worthy of doubt). The fact, similarly, that he could *not* baselessly or irrationally doubt a proposition *Q* would not imply or even faintly suggest that *Q* is true or even probable. A particular madman may be unable to doubt that he is invisible or made of glass, but his state of utter certainty and unshakeable conviction regarding his invisible or glassy person does not make it in the least likely that he is right.

3. Descartes' cogito

As I remarked earlier, Descartes said in his *Principles of Philosophy* that "this piece of knowledge – *I am thinking, therefore I exist* –

is the first and most certain of all to occur to anyone who philosophizes in an orderly way." The conclusion he mentions here has a confusing form, however: it could be an assertion or proposition that (in his opinion) he simply perceives to be true; it could be the conclusion of an argument; or it could be an argument, or "proof," itself. Since the sentence "I am thinking, therefore I exist" is a translation of Descartes' Latin sentence "*Cogito ergo sum*," it is natural to think of the sentence as formulating an argument, one whose conclusion follows "*ergo*": that is, "*sum*" or "I am" (= "I exist"). On the other hand, Descartes speaks of the sentence "*Cogito ergo sum*" as a conclusion, which suggests that it is part of an argument, something inferred from preceding premisses. Finally, in a reply he wrote to some objections, he said that when someone says "I am thinking, therefore I am or exist," he is not using a syllogism to deduce his existence from his thought, but is recognizing this as something self-evident, in a simple mental intuition.[9]

Descartes included *cogito* arguments in different works written at different times,[10] and it is possible that he did not always think of their form or structure in the same way. There can be no doubt, however, that such an argument emerges from his systematic doubt and is officially, in his words, "the piece of knowledge" he thereby obtains. If we consider that the doubting Descartes undertakes is at least intended, unlike the doubting of a madman, to be reasonable then it is natural to read him as being unable rationally to doubt that he exists *because* he is aware of his own thinking or doubting. This reading is supported by Descartes' remarks in the *Principles*, where he says that although he can doubt that there is a God or that he himself has hands or feet or a body, he cannot "in the same way conceive" (that is, doubt) that he who doubts these things is not, "for it is a contradiction to suppose that what thinks does not, at the very time when it is thinking, exist." In fact, in Principle 10, he said that when he stated that the proposition *I think, therefore I am* is the first and most certain that presents itself to those who philosophize in an orderly fashion, he did not "in saying that deny that one must first know what thought, existence, and certainty are, and it is impossible that that which thinks should not exist."[11] He did not mention these prior elements of knowledge because, he said, they are "very simple notions, and ones which on their own provide us of no knowledge of anything that exists."[12]

This background knowledge is vitally important not only for the questions it raises about the method of doubt but also for the interpretation of the *cogito* thought, "I think." When, in the *Meditations*, he concluded (or arrived at the conviction) that the proposition *I am, I exist* is necessarily true each time I pronounce or mentally conceive it, he had to admit that "I do not yet have a sufficient understanding of what this 'I' is, that now necessarily exists." Much of his uncertainty springs from the fact that he is still in a state of doubt about whether he has hands, feet, or indeed any body. As he says:

> I am not that structure of limbs which is called a human body. I am not even some thin vapour which permeates the limbs – a wind, fire, air, breath, or whatever I depict in my imagination; for these are things which I have supposed to be nothing. Let this supposition stand; for all that, I am still something.[13]

But how can he be *certain* that he exists if he has no idea what he is? The question is unnecessary because he really does have some idea of what he is. To the rhetorical question "But what then am I?" he promptly answers:

> A thing that thinks. What is that? A thing that doubts, understands, affirms, denies, is willing, is unwilling, and also imagines and has sensory perceptions.[14]

This last quotation underlines the fact that Descartes' certainty about his existence is based on his awareness of the thinking he is doing; he is immediately aware of that thinking. His claim that a thing that thinks is a thing that doubts, wills, imagines, feels, and the like is no doubt based on one of the "simple notions" that he acknowledged to be required for his *cogito*. The simple notion, which he does not specifically mention in Principle 10, would concern the nature of thinking. In a definition that he appended to his "Second Set of Replies," he specifies what he understands by the word "thinking" or "thought":

> *Thought.* I use this term to include everything that is within us in such a way that we are immediately aware of it. Thus, all the operations of the will, the intellect, the imagination, and the senses are thoughts.[15]

What is expressed by this definition is not, for Descartes, a mere verbal convention; it is the content of a concept or "simple notion."

A criticism of Descartes' cogito that calls attention to an additional presupposition has been made by Bertrand Russell:

> "I think" is his ultimate premiss. Here the word "I" is really illegitimate; he ought to state his ultimate premiss in the form "there are thoughts." The word "I" is grammatically convenient, but does not describe a datum. When he goes on to say "I am a *thing* which thinks," he is already using uncritically the apparatus of categories handed down by scholasticism. He nowhere proves that thoughts need a thinker, nor is there reason to believe this except in a grammatical sense.[16]

Russell is at least half right here. The word "I" does not describe anything that Descartes would acknowledge as a datum, and in concluding "I am, I exist" Descartes did tacitly employ the scholastic categories of substance and attribute. It is by no means obvious, on the other hand, that Descartes' initial premiss should have been stated in the form: "There are thoughts."

Having doubted that he has a body and not being consciously aware of something tenuous, like a wind or fire or ether, which he once imagined his soul to be,[17] Descartes was unable to put a mental finger on any distinct object or datum that he was prepared to call his self. His "natural light" assured him, however, that (as he put it in the *Principles*) "nothingness possesses no attributes or qualities" and that "wherever we find some attributes or qualities, there is necessarily some thing or substance to be found for them." [18] Since he conceived of thinking as a property or attribute, he had no doubt that the thinking of which he was immediately aware was attached to some thing or substance, some subject of attributes. He attempted to make his datum-less application of "I" credible to his readers by arguing that even in cases where a distinct subject of attributes seems most apparent, its identity is just as elusive and impossible to picture as his conscious self. He did this by attending to a yellow, fragrant, solid piece of wax, which becomes transparent, odorless, and liquid when it is heated. Although his readers would no doubt concede that the wax continues to exist throughout the change, they will be unable to picture a distinct subject that undergoes this change. In the case of both minds and bodies, the subject of the perceived attributes is not itself perceptible or picturable (no sensible image can be formed of it); it can be grasped only abstractly, in thought.[19]

When Russell claimed that Descartes' initial premiss should have been "There are thoughts" rather than "I am thinking," he was assuming that the phenomenon of thinking should be interpreted (or conceived of) as the occurrence of ultimately subjectless events rather than as the presence of an attribute to some subject. Russell's assumption here is debatable and requires supporting argumentation. Like Aristotle before him, Descartes conceived of the world as a system of substances possessing attributes; Russell, at least in his later career, conceived of the world as he thought contemporary physics required – as a system of "events." [20] The question of whose view is preferable can be adequately decided only when all the philosophical cards are on the table. Descartes' assumption that he is right depends largely on the case he could make for the truth of the principles he tacitly appealed to in his method of systematic doubt and in the *cogito* that he built upon it.

4. Descartes' fundamental principles

The avowed purpose of Descartes' method of systematic doubt was to identify a foundation of certain truth on which to build a system of scientific knowledge. My discussion in preceding sections has made it clear that, as a means of discovering primitive, uninferred truth, Descartes' method is seriously defective. The root difficulty concerns the nature of the relevant doubting. As Descartes himself seemed to recognize, some doubts are baseless or even insane; and if this sort of doubt is pertinent to the method, a proposition that can be doubted is not thereby doubtful, and one that cannot be doubted is not thereby certain to be true. If, on the other hand, the doubts relevant to the method must be reasonable doubts, they cannot be baseless and must be based on a reason. The reason, even if it has the status of a mere epistemic relative possibility (something not falsified by anything the reasoner actually knows), must be appropriately related to the doubted proposition – and the reasoner must be aware of this relation. More exactly stated, the requirement is that the reasoner must know what (relevant to the doubted proposition) *would be the case if the reason were true.* A reasonable doubt is, therefore, based on knowledge; it presupposes knowledge and cannot, as a consequence, provide a means of discovering primary truth.

My discussion of the *cogito* made it obvious that the first item of knowledge Descartes supposedly obtained by the method of doubt actually depended on a substantial fund of prior knowledge. The prior knowledge included:

1. The current operations of his intellect, will, imagination, and senses: the current "thoughts" of which he is immediately aware.
2. "Simple notions" such as the nature of knowledge, thought, existence, and certainty (what they are) and the fact that (as he put it) in order to think we must be.
3. Certain things of which he is assured by "the natural light" – for example, that "nothingness possesses no attributes or qualities" and that "wherever we find some attributes or qualities, there is necessarily some thing or substance to be found for them to belong to."

Later in the *Principles* Descartes said that he distinguishes all objects of our perception into two kinds, things that actually exist and "eternal truths" that exist only in our thought. The knowledge in groups 2 and 3 no doubt concerns eternal truths.

To explain what he meant about the mind-dependent status of eternal truths, Descartes said:

> when we recognize that it is impossible for anything to come from nothing, the proposition *Nothing comes from nothing* is regarded not as a really existing thing, or even as a mode of a thing, but as an eternal truth which resides within our mind. Such truths are termed common notions or axioms. The following are examples of this class: *It is impossible for the same thing to be and not be at the same time; What is done cannot be undone; [and] He who thinks cannot but exist while he thinks.*[21]

Existent things in the world must conform to eternal truths, but those truths do not themselves imply that any particular thing exists in the world. Although Descartes did not explicitly say so when he introduced his method of doubt, it is possible that he really intended to use the method only to discover foundational truths about existing things. But however this may be, his subsequent admissions leave no doubt that his *cogito* depends on truths of both kinds. The only knowledge of existent things (or semi-things[22]) presupposed by that argument concerns his current "thoughts" or occurrent mental states. The knowledge of both kinds presupposed here provides the ultimate basis for his system of knowledge; it is even more basic than his knowledge of his own existence.

How did Descartes justify this basic knowledge? How did he show that the propositions he regarded as expressing eternal truths and common knowledge are in fact true? The answer is that he did not attempt to show this at all. He occasionally spoke of certain propositions as self-evident: three examples are "The same thing cannot both be and not be at the same time"; "Nothingness cannot be the efficient cause of anything"; and "The number 2 is even and the number 3 is odd."[23] He made it clear that he cannot doubt such propositions – any more than he can doubt that he can be wrong about the thoughts he has when he has them. The fact that he could not doubt them does not, obviously, prove (or even provide respectable evidence for the idea) that they are true. They require defense because not every philosopher, particularly today, finds Descartes' eternal truths and all candid introspective reports equally acceptable.

Some readers of Descartes will dispute what I have said in this last paragraph; they will say that Descartes had a divine guarantee for propositions expressing what he took to be eternal truths and common knowledge. He obtained the guarantee, they will add, in the following way. Having ascertained his existence as a thing that thinks, he found that he had a very special idea that he could not have created himself. The idea is that of God, an all-perfect being. Since he was filled with unresolved doubts and had only the skimpiest idea of his own nature, he knew that he was a very imperfect being – one patently inadequate to create the idea of perfection. Considering that an idea of this kind could result only from a perfect being, he concluded that God must exist as the cause of his idea. Further reflection convinced him that he owed his own limited perfection to God as creator. As a perfect being, God is no deceiver, he reasoned; and if he uses his God-given faculties rightly, he will not err or make mistakes. What must he do to use his rational faculties rightly? His answer is that he must proceed cautiously and not affirm anything to be true that he cannot *clearly and distinctly* perceive to be so. Since common notions and elementary eternal truths are obvious instances of propositions that he can clearly and distinctly conceive to be true, he must have held that his confidence in these principles is supported by a divine guarantee.

I cannot deny that Descartes often wrote as if he held this position. At an early stage of his systematic doubting, he expressed a general doubt about "demonstrations" in mathematics and about mathematical principles that formerly seemed self-evident to him. These doubts were reinforced by the possibility of the malicious demon. When he was in the process of introducing this possibility, he said:

> since I sometimes believe that others go astray in cases where they think they have the most perfect knowledge, may I not similarly go wrong every time I add two and three or count the sides of a square, or in some even simpler matter, if that be imaginable? [24]

Since this kind of doubt would seem to apply to the premises he used in his argument for the existence of God, the conclusion by which he dispelled his doubts (that God exists and is no deceiver) would appear to rest on premises that he could defend only by circular reasoning.

In spite of appearances, Descartes' position does not actually contain the circularity that is alleged here. I have shown that the supposed "first certainty" of his system, his existence as a thinking thing, is actually based on prior certainties, which include "common notions," eternal truths, and the identity of his current thoughts. The reasoning by which he concluded that God exists is also based on prior certainties of the same kind, a significant example being the principle that there must be as much total reality in a cause as is contained, formally and objectively, in its effect. If Descartes really held that the certainty of *all* common notions and eternal truths can be known only by reference to God's existence and that God's existence can be known only by inferences from premises expressing both common notions and eternal truths, then his reasoning would be grossly circular – something a philosopher as shrewd as Descartes, and as compulsive in polishing his system as Descartes was, could hardly fail to appreciate. Since no serious philosopher would knowingly base a conviction on patently circular reasoning, I think it is reasonable to presume that

Descartes' system, as he understood it, does not actually possess the circular structure his critics suppose.

Although this patently fallacious reasoning is (nevertheless) so often attributed to Descartes that it has earned the name "the Cartesian circle,"[25] it also fails to accord with Descartes' explicit disavowal of the circularity. In reply to the charge that he argued in a circle in saying that the only secure reason we have for believing that what we clearly and distinctly perceive is true is the fact that God exists but that we can be sure that God exists only because we clearly and distinctly perceive such and such, Descartes said that he did not require the assurance of God's goodness to dispel doubts about what we clearly and distinctly perceive *when we perceive it.* In his view we are inherently incapable of having doubts in such a case. The assurance of God's goodness is needed, he said, only to dispel doubts about what we *remember* perceiving in this way. Since he assured himself of the existence of a non-deceiving God by a proof that he thinks we can understand without relying on memory,[26] his certainty that God exists and is not a deceiver is not dependent on the assumption that God has this character.

This reply effectively disposes of the circularity, but it indicates that Descartes has evidently lost track of an important task that his readers can reasonably expect him to be trying to carry out. Ostensibly, his method of systematic doubt was designed to identify primitive truths suitable as a foundation of scientific knowledge. A proposition so identified is supposed to be suitable for this purpose only because it is *certain to be true.* The fact that *we are certain* about something (in the sense of being unable to doubt it) obviously does not ensure that *it is true.* Yet Descartes' reply to the charge of circular reasoning is focused only on the certainty we feel for a proposition, not on the truth it must possess. Descartes, an unyielding opponent in philosophical disputation, seemed to recognize this defect in replying to another objection, but he brushed it aside, saying:

> What is it to us . . . that the perception we are so firmly convinced of may appear false to God or an angel, so that it is, absolutely speaking, false? Why should this alleged "absolute falsity" bother us, since we neither believe in it nor have the smallest suspicion of it? For the supposition which we are making here is of a conviction so firm that it is quite

15

incapable of being destroyed; and such a conviction is clearly the same as the most perfect certainty.[27]

But the point is not whether something we believe with utter firmness appears false to God or an angel; it is whether something we so believe *is* false. And something we believe is false if its subject is not as we believe it to be. The firmness or tentativeness of our belief has no bearing on this matter.

5. The development of Descartes' system

Having attained certainty about his existence as a thing that thinks, officially his primary certainty about the domain of existing things, Descartes turned to the task of building up the structure of his knowledge. His first step was to gain clarity about the nature of the certainty he had achieved. As he reflected on this certainty, he decided that there is nothing that assures him of its truth but the clear and distinct perception of what he states. Thinking that such a perception would be insufficient to assure him that what he thus perceived is true if it could ever happen that something conceived so clearly and distinctly is false, he felt entitled to lay it down as a general rule that all things which he perceives very clearly and distinctly are true.[28]

The inference Descartes drew here is pretty dubious. He may have been unable to doubt that he exists, and his perception that he does exist may have been clear and distinct; but his ignorance of his nature as a thinking thing was sufficiently great at this stage that he was hardly warranted in assuming that he would not be "assured" that what he perceived is true if it could happen that what he clearly and distinctly perceived is false. What could he know about the conditions in reality required to assure him about something? The answer should be "nothing." If he knew what he will eventually attempt to prove – that God exists, is his creator, and is not a deceiver – he may have been able to make a plausible case for this assumption; for a false assurance, or conviction, in a matter like this would then have been arguably a defect in his nature attributable to a deceptive (or at least imperfect) creator. As it was, Descartes' general rule is a very dubious guide or principle for a cautious, critical thinker.[29]

What are the properties of clarity and distinctness in an idea? Descartes defined them in his *Principles of Philosophy*:

16

I call a perception "clear" when it is present and accessible to the attentive mind – just as we say that we see something clearly when it is present to the eye's gaze and stimulates it with a sufficient degree of strength and accessibility. I call a perception "distinct" if, as well as being clear, it is so sharply separated from all other perceptions that it contains within itself only what is clear.[30]

He expanded upon this explanation by offering the example of a clear but indistinct perception – that of a severe pain. The sensation is very accessible to an attentive mind, but it is confused because it involves an "obscure judgment" that it is located in some part of the body. This judgment is actually false, Descartes thought, for pains actually occur in the soul and may be "felt" in limbs that have been amputated.

Thus understood, clear and distinct perception is closely related to (if not the same as) what Descartes called "intuition" in an earlier work. His definition was:

By "intuition" I [mean] . . . the conception of a clear and attentive mind, which is so easy and distinct that there can be no room for doubt about what we are understanding.[31]

Intuition, so understood, is closely related to another operation of the mind from which Descartes thought certainty can be attained. He called this other operation *deduction*.[32] As he understood it, deduction is "the inference of something as following necessarily from some other propositions which are known with certainty." [33] Such inference is based on an intuitive apprehension of the connection between a premiss (known with certainty) and some immediate consequence of it. Descartes implied that the certainty conferred by deduction is transitive, so that if a conclusion C is deduced from a premiss B that has been deduced from an intuited axiom A, then C is certain if "each individual proposition [in the process] is clearly intuited." In some cases, when a conclusion is obtained as the last link in a long chain of necessary inferences, a clear vision of this kind is not possible, and the thinker's certainty will depend on his or her *memory* of the certainty-conferring deductive links.[34]

Descartes said in his *Rules* that the methods of intuition and deduction are the most certain routes to knowledge that we have, and that we should "reject all others as suspect and liable to error." [35] Although he spoke of clear and distinct perception rather than intuition in his *Meditations* and *Principles*, his basic position in this regard did not change: knowledge can be achieved only by the immediate apprehension of indubitable certainty and by "necessary inferences" therefrom. As I have shown, both methods are founded on subjective conviction and subjective indubitability. The index of what is certain is what we cannot doubt: this holds for axiomatic certainties and for the inferential certainties obtained by mental transitions of the kind "Since P is certain, Q is certain" or "P; therefore, Q."

6. Descartes' approach to the external world

The subjective basis of Cartesian certainty deserves to be emphasized because it generates a characteristically Cartesian problem about our knowledge of the external world. In spite of the "revolutions" that have occurred from time to time in modern philosophy, this problem has stubbornly remained alive, and it is therefore important to understand it and to appreciate the strategy of the solution that Descartes' offered. I shall comment critically on both the problem and Descartes' solution.

Having obtained, in his *Meditations*, the certainty of his existence of a thing that thinks, and having decided that the mark of this primitive certainty (concerning things that exist, at least) is clear and distinct perception, Descartes looked to his own consciousness for clues to other existing things. His epistemological problem about the external world thus began with the here-and-now certainty of his mental existence and the here-and-now uncertainty of anything else – in particular, of anything external to his "inner" domain. The basic problem was how, starting from the here-and-now certainty of his current existence and state of mind, he could gain certain knowledge of an ambient world.

As he considered the ideas he currently had, he found that some seem to be innate, some seem to have been produced in his mind by an external cause, and some seem to have been invented by him. The seemingly innate ones include his idea of a thing, a thought, or a truth: his ability to conceive of such things seems to be owing to his nature as a thinking thing. This is not true of the ideas he has when (as he thinks) he hears a sound, feels heat, or sees the sun:

18

these ideas seem to be produced by things external to his mind. The final group of ideas, the ones he seems to have invented himself, include *siren, hippogriff,* and the like: he seems to have invented them by putting simpler ideas together.

If any of his ideas actually represent things external to his mind, it is no doubt ideas of the second class: these seem to represent things that produce them in his mind. Does he have adequate grounds for believing that some of these ideas, at least, really do represent things existing outside his mind? In the past he has believed in such things for two basic reasons. The first is that he seems to have been "so taught by nature." To be so taught that certain of his ideas have external causes only means, he realized, that he has a "spontaneous impulse" to accept this belief. But he can easily doubt the truth of things he merely believes on impulse: he has, in fact, often been misled by spontaneous impulses when he has had to choose between right and wrong. A natural impulse provides poor evidence, therefore, that the relevant belief is true. It falls far short of clear and distinct apprehension. His other reason for believing that certain of his ideas are caused by external things is that these ideas arise in his mind independently of his will: he has them whether he wants them or not. But this reason is equally poor. When he dreams, ideas arise in his mind independently of his will, but he does not suppose that those ideas have external causes, let alone causes that those ideas adequately represent.

Since his previous reasons for believing in the existence of external objects of perception are woefully inadequate to yield scientific knowledge, he moves on to consider another means of determining whether some of his ideas adequately represent something outside himself. This new strategy is based on what he calls an idea's degree of perfection or reality. In adopting this strategy Descartes shows himself to be only partially liberated from the world of the medieval philosophers, who believed in a Great Chain of Being, a cosmic order of perfection in which each thing occupies some determinate position. The most perfect thing in the order is God, a being perfect in all respects; the opposite extreme is nothingness, the utter absence of reality; and in between fall imperfect, finite things, with "substances" (complete individual things) more perfect or real than their activities or characteristics. In adopting the new strategy Descartes is not assuming that this cosmic order actually exists; he is assuming that it is represented in his thinking, different things represented as having this or that degree of "reality or perfection." If a thing conforming to one of his ideas actually exists, it will have the degree of perfection specified by that idea; if nothing conforms to a certain idea, or class of ideas, nothing may actually exist with the specified degree of reality.

Making use of the principle that the perfection represented in an idea must be owing to the idea's cause, Descartes quicky moved to the conclusion that his idea of God must have been caused by God Himself. His idea of God, he said, is the idea of a perfect being, and such an idea represents infinite perfection. Since he, Descartes, is certain that he is imperfect, too limited in his understanding to be perfectly wise, too limited in realizing his desires to be omnipotent, and so on and so forth, he was assured that he cannot have caused his idea of God. In fact, nothing less than a perfect being could have caused that idea. Since his idea must have a cause, he concluded that God must exist as the cause of his idea.

What about the external world, the world of physical bodies? Although Descartes is convinced that God, being all-perfect, is not a deceiver, and although he concedes that the existence of a body would provide a convenient means of explaining the mental imagery and perceptual experiences he often has, he acknowledges that these convictions do not yield an argument from which the existence of external objects, or bodies, can "necessarily be deduced." To be sure, a convenient means of explaining a phenomenon supports a probable conjecture, and the existence of body does have, at the very least, this limited support. But Descartes is after rational certainty, *scientia* or scientific knowledge as he understands it, and he cannot truthfully say that he now has this respecting the existence of any things but God and himself.

Although the premisses I have mentioned do not yield the conclusion Descartes is after, he thinks he can reach that conclusion by a different route. His first move is to argue that his nature as a thing that thinks is purely mental, and that he is, therefore, really distinct from his body and can exist without it.[36] He observes, however, that he possesses a passive faculty of receiving and recognizing sensory experiences, and he realizes that this faculty would be useless to him if he or something else did not possess a corresponding active faculty that formed and produced the ideas (or experiences) that he receives. Since an active faculty of this kind does not "presuppose an intellectual act on his part" and often produces its effects contrary to his will, he concludes that it must reside in a substance different from his self. In what sort of substance might it reside? He thought there were just three possibilities: either it resides in some body or bodies, which the evoked experiences (or "ideas") represent; or it resides in some thing nobler than a body in which the content of the experiences is also represented; or it resides in God, the sustaining cause of all things.[37] His conclusion was that only the first possibility is admissible: the others would require God to be a deceiver – something he knows to be false.

If bodies must exist as active causes of our sensory experiences, what are they like? Descartes' answer is that their basic features are wholly geometrical and kinematic: they are invariably extended (spatially spread out) in three dimensions, divisible into parts, and have (as their parts do) some determinate size, shape, and quantity of motion. We can clearly and distinctly conceive these features, and because God is not a deceiver we can be certain that external bodies actually have them. These features are basic to bodies in the sense, Descartes said, that all other corporeal qualities can be "reduced" to them.[38] The hardness or heaviness we attribute to a body is really a disposition it has to resist (by the motions of its parts) the contrary motions of other things in a certain way; and the qualities of light, color, smell, taste, sounds, and touch are really dispositions of objects to affect our nerves in certain ways and thereby to produce certain "confused ideas" (sensory experiences) in our souls. The whiteness or greenness or bitterness or heat that we perceive do not actually belong to external bodies; like the pain we may also perceive, they are confused ideas produced in our souls by (ultimately) the physical interaction of our bodies with others.[39]

Having based his claim that external bodies have geometrical qualities on God's non-deceptive nature, Descartes takes pains to insist that God is not deceptive in creating us to have confused perceptual ideas. To support his stand on this matter, he mentions a sense in which we can be regarded as composite beings, having bodies as well as minds. Nature teaches him, he says, that he is not only present in a body "as a sailor is present in a ship," feeling pain when there is something wrong with the body or feeling thirst when the body needs water, but so "intermingled" with it that he and the body form a unit. Nature also teaches him that many other bodies exist around his, some of which are to be avoided, others to be sought after. The fact that he is aware of different sorts of colors, sounds, tastes, and the like entitles him to conclude that the bodies producing the perceptions of them possess certain differences corresponding to the perceptions, but the differences need not be similar to those perceptions – any more than the hardness and weight of a hammer have to be similar to the pain it causes. The purpose of the perceptions is to signify to his mind "what things are beneficial or hurtful to the composite whole of which it is a part." [40] Since he has the God-given ability to ascertain this purpose, God is clearly not a deceiver in giving us indistinct (or confused) perceptions. For the purpose they serve, they are as distinct as they need to be.

7. Criticisms and prospects

The reasoning leading to Descartes' conclusion that a world of geometrically characterized bodies exists external to his consciousness is supposed to have the structure, at least when fully spelled out, of a mathematical proof. It begins, ultimately, with intuitions – that he has certain thoughts, perhaps that he exists[41] – and proceeds to the conclusion by a series of "necessary inferences" or deductions in which additional intuitions are occasionally introduced as premisses. (One such intuition is the premiss that there must be as much reality in a total cause as is contained in the effect.) In my exposition I gave only the highlights of Descartes' reasoning, and Descartes himself omitted many necessary details, since a fully explicit proof would not have been suitable for the audience he had in mind. I want to dig into some of the details now, so that the acceptability of his "proof" can be responsibly assessed.

From a contemporary point of view, the inferential steps by which Descartes supported his principal contentions (or intermediate conclusions) vary in plausibility. His first principal contention – the lemma that he is entirely and absolutely distinct from his body – is based on the premise that all things that he apprehends clearly and distinctly can be created by God just as he apprehends them and that if he can clearly and distinctly apprehend a thing A apart from a thing B, then A is different from B. He concludes that, since he knows with certainty that he exists and yet does not clearly and distinctly perceive that anything necessarily pertains to his nature except that he is a thinking thing, his nature dóes not include anything non-mental and that he is, consequently, entirely distinct (or different) from anything physical, however "intimately conjoined" he may be with the special physical thing he has formerly considered his body. This conclusion is highly questionable because, in (supposedly) clearly and distinctly apprehending himself as a thinking thing without, at the same time, apprehending himself as having any physical features, he does not thereby (clearly and distinctly) apprehend himself as a thing that *does not have* physical features.[42]

If Descartes' views on clear and distinct apprehension are accepted, we might allow that the latter apprehension – that he *does not have* physical features – does prove that Descartes is distinct from anything even partly physical. But the apprehension Descartes says he has does not prove this at all. What it does prove is only that he can be *thought of* (however clearly and distinctly) as the subject of one attribute, thinking, without being *thought of* as having any physical attributes. The possibility of thinking of him in this last way may be owing the fact that *a thing that thinks* is a very abstract idea, comparable to *an X that thinks*, which represents a subject, *whatever it might be*, that thinks. For all Descartes actually knows at this point, all X's that think are (if finite) rational animals.

Another principal contention inadequately supported by Descartes is that the substance possessing the active faculty of producing sensory experiences in him must be other than himself because it does not "presuppose" thought and it produces experiences contrary to his will. This is dubious for a reason close to one that he himself identified earlier – namely, that the cause of his dreams does not presuppose thought, does produce dreams often contrary to his will, and yet is presumably himself. As for the contentions based on the conviction that God is not a deceiver, Descartes is open to the reply that "the Lord moves in mysterious ways His wonders to perform," and that what may look like a divinely deceptive act to a finite mind may be a necessary means to some higher purpose. This kind of reply may seem lame to someone who complains about the starving children in Ethopia; but when it is made in response to the more tenuous academic claim that divine benevolence requires our sensory experiences to have extended bodies as causes, it is certainly effective. Descartes is attempting to obtain his conclusion about extended bodies by "necessary reasoning" from indubitable premises, and doubts about the scrutibility of divine purposes are adequate to undermine the necessity of his reasoning at this point.

In his *Principles of Philosophy* Descartes attempted to provide strict proofs for the laws of physics, saying: "The only principles which I accept, or require, in physics are those of geometry and pure mathematics; these principles explain all natural phenomena, and enable us to provide quite certain demonstrations regarding them." [43] Some of his "laws of nature" are these:

1. Each and every thing, in so far as it can, always continues in the same state; and thus what is once in motion always continues to move.
2. All motion is in itself rectilinear; and hence any body moving in a circle always tends to move away from the center of the circle which it describes.
3. If a body collides with another body that is stronger than itself, it loses none of its motion; but if it collides with a weaker body, it loses a quantity of motion equal to that which it imparts to the other body.[44]

Contemporary philosophers are generally very doubtful about Descartes' project of providing demonstrative proofs for the laws of physics; it is now a common assumption that natural laws (physical, chemical, or psychological) can be discovered only *a posteriori*, by experimental reasoning.

As it happens, Descartes actually offered a kind of *a posteriori* defense for some of his basic convictions about the world, but he did not include it in his official program because it did not render the convictions demonstrably certain and thus, in his view, legitimate elements of scientific knowledge. The most significant conviction that he defended in this way was one of his last "principles of philosophy," the principle that "there are corporeal particles which cannot be perceived by the senses." [45] His defense of this principle amounted to what is now called an inference to the best explanation – a kind of inference considered by some philosophers as the fundamental form of induction.[46]

When Descartes introduced his principle about insensible particles, he said that the existence of such things cannot be doubted by anyone who considers how a tree grows: bodies must be added, though they are too small to be perceived.[47] He expanded upon the reasoning by which he arrived at this hypothesis in his gloss on Principle 203:

> First . . . I took the simplest and best known principles, knowledge of which is naturally implanted in our minds; and working from these I considered, in general terms, firstly, what are the principal differences which can exist between the sizes, shapes, and positions of bodies which are imperceptible by the senses merely because of their small size, and, secondly, what observable effects would result from their various interactions. Later on, when I observed just such effects in objects that can be perceived by the senses, I judged that they in fact arose from just such an interaction of bodies that cannot be perceived – especially since it seemed impossible to think up any other explanation for them.[48]

His confidence in the hypothesis was increased, he said, by a consideration of how the constituent parts of automata (such as clocks) provide a similar explanation of observable effect.

How confident is Descartes that his explanatory hypothesis is true? In his gloss on Principle 204 he expresses less confidence than he did in his gloss on Principle 201. In reply to the fancied objections that there is an infinity of different ways in which all things that we see could, for all we know, be formed by "the great Artificer," Descartes replied:

> I am very happy to admit this; and I think I shall have achieved enough provided only that what I have written is such as to correspond accurately with all the phenomena of nature.

He then added:

> This will indeed be sufficient for application in ordinary life, since medicince and mechanics, and all the other arts which can be fully developed with the help of physics, are directed only towards items that can be perceived by the senses and are therefore to be counted among the phenomena of nature.[49]

This last remark accords with what is now called an "instrumentalist" interpretation of explanatory hypotheses. Philosophers who accept this interpretation of explanatory hypotheses say that even the best of such hypotheses do not have to be regarded as true; they merely have to be regarded as "observationally adequate." [50]

The proper attitude to take to explanatory hypotheses is one of the most important questions of epistemology, and I shall return to it again and again in what follows. Descartes, near the end of his *Principles of Philosophy*, attempted to cope with it by introducing a distinction between two kinds of certainty. One kind, new to his discussion, is *moral certainty*: this suffices for the conduct of life, though if we regard the absolute power of God, what is morally certain may be uncertain.[51] In view of this last qualification, the contrasting kind of certainty might be called *metaphysical certainty*. Descartes indicates by an example that moral certainty can be very great in theoretical matters. The example concerns a letter written in Latin characters that are not placed in their proper Latin order. If a person attempting to read the letter takes it into his head to read *B* whenever he finds *A* and *C* wherever he finds *B* and so on (thus substituting for the letters he sees the ones following it in the alphabet) and finds that the substitutions yield a proper Latin letter, he will be convinced that he has interpreted the letter correctly, finding an alternative possibility so unlikely, if the cipher contains many words, as to seem incredible.[52]

Although Descartes was a very self-assured philosopher who expressed great confidence in the basis on which he founded his system, he remarked in one of the final glosses in *Principles* that his basic contentions can be seen to be morally certain even if his grounds for holding them are unknown or disregarded:

> If people look at all the many properties relating to magnetism, fire, and the fabric of the entire world, which I have deduced in this book from just a few principles, then, even if they think my assumption of these principles was arbitrary and groundless, they will still perhaps acknowledge that it would hardly have been possible for so many items to fit into a coherent pattern if the original principles had been false.[53]

If, as I have argued, the chain of deductions on which Descartes founded his system has many fatally weak links, its coherence and explanatory fertility may add a special credibility to it. I shall discuss this means of supporting a system of principles in Chapter VII.

CHAPTER II

Locke and Berkeley

The road to solipsism, at least as it was created in Great Britain, began with Locke's *Essay Concerning Human Understanding* (1690), took a sharp turn at the hands of George Berkeley, and, guided by David Hume, moved relentlessly toward its lonely end. Locke offered a theoretical picture of the natural world which fitted together nicely with current views in chemistry and physics and which, in large-scale features, is plausible even today. Berkeley attacked Locke's picture as rationally ill-founded and conceptually incoherent, basing his idealist alternative on subtle critical observations. Hume criticized Berkeley almost as effectively as Berkeley criticized Locke, making a powerful case for a "mitigated" skepticism that was nevertheless solipsistic. I shall discuss the contributions of Locke and Berkeley in this chapter, the revolutionary arguments of Hume in the chapter that follows.

1. Locke on knowledge

Although Locke is considered an empiricist, he was close to Descartes in his conception of knowledge. This is evident in his official definition of "actual" or occurrent knowledge, which is "the perception of the connection and agreement, or disagreement and repugnancy, of any of our ideas." [1] When we perceive that the three angles of a triangle are equal to two right ones, we perceive, he says, that equality to two right ones "necessarily agree[s] to, and is inseparable from, the three angles of a triangle." And when we perceive that white is not black, we perceive that the ideas of white and black do not agree. As with Descartes, the perception involved here is either direct or mediate. If it is direct, Locke called the knowledge "intuitive"; if it is mediate, he called it "demonstrative."

27

The latter is dependent, he said, on the former, for the aim of demonstration is to ascertain the relation between ideas A, B, C . . . by means of their perceived relation to intermediate ideas X, Y, Z . . . – something that must be perceived intuitively. As in Descartes' account, a demonstration thus consists of a sequence of intuitions. Intuitive knowledge is, as it was for Descartes, "the clearest and most certain that human frailty is capable of."

Knowledge thus understood is typically general and restricted to the mere relations between ideas, telling us nothing about matters of fact and existence (as Hume would later put it). Thus, if one's idea of snow is the idea of a cold, white, powdery substance that falls from the sky in winter, then one will know intuitively that snow is white. But this knowledge, like one's knowledge that a centaur is half-man and half-horse, does not have existential import: in both cases the knowledge concerns the content of an idea and does not imply that the idea applies to something real or existent.[2] I said that knowledge as Locke understood it is *typically* like this because he identified two important exceptions. One concerns a thinker's own existence: this is known intuitively by that person, though the nature of his or her self is not thereby understood in any clear way.[3] The other concerns the existence of "a God," which Locke thought we can know by demonstration.[4]

Although Locke's definition of knowledge is clearly applicable to general truths of the sort I have mentioned, it is not equally applicable (at least in an unproblematic way) to one's own existence and the existence of God. The reason is that his definition concerns the relation between ideas – their agreement or disagreement – rather than the relation between ideas and the non-ideas that they represent. If my idea of existence merely "agrees" with my idea of myself or my idea of God, then I might be inconsistent in thinking of myself or God as not existing, but it does not follow (from the inconsistency) that I and God must therefore exist.[5]

However this last point may be, Locke claimed that there is another sort of knowledge to which his definition clearly does not apply, a sort that he called "sensitive knowledge." This concerns the existence of objects that affect our senses: the things we see and feel when we see and feel them. I did not identify this kind of knowledge as one of the exceptions Locke admitted to his definition because he seemed to regard it as knowledge in a different sense of the word, not the sort of thing he was attempting to pin down with his formula concerning the agreement or disagreement of ideas. In the paragraph in which he introduced the notion of sensitive knowledge he said that "whatever comes short of . . . [intuition and demonstration] is but *faith* or *opinion*, but not knowledge, at least in all general truths."[6] He offered five reasons why the assurance we get from our senses deserves the name of *knowledge*; but then, realizing that the five reasons are far from conclusive, he disparaged the need for greater certainty, claiming that the certainty we have "is as great as our condition needs."

The attempt to defend a claim to knowledge by disparaging the need for a justification we cannot give has become popular in recent epistemology where, instead of showing why claims of certain sorts are apt to be true, philosophers attack the position of some fancied skeptic, attempting to show that his doubts or criticisms are unwarranted. The strategy smacks of theoretical incompetence or desperation. The claims in question are epistemically interesting because their credentials are uncertain, unknown, or poorly understood – not because someone has doubts about them or has offered arguments in support of their falsity or improbability. Locke, considering the possibility that everyday perceptual experiences (of sitting in a chair, or even of being in a fire) could be as unrelated to an external world as a series of dream experiences, defended his realist convictions by asking anyone who takes the possibility seriously to "dream" that he gives this two-step answer: If eveything is a dream, no answer is needed because reasoning and arguments are of no use in a dream; and second, even a dreamer will want to allow that there is "a very manifest difference" between dreaming of being in a fire and actually being in one. The certainty Locke felt that the reality is far more painful than a mere dream is, he insisted, as much as he needs in a matter like this.

Part of Locke's reply here was echoed in recent years by J. L. Austin, who asked: "Could it be seriously suggested that having this dream [of being presented to the Pope] is 'qualitatively indistinguishable' from *actually being* presented to the Pope? " "Quite obviously not," he replied triumphantly.[7] This reply is, alas, irrelevant to the traditional dream argument – as Locke's was too. The argument does not allege that the dream (of being presented to the Pope, of being in a fire) is indistinguishable from the reality; it alleges that the dream is, or the dream experiences are, indistinguishable from the experiences one might (or could conceivably) have in a real-life case. And the falsity of this allegation is not obvious. My belief on this matter, for what it is worth, is this. The experiences I have in some real-life cases (when I am excited) seem to flash by, blurry and confused; the experiences I have had in some dreams are amazingly sharp and distinct. A phenomenal difference between the two cases is not *always* evident when I am experiencing them.

The pertinent philosophical question to ask here is not, in any case, whether we believe there are decisive differences between dreaming and waking experience. It is what reasons can be given for the thesis that our sensory experiences yield true or even mostly true beliefs about objects external to our consciousness. As I mentioned, Locke identified four reasons in response to this question. His first reason follows an initial argument (possibly a restatement of his reply to the skeptic) [8] to the effect that, since the testimony of our senses yields reliable predictions about conditions that produce pain and pleasure in us, they provide "assurance enough" of the existence of things outside us.[9] The reason is that "those who want [lack] the organs of any sense never can have the ideas belonging to that sense" and that "the organs themselves . . . do not produce them, for then the eyes of a man in the dark would produce colors." [10] The second reason is that sensations are produced in him independently of his will: "If I turn my eyes at noon towards the sun," he said, "I cannot avoid the ideas which the light or sun then produces in me." [11] The third reason is that "many ideas are produced in us with pain, which after we remember without the least offense." [12] The final reason is that the testimony of different senses generally corroborate one another: "He that sees a fire may, if he doubt whether it be anything more than a bare fancy, feel it too, and be convinced by putting his hand in it."[13]

These four reasons obviously vary in cogency. If, as Locke claimed, we can know that physical things exist "only by sensation," his first reason is question-begging. To know that there are sense organs, we have to have sensitive knowledge – and this is the conclusion the first reason is supposed to support. If this first reason is restated so that it concerns only the perceptual impressions we have when we believe we are observing the behavior of people with and without healthy sense organs, then it can, I should say, when conjoined with the other three reasons and an analogous restatement of the initial argument, provide some confirming evidence for an explanatory theory that postulates a world of observers and perceptual objects, the latter producing experiences in the former by stimulating appropriate sense-organs. The confirming evidence thus provided would be fairly weak, but nothing stronger can be extracted from the reasons Locke offered.

Locke may have exaggerated the cogency of his reasons because he regarded sensitive knowledge as being very limited in content. "It is the actual receiving of [certain] ideas from without," he said, "that gives us notice of the existence of other things and makes us know that *something* doth exist *at that time* without us which causes that idea in us, though perhaps we neither know nor consider how it does it" (italics mine). In fact, he added, when an idea (= an awareness) of whiteness is produced in his mind, he knows that an external object exists that has a "quality or accident . . . whose appearance before [his] eyes always causes that idea." [14] This knowledge is very limited because it does not extend to the nature of the quality or accident that supposedly produces his awareness of whiteness (his "idea") and it is limited to the present moment, the time when the whiteness is being experienced.[15]

2. Locke on judgment and opinion

Although Locke was basically Cartesian in his conception of knowledge, he thought that our stock of knowledge is extremely limited and that it is "folly to expect demonstration in everything."[16] Insisting that "our knowledge being short, we want something else,"[17] he identified the desired alternative as belief, assent, or opinion. We attain this alternative by our faculty of judgment, which, when rightly conducted, yields probability. For Locke, probability, not certainty, is the guide to life and the rational basis for natural philosophy. Post-renaissance science is founded on this conviction.

What is probability? When Locke talked about it, he did not have a modern conception in mind, though a modern conception had emerged before his *Essay* was completed.[18] Locke's description of probability is confusing; his most explicit words are: "Probability is likeliness to be true, the very notation of the word signifying . . . a proposition for which there be arguments or proofs to make it pass or be received for true." Our mental attitude to a probable proposition, he added, is belief, assent, or opinion, "which is the admitting or receiving any proposition for true upon arguments or proofs that are found to persuade us to receive it as true, without certain knowledge that it is so."[19] To a modern reader, the striking defect with Locke's description lies in the words "likeliness to be true," for "likeliness" is apt to be taken as a synonym for "probability." Yet in Locke's time "likeliness" could mean either "similarity" or "sign of," and either of these readings is appropriate to Locke's discussion.[20] As it happens, on the page preceding the one from which I took the quotation above, Locke described probability as the "appearance" of demonstrative knowledge, so "similarity" is no doubt what he meant. Probable propositions, for him, are thus things we believe to be true on the basis of arguments similar to (but falling short of) proofs or demonstrations.

What sort of arguments did Locke have in mind here? Obviously, they cannot be demonstrations. Was he thinking of inductive arguments? Strictly speaking, the answer is no: he did not have a determinate conception of an inductive argument. When he spoke of belief or opinion as the attitude appropriate to a probable proposition, he was following a tradition begun with Plato, perfected by the scholastics, and retained by seventeenth-century philosophers such as Descartes. According to this tradition, knowledge is *scientia*, something requiring rational demonstration; probable opinion or belief is *opinio*, what authorities and intelligent people accept or take to be true but do not know. Thinkers in this tradition lacked a concept of inductive evidence.[21] The tradition began to fall apart in Locke's day, when "natural philosophy" (what we call natural science) became experimental and a modern concept of probability came into existence. A concept of inductive or experimental inference and a related concept of evidence had to be created at this time, and Locke, led by Boyle and Newton, took important steps toward creating it.[22] The arguments Locke had in mind when he spoke of probability are the sorts of non-demonstrative arguments that he and his scientific colleagues regarded as acceptable.

According to Locke, probable beliefs concern either matters of fact or matters of speculation. Matters of fact, as he understood them, are the sorts of thing that, being observable, can be supported by human testimony. Probability has degrees, Locke said, and the highest degree is found

when the general consent of all men in all ages, as far as can
be known, concurs with a man's constant and never failing
experience in like cases to confirm the truth of any particular
matter of fact attested by fair witnesses: such are the stated
constitutions of bodies and properties of bodies [e.g. that fire
is hot, that water freezes at a certain temperature] and the
regular proceedings of causes and effects in the ordinary course
of nature.[23]

He remarked that this sort of probability is "from the nature of
things themselves," adding that

what our own and other men's constant observation has found
always to be after the same manner . . . we with reason
conclude to be the effects of steady and regular causes, though
they come not within the reach of our knowledge.[24]

This last remark is informative and highly significant: it is a
succinct, informal statement of a now familiar inductive principle.
Though vague in important respects, the principle supports a wide
variety of non-deductive inferences. For example, it permits us to
infer that if something of kind A is invariably observed by a large
and varied group of people to be followed by something of kind B,
then B is very probably a causal consequence of A, arising from it
by "steady and regular causes."

In an earlier passage Locke mentioned a number of factors that
should be considered in assessing human testimony. These factors
include (a) the number of people who claim to have observed
something; (b) the integrity of the observers; (c) the observers' skill
in making the relevant observations; (d) the design or purpose of an
author, when the testimony is taken from a book; (e) "the constancy
of the parts and the circumstances of the relation" – by which he
probably means such things as the consistency of the testimony, its
coherence, its "constancy" as to voice, competence, information,
and so forth, and the presence of circumstances that may have a
bearing on these things, such as fear, sorrow, love, or hate; and (f)
the presence, nature, and circumstances of "contrary
testimonies." [25] Noting that many factors are commonly relevant to
a reasonable opinion, Locke said that, to be rational, we ought to
examine all the grounds of probability bearing on a proposition
before we assent to it, or dissent from it; and then, "upon a due

balancing of the whole, reject or receive it with a more or less firm assent proportional to the preponderancy of the greater grounds of probability on one side or the other." [26]

As we shall see in later chapters, there is a serious theoretical problem about how these various grounds of probability can be ascertained. According to many later empiricists, the basic rule is (roughly) generalization from experience; but as Locke well knew, experience itself has to be assessed for reliability (even one's own experience), and it is not entirely clear that experience can always be assessed by other experience without objectionable circularity. (How, by appealing to experience, can one show that there exists at least one reliable observer?) Evidently, Locke was unaware of this problem, but he is in good company: few philosophers have realized that it exists.

The probabilities I have been discussing concern matters of fact, as Locke called them; the other sort that he recognized concern matters of "speculation" – things we cannot observe by our senses. Locke divided these matters into two classes. The first includes the existence, nature, and operations of "finite immaterial beings without us," such as spirits, angels, or devils; and also the existence of material beings that are either too small or too remote to be observed. The other class includes the unobservable causes of observable effects. We see animals generated, nourished, and growing; we see magnets attract iron; we see the parts of a candle successively melt, turn to flame, and give us both light and heat. "These and the like effects we see and know," Locke said; "but the causes that operate, and the manner they are produced in, we can only guess and probably conjecture." The only help we have here, he concluded, is analogy: it is from analogy alone that we find our grounds of probability.[27]

The claim that a principle of analogy is needed in experimental inference has been persistent in modern philosophy; it was made in the late seventeenth century by Newton, in the final edition of his famous *Principia*;[28] its importance was emphasized in the eighteenth century by Hume;[29] and in our century it was declared essential to scientific inference by Bertrand Russell (among others).[30] As we shall see when we discuss Hume's views on experimental inference, there is a serious problem about how inductive rules and principles can be justified. Locke himself did not attempt to justify a principle of analogy; he merely said that analogy is the only help we have in thinking about "things which sense cannot discover." [31]

Assuming that we are rationally entitled to employ a principle of analogy in our probable reasoning, we may ask how the principle can be used to support beliefs about things not open to our senses. Perhaps the most obvious way of answering this is in connection with the minds or experiences of others. Since their minds, experiences, or "ideas" are not sensibly apparent to us, we cannot know (or have sensitive knowledge) that they exist. On the other hand, the words and actions of other human bodies give us reason to be "satisfied" (Locke said) that there are "minds and thinking beings" in them.[32] Evidently, analogy is the basis for our conviction here. We have intuitive knowledge of our own existence as thinking things or "spirits," and we perceive the motions and noises our bodies make in response to experiences and purposes that we have. When we observe other human bodies behaving (moving, making verbal noises) in ways similar to the behavior of our own bodies, we form the belief that the cause of their behavior is analogous to the cause of our behavior and, consequently, that there are minds or thinking beings in them. From like effects (as Hume put it)[33] we infer like causes.

Although Locke was a convinced atomist, he did not (so far as I know) explicitly attempt to explain how the existence of atoms can be supported by analogical reasoning. It is not difficult, however, to see how this kind of support could be given. If we have a jagged board, we can make it smooth by cutting off its rough edges: when we do this, we remove small but visible parts. If we proceed to sand the board, we can make it even smoother, and we remove smaller parts in the process: these small parts are the constituents of sand dust, which we can observe to be granular. When we observe the sharp edges of statues become smooth over a long period of time, we will expect that an analogous process of erosion has taken place, though the eroded parts are too small to be seen or felt. A similar argument was given by Descartes when he said, "We day by day see a tree grow, and it is impossible to comprehend how it becomes larger than it was before unless by conceiving that some body is added to it. But who has ever observed by means of the senses what are the small bodies which are each day added to the plant that grows?" [34] Neither Descartes nor Locke would pretend that we can obtain certain conclusions by such reasoning; they agreed, however, that it was an acceptable source of reasonable (or probable) opinion.

3. *Locke on the nature of external objects*

Berkeley's attack on Locke was directed more to his views on material objects than to his epistemological principles. Since I shall be discussing Berkeley's criticism in the next section of this chapter, I shall devote this one to a general description of Locke's views on material objects. Like Descartes, Locke thought of such objects as spatially extended substances; his conception or complex idea of them was nevertheless novel in important respects.

As his examples indicate, Locke applied the term "substance" to a wide variety of things and materials – for example, to sticks, stones, plants, animals, spirits, artifacts, and stuff such as gold and water. Although such things are describable in a great many ways, they fall into the category of material or spiritual things because of certain basic qualities. A particular thing may be describable as a piece of furniture – specifically, a lacquered desk – by virtue of its function and finish, but it is a material thing because it has the basic qualities of things of that category. For Locke, the basic qualities of material things are both occurrent and dispositional. A piece of gold has at a given time a particular size and shape: these are examples of its occurrent qualities. But it also has distinctive powers, as Locke put it. Gold not only has the power or disposition (as we are apt to say today) to dissolve in *aqua regia*; it is also malleable, or capable of being hammered into a different shape, and visible: it will look yellow to normal observers who view it in good light.

Locke claimed that, "rightly considered," bodies have three sorts of qualities.[35] The first sort he calls "primary": these include the size, shape, motion, number, and situation (or arrangement) of an object's "solid parts." A body has these qualities, Locke said, whether we perceive them or not. If the parts they qualify are large enough to be perceived by us, our ideas of them represent them as they really are: parts conceived to be spherical may actually be spherical. In this respect primary qualities differ fundamentally from those Locke terms "secondary." A body's secondary qualities include its color, smell, taste, and the sounds it makes. "Rightly considered," these qualities are powers of the object to produce certain ideas (or sensory effects) in us. We are prone to think of colors, smells, sounds, and tastes as being similar to the sensory qualities we are aware of when (under good conditions) we see, smell, hear, and taste an object, but we are mistaken in this. The color we are aware of when we see the sun is no more in the sun (as an occurrent quality) than the changes it makes in wax, when it blanches or melts the latter, are in it: in both cases, the qualities in the sun are powers that depend on the sun's primary qualities. The sun's power to melt wax is an example of the third sort of quality that Locke recognized. It differs from a secondary quality in the kind of effect it brings about. Instead of producing certain ideas in a perceiver, it produces changes in a body's primary qualities.

In addition to encompassing qualities of these three sorts, our idea of a substance includes the idea of something that supports these qualities. The idea of this support for qualities, this *substratum* as Locke called it, is very obscure in his opinion. When we think of a particular thing, we think of various qualities existing together; and "not imaging how these . . . ideas can subsist by themselves, we accustom ourselves to suppose some *substratum* wherein they do subsist, and from which they do result." [36] The idea of this *substratum* is nothing more, he insisted, than the supposition of a thing "he knows not what" that supports qualities. "We call that support *substantia*," he added; "according to the true import of the word, [it] is, in plain English, standing under, or upholding."

Locke inherited the notion of a *substratum* from medieval philosophy – also the source of the term "accident," which he applied to the qualities inhering in a *substratum*. Another term that he inherited from his medieval forebears and that complicates his notion of a substance is "essence." Locke used this word in two senses. In one sense, marked by the adjective "real," Locke referred to what he regarded as the generally unknown "constitution" of things on which their observable qualities depend. Like his friend Robert Boyle, Locke was convinced that visible bodies are complex aggregates of invisible atoms and that their discoverable qualities (their powers and large-scale occurrent features) depend on the primary qualities of these constituent atoms – their number, arrangement, motions, and the like. In Locke's day the nature of a visible object's constituent atoms and the manner in which those atoms accounted for the object's observable features were substantially unknown. Although Locke had to acknowledge that visible objects had "real" essences, he insisted that objects could not be classified by reference to them. For this latter purpose – for the classification of objects into sorts or kinds – it is necessary to appeal to the other sense of "essence," the sense marked by the adjective "nominal."

A nominal essence, for Locke, is nothing but an abstract idea, which we form and associate with a general term or sortal noun. If our abstract idea of gold – the idea we happen to associate with the word "gold" – is the idea of a soft, heavy, valuable, yellow metal soluble in *aqua regia*, then anything having these qualities is rightly classifiable as gold. Understood as an idea of this kind, a nominal essence serves as a criterion or standard by which classificatory predicates (sortals) are correctly applied to objects. The basis for classification is not some natural boundary, some "joint" in the body of nature (as Plato seemed to think),[37] but an idea formed in the human mind and annexed to a name (a sortal expression) that enables human beings "to consider things, and discourse on them, as it were in bundles, for the easier and readier improvement and communication of their knowledge, which would advance but slowly were their words and thoughts confined only to particulars."[38]

Locke's conception of an observable physical body or "substance" is very plausible if it is properly understood. A common source of misunderstanding can be traced to his unfortunate remark that "the ideas of primary qualities are resemblances of them, and their patterns do really exist in the bodies themselves; but the ideas produced in us by these secondary qualities have no resemblance of them at all."[39] This remark is unfortunate mainly because of the word "idea," which Locke used in a loose and peculiar way. As he explained in his introduction to the *Essay*, he used "idea" as a catch-all term for "whatever is the object of the understanding when a man thinks," this including "whatever is meant by *phantasm, notion, species,* or whatever the mind can be employed about in thinking."[40] These last words make it clear that a Lockean idea is best understood as anything "present to a mind": it covers occurrent thoughts, conceptions, mental images, and sensory impressions.

When Locke said that ideas of primary qualities (unlike ideas of secondary qualities) are "resemblances" of qualities bodies actually have, his point can be explained as follows. Consider the experience of seeing a large scarlet disk in good light. If your eyes are good, you will be visually aware of an expanse that is naturally describable as both scarlet and circular. If there is an actual physical disk before you, it is not "united to your mind"; the perception you have is produced in your mind by "singly imperceptive bodies" that come from the physical disk to your eyes and "thereby convey" to your brain a proximate stimulus.[41] The scarlet you are immediately (or non-inferentially) aware of is not actually spread out over the surface of the physical disk, and there is nothing on that surface (or in the disk) that in any way resembles the scarlet you are thus aware of. By contrast, the physical disk is actually circular (or approximately so) and thus "resembles" the expanse you are immediately aware of. The circularity of the disk is a primary quality of it; its power to produce an awareness of scarlet in you is a secondary quality. The power, a causal property, in no way resembles the expanse you are non-inferentially aware of.

Why was Locke convinced that physical objects do not have qualities resembling the colors and so forth that we are aware of when we perceive them? The fact (assuming it to be such) that the colored expanses we are immediately aware of do not belong to the surfaces of physical objects does not show that those objects do not have qualities like the qualities of those expanses. If the physical disk has a primary quality resembling the circularity of the non-physical scarlet expanse, why can't it have a quality resembling the scarlet of that expanse? Locke's answer seems to be based on his atomism. In one passage he said this:

> If we had senses acute enough to discern the minute particles
> . . . I doubt not that they would produce quite different ideas
> in us, and that which is now the yellow color of gold would
> then disappear, and instead of it we should see an admirable
> texture of parts of a certain size and figure. This microscopes
> plainly discover to us; for what to our naked eyes produces a
> certain color is, by thus augmenting the acuteness of our
> senses, discovered to be quite a different thing. . . . Blood to
> the naked eye appears all red; but by a good microscope,
> wherein its lesser parts appear, shows only some few globules
> of red swimming in a pellucid liquor; and how these red
> globules would appear, if glasses could be found that yet could
> magnify them one thousand or ten thousand times more, is
> uncertain.[42]

His idea was that a microscope gives us a better idea of what a body is really like than our unaided senses do, and that what appears red to our naked eyes is really very different: it consists of some red globules swimming in a pellucid liquor. Evidently, he thought the red globules were not themselves atoms but aggregates of spatially separated micro-bodies. Thus, their redness is an appearance, too.

But couldn't the atoms be colored? Locke, to my knowledge, did not discuss this matter; but if the question had been put to him, he might have responded with two further arguments. First, the colors that we are aware of are invariably mere appearances, however far we proceed with magnification. In the absence, therefore, of clear evidence to the contrary (which we lack) we have no basis for supposing that colors are ever anything but mere appearances. This argument is equally applicable to tastes, sounds, and smells; and it is sufficient to remind us that we have no positive evidence that bodies have qualities that are anything like these appearances. The surface that looks smooth and scarlet to the naked eye is seen to be discontinuous and largely pellucid under the microscope: the latter shows us that the physical surface does not really have large-scale qualities similar to perceived-scarlet and perceived-smoothness. The second argument he might have employed is that, as far as the evidence we have is concerned, qualities like perceptible-color, perceptible-smell, and perceptible-taste exist only in connection with minds and medium-sized objects. An object's color, smell, and taste are diminished as its size is diminished; and micro-objects cannot be seen, smelled, or tasted at all. It is reasonable to conclude, therefore, that micro-objects do not have these qualities at all – or any qualities like them (since we have no evidence for such things).

Don't these arguments apply to primary qualities as well? Locke would have conceded that they do in part: the primary qualities we are perceptibly aware of when we perceive a physical thing are not actually possessed by those bodies. This is, in fact, his view anyway. When he spoke carefully, he always made it clear that an object's primary qualities are such things as "the bulk, figure, number, situation, and motion of [its] parts" [43] – and by parts, he meant its micro-parts. Locke could, of course, have been pressed to explain how he knew that an object's micro-parts have size, shape, motion, and geometrical arrangement. He would have answered that he did not, strictly speaking, *know* this at all but that it is a probable opinion that gets its support from experimental reasoning. An atomic (or "corpuscularian") theory of matter provides the best available account of the nature of the bodies whose existence is *known to us* by sensation. "Sensitive knowledge" assures us of their existence; we must speculate about their nature.

4. Berkeley on secondary qualities

George Berkeley attacked Locke's view of the natural world in two famous books, *Principles of Human Knowledge* (1710) and *Three Dialogues Between Hylas* and *Philonous* (1713), the latter officially written in opposition to skeptics and atheists. Berkeley did not believe that Locke was a skeptic or atheist, but he was convinced that Locke's philosophy led to skepticism. He was also convinced that if the errors he saw in Locke's philosophy were adequately appreciated, the principles of natural religion would be convincing and the case for atheism would be seriously undermined. Attacking the foundations of Locke's philosophy was thus, for him, a significant means of opposing both skepticism and atheism.

In spite of his serious disagreement with Locke, Berkeley shared some of his basic assumptions. One assumption on which much of his criticism was based is that the characteristic qualities we are immediately aware of when we see, hear, smell, or taste something exist only "in our minds." Locke described these subjective objects of awareness as ideas, saying that their correlates in perceived bodies are mere powers – powers to produce such ideas in suitably situated perceivers. Berkeley did not believe in purely physical powers, but he emphasized that the qualities we are aware of in perception and normally regard as colors, sounds, smells, and tastes are actually mental. The "beautiful red and purple we see in the clouds" are not really in them; the sonorous *do, mi, so, do* we hear is not really in the air around us; the sweet smell we inhale is not really in the rose; and the bitterness we taste is not really in the mustard. These qualities really exist "in" our minds. They may or may not correspond to powers in clouds, air, roses, and mustard; it is they, rather than these alleged powers, that we perceive and consider sensible qualities.

Berkeley's insistence that we perceive mind-dependent occurrent qualities in these cases rather than objective powers is not contrary to Locke's explicit doctrine, but it puts his doctrine in an awkward light. Anyone who has grown up with a micro-theory of matter finds it natural to follow Locke and think of the colors, sounds, smells, and tastes of external objects as dispositional properties, or "powers" that they possess. But this natural view has awkward consequences. We ordinarily think of colors as visible qualities – qualities we can directly observe in colored bodies – and we think of sounds, smells, and tastes as directly perceptible in analogous ways. But Locke's powers are iffy qualities: they are dispositions to produce discernible effects *if and when* certain conditions obtain. Not being occurrent, such qualities are inappropriate objects of direct perception. Berkeley found this more than paradoxical; he thought it marks a serious error in Locke's conception of a secondary quality.

Berkeley approached the issue by attacking a related view of physical qualities, one that identifies them not with powers but with the supposed physical basis for powers: certain "motions" of the atoms composing visible bodies. The problem with these motions is that they are not visible: they are too minute to be seen. If some of these motions are to be considered real colors, they will be colors that *cannot be seen*. If other such motions are to be considered sounds, they will be sounds that cannot meaningfully be said to be *loud, sweet, acute* or *grave*. Since motions are appropriate objects of sight or touch but not sound (we hear noises!), these micro-motions may possibly be *seen* or *felt* (if they could be detected at all) but never *heard*.[44] But how could something that cannot be heard be a sound? The same difficulties arise, obviously, for Locke's view of physical colors, sounds, and the like. Since powers, being iffy, are never, strictly speaking, seen, heard, smelled, or tasted, his view also has the consequence that a cloud's colors are not seen, a tenor's sounds are not heard, a rose's odor is not smelled, and mustard's flavor is not tasted. It also has the consequence that sounds cannot be sweet or grave, colors cannot be intense or saturated, smells cannot be fragrant, and tastes cannot be bitter. (How could a power have any of these qualities?)

Although Berkeley thought that these paradoxes disclosed a definite error in Locke's view, he was mistaken: they merely show that Locke's scientifically inspired conception of an object's second-ary qualities is different from a scientifically more naive one. To remove the perplexity these paradoxes might produce, it is sufficient to make some minor adjustments in the way we customar-ily speak about secondary qualities. Instead of speaking about seeing, hearing, smelling, or tasting an object's color, sounds, odor, or taste, we can speak of seeing *that* the object has this or that color, odor, or taste, or is making this or that sound. To perceive such a thing, one has an appropriate sensory experience (visual, auditory, or whatever) and, on the basis of the experience, takes the object to have this or that sensible power. One would take an object to have a certain power on the basis of having a certain experience if that experience made one believe that the object had that power – that the object would produce (perhaps) similar experiences in normal observers. This belief would naturally arise in observers when they have a certain experience if they think of themselves as normal: they would expect other normal observers to experience what they experience in the circumstances.

This adjustment in the way one speaks about sensible qualities is not very dramatic; in fact, it is arguable that careful thought requires this adjustment even for a scientifically less sophisticated view of such qualities. Take color, again. Even if colors are thought to be non-iffy features occurrently spread out over the surface of an object (or permeating its entire volume), a distinction must be drawn between an object's apparent color (the color it actually presents to Tom, Dick, or Mary under these conditions) and the color it really has. Only in special cases would the color actually seen by someone be a thing's actual color; in the usual case, the color a person sees corresponds only approximately with that color. What an observer sees depends not only on the object but on the condition of his or her optical system (eyes, nerves, etc.) and the conditions under which the object is viewed. Seeing that an object is scarlet would amount to taking the object, on the basis of one's current visual experience, to have an objective visual quality that is either similar to or related in a special way to the color apparent in one's current experience. One would expect the color to be very similar to the quality one directly experiences only when one is a highly reliable observer viewing the object under ideal conditions of visual perception.

As for the objection that the distinctive features of sensible qualities (sweetness, fragrance, saturation, etc.) cannot reasonably be attributed to mere powers, the proper reply requires us to appreciate that when we have changed our conception of a thing, we must change our conception of what we can truly say about it. The point seems trivial, but it is related to an important twentieth-century development: the concept of a contextual defini-tion.[45] Definitions of this kind were introduced into philosophy by early practitioners of linguistic or conceptual analysis. Bertrand Russell was particularly influential in this respect. When he attempted, with A. N. Whitehead, to reduce mathematics to logic, he defined natural numbers as classes or sets: the number 2 was defined as the class of couples; the number 3 was defined as the class of triples, and so on. These definitions served their purpose only because they were accompanied by definitions in set-theoreti-cal terms of numerical operations – of addition, subtraction, multiplication, and division. The result of these definitions was that an arithmetical statement was shown to be equivalent to another statement containing only set-theoretical terms. Instead of saying, then, that sets could be added, divided, and the like, which would mix defined and undefined terms in unacceptable ways, one would say that certain sets could be related to others by certain set-theoretical operations in terms of which the arithmetical ones are defined.

Consider the claim, now, that a physical sound is a power to produce auditory "ideas" in an observer. In so far as this claim expresses a new idea of what a sound is, we can continue to speak of sounds as high, low, sweet, or grave only if we reinterpret these predicates. Since the meaning of predicates belonging to a certain class is intimately related to the meaning of nouns they can modify, the required reinterpretation must be contextual, sentences contain-ing both kinds of words reinterpreted as units. One sentence requiring reinterpretation might be "Body B emits a loud or grave sound." An appropriate definition will not necessarily assign a property corresponding to "loud" or "grave" to a power; a more satisfactory definition will assign a new property to the sensory experience that the power produces in a normal observer. Such a definition will be more satisfactory in the sense that it will better accord with the intent of Locke's theory. A sweet sound, as he understood it, would be a short-term power (perhaps of a ring of air expanding around a source) to produce sweet* sound-experiences in suitably situated, normal sound-observers. A sweet* sound-experience is one that an intelligent speaker would describe by "sweet" or some equivalent, or at least acknowledge to have a quality that is aptly describable by such a word.

5. *Berkeley on primary qualities*

The point of Berkeley's major criticism of Locke pertains to his view of primary qualities and the *substratum* in which they supposedly inhere. I shall begin with what he said about primary qualities. His remarks on these qualities were based partly on his conception of a secondary quality, and I shall have to refer to the latter in the course of my discussion. To make things easier for myself, I shall use the term "secondary quality" as Berkeley did – to refer to the mind-dependent qualities produced by the powers that Locke called secondary qualities. The difference in their terminology here will not be confusing if it is carefully noted. Evidently, Berkeley did not regard secondary qualities as Lockean powers because he did not believe that such things existed. In his view all genuine qualities are mind-dependent.

Agreeing with Locke that secondary qualities (as Berkeley understood them) exist only in the mind, Berkeley argued that primary qualities must also exist in the mind because the arguments showing secondary qualities to be mind-dependent also hold for primary qualities. What are these arguments that apply to both sorts of qualities? The answer is relativity-of-perception arguments.[46] Different observers with different perceptual apparatus perceiving a body from different positions will generally be aware of different primary qualities – different sizes, different shapes, different motions, and the like. But a particular object cannot have different sizes, shapes, or motions at the same time. Therefore, the varying primary qualities perceived in an object cannot be qualities of that object; they must be dependent on the nature of the observer. This conclusion is reinforced by the fact that the primary qualities we perceive in observing an object can be changed by an alteration in us or in our position. Obviously, a "real inherent property of any object" cannot be changed without changing that object – without a change that accounts for the alteration.[47] Since the primary qualities we observe can be changed without causing an underlying change in the object, those qualities must be every bit as observer-dependent as the qualities we call secondary.

Relativity-of-perception arguments have been hotly criticized in the contemporary period, but they deserve the attention they have been given. As against the first part of the argument, it has been objected that, although an object cannot have at any one time all the shapes and sizes that a variety of observers may discern in looking at it, it does not follow that it does not have as real, inherent properties a jointly compatible set of such properties. This objection is well taken, but its force is weakened by Berkeley's additional claim that changes in real, inherent properties require underlying changes in an object and that perceived primary changes can always be altered by changes in the observer or the observer's perspective. This additional claim, if true, does not prove that bodies do not have shapes, sizes, and motions as real, inherent qualities, but it does cast doubt on the idea that the shapes, sizes, and motions that observers immediately apprehend in their perceptual experience are the real, inherent qualities of existing physical bodies. The shapes and so forth that they apprehend seem to be as dependent on them and their circumstances as on anything in the bodies they perceive.

Some philosophers have claimed that an object's primary qualities (the qualities it actually has) are distinguished from its many apparent qualities by the special conditions in which they are discernible and by the judgment of special observers. The edge of a razor may appear serrated when viewed under a microscope, but if it looks straight to the naked eye, it is straight. Similarly, if the top of a desk feels smooth and solid to a normal observer, then it is smooth and solid – no matter what physicists may tell us about the gaps between its minute parts.[48] Berkeley had several replies to this sort of claim. He made one of them in connection with an analogous claim about color. His reply was cast in the form of a request that Philonous, his protagonist in *Three Dialogues*, puts to Hylas:

> I would fain know . . . from you what certain distance and position of the object, what peculiar texture and formation of the eye, what degree or kind of light is necessary for ascertaining [an object's] . . . true color, and distinguishing it from apparent ones.[49]

Although we now have (for semi-technical purposes) conventions about the sort of light in which an object's true color is discernible ("white light") and tests by which normal color-observers can be identified, we do not have anything like precise criteria for determining the true primary qualities of objects. For practical purposes, we can usually reach agreement about an object's shape, size, and motion, but we should not suppose that the informal, practical conventions we tacitly employ in such cases are theoretically satisfactory and can solve the problems Berkeley raised.

The theoretical limitations of our informal conventions stand out sharply when we consider that many highly significant features of an object's surfaces are admittedly not apparent to the naked eye. A surface may have become contaminated and will cause illness in those who touch it unless certain measures are taken. How is it contaminated? Perhaps by a harmful mold, which microscopic examination shows to be growing on its surface – a surface that supports the mold because its minute *irregularities* retain moisture. A more minute examination conducted with devices available today (for example, an electron microscope) will show the surface to be even more irregular; and the continuities apparent to the naked eye and the ungloved hand, however objective they may be said to be, will be declared to be mere objective appearances. Far from being "real inherent qualities," these objective appearances will be powers – powers to produce impressions of continuity, both visual and tactile, in normal observers. The shapes and sizes *immediately apprehended* are thus as mind-dependent as any secondary quality.

Perhaps Berkeley's most striking argument against the view that the primary qualities immediately perceived are sometimes objective, mind-independent attributes of physical things is based on the premiss that primary qualities cannot be perceived apart from secondary qualities. The premiss seems correct: any primary quality one actually perceives is distinguished by some associated secondary quality. This can be illustrated by the scarlet disk I mentioned earlier. In apprehending the disk one is visually aware of a circular expanse of scarlet; yet if all color were to disappear from one's perceptual field, the perceived circularity would disappear too. One might attempt to ascertain the presence of the disk by touch, but any circularity one might become aware of in this way will be distinguished by a tactile quality, a feel, that is as mind-dependent as a color-expanse or a pain. As a general matter, then, geometrical features (of which shapes and sizes are instances) are invariably distinguished in our experience, at least ultimately,[50] by some kind of "content quality" that is classifiable as secondary. If, as seems reasonable, we can perceive primary qualities only by perceiving items that are spread out in this or that way and have this or that shape,[51] then we shall always perceive primary qualities as features of mind-dependent realities that are occurrently colored, felt, or otherwise sensed. Features thus perceived are as mind-dependent as the realities they qualify.

Even if the primary qualities we immediately perceive are invariably mind-dependent, it does not follow that mind-independent bodies do not have mind-independent primary qualities. Berkeley recognized this, and met it with an argument about similarity. Since we are never aware of a mind-independent primary quality, we can conceive of such a quality only as something similar to qualities we are aware of. Having convinced himself that the latter exist only in the mind, Berkeley adopted Locke's terminology and spoke of them as ideas. In response to the suggestion that mind-independent objects may have qualities like the mind-dependent qualities we identify as primary, Berkeley (in the guise of Philonous) asked the rhetorical question:

> But how can that which is sensible be like that which is insensible? Can a real thing, in itself *invisible*, be like a *color*; or a real thing, which is not *audible*, be like a *sound*? In a word, can anything be like a sensation or idea, but another sensation or idea? [52]

His opponent, Hylas, had no answer to this, and Philonous felt that he had thereby disposed of the suggestion that mind-dependent sensible qualities could be like mind-independent ones, and vice versa.

To refute Berkeley's claim here, one has to provide acceptable reasons for thinking that a mind-independent quality may be relevantly like a mind-dependent one. I say "relevantly like" because entities may be like one another in various respects, some irrelevant to a given investigation. In the present context it cannot be assumed that a quality B is like a mind-dependent quality A only if B is mind-dependent as well, for the possibility of this kind of dissimilarity between otherwise similar qualities is assumed by the question at issue. That question is: Given a mind-dependent primary quality A and a mind-independent quality B, how could B be sufficiently similar to A in relevant respects (or vice versa) to count as a primary quality? To answer this question one has to explain how the relevant similarity is possible.

As a prelude to answering the question, it is useful to observe that if there are, as Locke thought, mind-independent objects with mind-independent geometrical features, then those objects must have qualities that are analogous, in significant respects, to Berkelean secondary qualities. The analogy concerns what I earlier referred to as the "content" needed for the exemplification of form. A geometrical feature like circularity can be exemplified by a thing only if that thing has some content quality that is spread out in two dimensions and is terminated circularly. If a color expanse is terminated circularly, it is a circular expanse. The primary qualities present in our immediate perceptual experience are distinguished by the sort of content that Berkeley calls a secondary quality, but primary qualities could conceivably be exemplified in and distinguished by qualities that are as different from the secondary qualities we are aware of as they are different among themselves. On the other hand, any qualities that could play the content role necessary for the exemplification of primary qualities are analogous (or similar) in an important respect. This respect gives us some understanding of what may be involved in a similarity or likeness between items that in certain respects are very dissimilar indeed.

We can now turn to the question about primary qualities: Could a mind-independent quality be sufficiently similar to a mind-dependent primary quality to be considered a primary quality as well? What is crucial in this question is the need to explain how a quality of the first sort could be similar to a quality of the second sort. Berkeley denied the possibility of such a similarity, asking, "What could be similar to an idea but another idea?" Considering the very broad sense in which the term "idea" was being used here, one might initially wonder why Berkeley should have been so confident that nothing could be similar to an idea but another idea. Surely, diagrams and pictures are similar to the things they represent, even when the latter are not themselves diagrams or pictures. If the colored and lined expanses we are aware of when, speaking with the vulgar, we say we are seeing diagrams and pictures are really mind-dependent (or ideas), then those expanses may still be similar to the things they represent even when these things are not themselves mental expanses.

Berkeley would have objected to this last comparison on the ground that if the objects supposedly represented by the diagrams and pictures are non-mental and mind-independent, they are fundamentally different from any idea or purely mental representation, which the diagrams and pictures are now assumed to be. Berkeley's claim that the two sorts of entity here are fundamentally different did not prove that a relevant similarity may not be present among the differences. A slightly wavy line written on paper may be "fundamentally different" from the path of a photon, yet the former could be used to represent the latter and is arguably similar to it in a relevant abstract respect. Berkeley had little patience with talk about abstract similarities, and he would not have been daunted by this last observation. The fact remains, however, that he did not succeed in ruling out the possibility of a relevant similarity between "mental" and non-mental geometrical features. Such a similarity may well be problematic; the point is simply that Berkeley did not demonstrate its impossibility.

As I explained earlier, Locke did not actually hold the view of primary qualities that Berkeley was attacking here. Locke did believe that physical things had occurrent primary qualities, but he thought that their real primary qualities were significantly different from (and not truly similar to) what we perceive. In his opinion, observable objects were aggregates of microscopic atoms, and the determinate primary qualities of these atoms (their size, shape, weight, motion, and arrangement) collectively account for the attributes (the powers and interactions) of the wholes. These aggregates do have primary qualities, but they are not what we perceive. Microscopes show us that pieces of furniture do not really have sharp edges or flat surfaces: they merely appear to have these qualities. Their real qualities are very complex and, in detail, unknown to us. Our general convictions about them are mere "probable opinions," based largely on "speculation."

It is interesting to observe that Cartesians typically take a position on primary qualities that is the opposite of Berkeley's. As they see it, the physical world is characterized by geometrical features, and the mental world lacks these features entirely. But what about the triangular expanses apparent in our experience? No such expanses are actually there, they say. Granted, we often seem to see such expanses, but we are not seeing a physical expanse, we are merely "sensing in a certain way" or having "confused ideas." When we are aware of color expanses, we are always having confused ideas in Descartes' opinion; for he did not believe that the beautiful red and purple we see in the clouds is really there: extended reality is, for him, occurrently colorless. Since external surfaces are not "united to our minds," as Locke put it, we cannot object to a theoretical relocation of the beautiful red and purple that we see. But these occurrent features should fit into the picture somewhere, and the geometrical features tied to them (their perceptible shape and size) should fit in *along with them*. This is one of the points Berkeley rightly insisted upon. Locke did not disagree; the geometrical qualities he claimed to be non-mental were the inferred qualities (individual and collective) of physical atoms.

6. *Berkeley's idealism*

According to Locke, the physical world consists of physical bodies, which are things having primary qualities and two sorts of powers: one to bring about or undergo physical changes as the result of physical interactions; the other to cause ideas in a mind by stimulating the senses of the body that it animates. Both sorts of powers are consequences, Locke thought, of the primary qualities of a thing's minute parts. Primary qualities are thus basic to physical bodies; fundamentally, bodies are *substrata* in which primary qualities inhere. Berkeley, finding the notion of a *substratum* incoherent or empty and regarding primary qualities as existing only in the mind, came to the conclusion that physical bodies are nothing but "bundles" of qualities (or "ideas") existing in some mind.

Although Locke confessed that his idea of a *substratum* was very obscure and imperfect, he thought that such things must exist because qualities exist. Qualities, he reasoned, are attributes, and attributes are things attributable to a subject. A *substratum* is simply a subject of attributes – something in which the attributes of a single thing are united: they "inhere" in it, and it "supports" them. If Berkeley was right in thinking that a thing's ultimate qualities (the qualities underlying and accounting for its observable powers) exist only in some mind, then the fact that a thing has a quality would not imply that a mind-independent *substratum* exists. Berkeley saw this point clearly,[53] but he opposed the conclusion with additional arguments. According to one, the conclusion is baseless, lacking all positive support; according to the other, it is inherently false or else meaningless.

It is admitted that a *substratum* is not perceived: the only things directly observable about a sensible object are its sensible qualities. As far as our observations are concerned, a sensible thing is, in fact, nothing but a "combination" of sensible qualities. Thus, we have no observational evidence for the existence of a *substratum*. If we attempt to demonstrate the existence of such a thing, we find that the idea of a *substratum* is either empty or inherently confused. The latter is true if we take the notion of a "support" for qualities literally. *S* can literally support *P*, or *P* can literally inhere in *S*, only if *S* is spatially extended: an unextended pin-cushion could not support a cluster of inhering pins. Yet extension is a primary quality and, as such, exists only in the mind. A mind-independent support for primary qualities is therefore an impossibility. On the other hand, if we do not take "support" and "inhere" literally, we do not know how to understand them, for no alternative account is offered. The idea of a non-extended support or a non-extended subject of inherence is then empty for us, and we have no determinate hypothesis to consider.

When Bertrand Russell commented on Berkeley's philosophy, he said that Berkeley was at least on firm ground in adopting his bundle theory of particulars:

> Things as we know them are bundles of sensible qualities: a table, for example, consists of its visual shape, its hardness, the noise it emits when rapped, and its smell (if any). These sensible qualities have certain contiguities in experience, which lead common sense to regard them as belonging to one "thing", but the concept of "thing" or "substance" adds nothing to the perceived qualities, and is unnecessary.[54]

This comment may seem level-headed and austere, but it actually contains some extravagant metaphysics. Are tables really composed of qualities, or of legs and a top? I should say the latter. Russell thought that a substantial thing is nothing but an imaginary hook on which attributes are hung;[55] but if attributes are treated as things that might (even figuratively) be hung on something, they will be subjects of attributes themselves – and therefore be higher-order imaginary hooks or higher-order bundles.[56]

However this last point may be, Berkeley's considered view of a particular is more difficult to interpret than Russell's remark indicates. He did speak of a particular thing as a "combination of sensible qualities or ideas," [57] but the disjunction is problematic: as he described them, qualities seem quite different from ideas. When he replied to the charge that if extension and figure exist only in the mind, the mind must itself be extended and figured, he said that these qualities are in the mind "not by way of *mode* or *attribute*, but only by way of *idea*." [58] This remark is not transparent in meaning, but it strongly suggests that a particular quality – for example, the bright yellow I am aware of when I view the notepad before me – cannot be the same, for Berkeley, as the "idea" of this quality. As an object before my mind, the yellow expanse is probably best described as the "content" of my idea: it is what the idea is "of," and it is present to mind "by way of idea," not "by way of attribute."

If particular colors are not present to mind by way of attribute, it would appear that they are not present to anything by way of attribute. Strictly speaking, nothing then should actually be colored, according to Berkeley's view. This sounds very dramatic, but it makes sense. According to Berkeley's form of idealism, the only things that actually exist are spirits and their ideas. Spirits are indivisible, unextended, immaterial beings, and neither they nor their ideas are colored or extended. Berkeley wrote as if particular things – cows, trees, and windmills – are combinations of ideas, but this is a rough-and-ready statement that needs careful qualification. One needed qualification concerns the attributes of particular things: we do not want to say that since cows give milk, certain combinations of ideas give it. As I pointed out in connection with Locke's views,[59] a new conception of an object often requires a new conception of the object's attributes or, more generally, a new interpretation of statements about the object that are still considered true. Berkeley's theory is not worked out in the kind of detail needed for an across-the-board interpretation of common-sense discourse, but he would probably say that a properly founded idea of a cow is the idea of a milk-giver. The content of this latter idea can be clarified, presumably, in terms of appropriate primary and secondary qualities. These qualities are not ideas, he would have to add, but idea-contents: our ideas are naturally supplied with such things.

It is worth mentioning here that, unlike Russell, Berkeley did not believe in abstract qualities: for him, "everything which exists is particular." [60] Properties such as *extension* or *redness* do not therefore exist, in his opinion. (He even denied that we can form ideas of such qualities: an abstract idea is as fictional in his view as an abstract quality.[61]) When he spoke of qualities, he had highly determinate features in mind, and he emphasized that they normally exist blended together in single objects.[62] The bright yellow I spoke about is no doubt a case in point: it is joined to a particular quality of extension, being spread out rectangularly in my visual field. I should naturally describe the yellow rectangle I am immediately perceiving as a piece of paper, but it must be something else because it lacks weight and texture, which a piece of paper properly possesses. (Berkeley insisted that things immediately perceived have only the qualities they are perceived as having.[63]) The thing I am immediately perceiving, evidently, is the facing surface of a piece of paper – something that should belong to the bundle that the paper officially is. The facing surface exists "in my mind" as the content of a perceptual idea; and this content is a "combination" of determinate qualities.

If Berkeley is best understood as saying that sensible objects are bundles of idea-contents, in whose mind are the ideas best understood as existing? Berkeley's answer is "all minds whatsoever." [64] In an early passage of his *Principles* he wrote:

> The table I write on I say exists; that is, I see and feel it: and
> if I were out of my study I should say it existed; meaning
> thereby that if I was in my study I might perceive it, or that
> some other spirit actually does perceive it. There was an
> odour, that is, it was smelt; there was a sound, that is, it was
> heard . . . [and so on].[65]

According to this passage, a sensible thing exists when it is perceived or might be perceived. Berkeley emphasized this last possibility in a later passage, saying that the question whether the earth moves when it is not perceived to do so amounts to no more than "whether we have reason to conclude . . . that if we were placed in such and such circumstances, and such or such a position and distance both from the earth and the sun, we should perceive the former to move." [66] In his *Three Dialogues* he developed the view that sensible things not dependent on the thought of Tom, Dick, or Mary are perceived by God.[67]

These views of the existence of sensible things raise a number of problems that Berkeley did not consider or attempt to solve. One concerns the identity conditions for a particular sensible object. The idea-contents that compose the bundle with which Berkeley identifies a particular sensible thing are both actual and merely possible (= what would be perceived if . . .) and they are distributed among various minds, both finite and divine. How is a given bundle unified? Which ideas from which minds belong to it? Berkeley did not deal with these questions. Another problem (widely discussed in the twentieth century) concerns the idea of a possible or conditional perception. In discussing the movement of the earth, Berkeley spoke of the perceptions we would have if we were in such and such circumstances, related in such and such a way to the earth, and so on. Since physical circumstances and spatial relations exist only in the mind on his view, a possible perception is ultimately identifiable only in relation to some actual perceptions that are sufficient to specify the conditions of its occurrence. But can a possible perception actually be identified this way? Are any actual perceptions sufficient for this task? Berkeley did not deal with these questions either.

Some equally important questions to ask about Berkeley's system concern his notion of a mind or spirit. How are we to conceive of such a thing? In a famous notebook entry written in preparation for his *Principles*, Berkeley adopted a bundle theory of mind, saying:

> Mind is a congeries of Perceptions. Take away Perceptions and you take away the Mind; put the Perceptions and you put the Mind.[68]

Obviously, this view accords with his bundle theory of sensible bodies: perceptions (or ideas) are the correlates of sensible qualities, and neither inheres in a distinct subject or *substratum*. Although Hume developed this sort of view about twenty-five years later, Berkeley retreated to a more Cartesian view in his *Principles* and *Three Dialogues*. In these works he said that a mind is a spirit, an unextended, indivisible, and therefore immaterial thing, which thinks and acts and perceives.[69] He admitted that he does not have an actual idea of his mind or any mind, but he has, "by a reflex act," an immediate and intuitive knowledge of his own mind that is comparable to his knowledge of his own ideas. He lacks an idea of a mind because ideas must be like the things they are of (or represent) and "nothing can be like an idea but another idea." Minds, as he knows from his own case, are very unlike ideas: they are essentially "active," whereas ideas are "inert" or "passive." Though his "reflective" knowledge of his nature as an active thing cannot, strictly speaking, be represented by an idea, it does give him a "notion" of his self. The notion is legitimate because it is supported by immediate, reflective knowledge.

Though highly imaginative and based on subtle arguments, Berkeley's idealism is a shaky doctrine open to attack on several fronts. One obvious point of weakness concerns the existence of unperceived objects such as the back of one's head or a tree in the quad. Berkeley argued that sensible things do not depend on us for their existence because it is not in our power "to determine at pleasure" what perceptions we shall have when (as we believe!) we open our eyes and ears, or look in a mirror.[70] The argument is weak because, as Descartes observed, we lack the power to determine the course of our dreams. Given the existence of unobserved sensible things, Berkeley argues that an infinite mind, God, must exist to perceive them. Since they are, in his view, mere bundles of ideas, they are inert, inactive things, and they cannot therefore be causes.[71] What causes the perceptions whose independence of our will assures us that unperceived sensible objects exist? Not those objects, but God. Yet if they are powerless to account for our unchosen perceptions, we have no rational basis for accepting their existence in the first place. Do the unchosen perceptions I myself have justify the conclusion that an infinite mind exists? Hardly. They could conceivably be produced by a Cartesian demon or a mad scientist with a super-super computer. Skepticism looms – the specter that, along with atheism, Berkeley's Idealism was officially constructed to oppose. Hume, the subject of the next chapter, drew the necessary conclusions.

CHAPTER III

Hume and Solipsism

It is often said that Hume carried the epistemological principles of British empiricism to their logical conclusion. This is no doubt close to the truth, but it is not exactly right. Hume's epistemological conclusions were consequences of principles that he was the first to formulate precisely. There is a family resemblance between them and the principles employed by Locke and Berkeley, but they are not exactly the same. Hume is the first clear example of a modern empiricist.

1. Hume's epistemic principles

According to Hume, the matters we can think about and attempt to ascertain fall into two mutually exclusive groups: "relations of ideas" and "matters of fact and existence." [1] This division in what Hume called the objects of human inquiry was implicit in Locke's discussion of knowledge,[2] and Hume was clearly indebted to that discussion. Nevertheless, his aim in introducing the distinction was to clarify a wider subject than knowledge: his target was what we would call rational opinion. Recognizing that the various "objects of inquiry" are ascertained in fundamentally different ways and that our evidence of their truth is correspondingly different as well, Hume traced these differences to a distinction his recent admirers have identified with the analytic–synthetic distinction first drawn by Kant.[3] Hume's distinction is not the same as the analytic–synthetic distinction, but it is drawn in a comparable epistemic spirit and it has similar consequences.

Like Locke, Berkeley, and other philosophers of their time, Hume thought that we think by means of ideas, which we form from experiences of a more primitive kind. These ideas constitute

57

the meanings of our words: words express them and "convey" them to others. Although Hume acknowledged that some of our ideas are faint or obscure, he thought we can generally ascertain their nature or content if we attend carefully to them. Our ability to do this is the foundation for the sciences of geometry, algebra, and arithmetic – in short, for "every affirmation which is either intuitively or demonstratively certain." These affirmations, because they concern mere relations among our ideas, can be discovered to be true "by the mere operation of thought, without dependence on what is anywhere existent in the universe." Even if a triangle or circle never existed in nature, "the truths demonstrated by Euclid would for ever retain their certainty and evidence." [4]

Hume's view here is essentially the same as Locke's. Like Locke, he thought that certain relations between our ideas are immediately or intuitively apparent to us, and that we can know other relations by demonstration. Hume did not mention the relevant relations in his later, ostensibly definitive *Enquiry Concerning Human Understanding* (1748), but in his *Treatise of Human Nature* (1739) he cited three relations between our ideas that are "discoverable at first sight" and thus "fall under the province of intuition – namely, *resemblance, contrariety*, and *degrees of quality*." [5] He allowed that it is impossible to judge exactly when an idea-quality of color, heat, or cold exceeds another in a minute degree, but he thought there could be little problem judging such a thing immediately when the degree of difference is large. As for "demonstratively" knowable relations, the case he cited was *proportions in quantity or number*. He noted that we can achieve certainty about this relation because we have a precise standard for estimating quantities. The standard concerns the "equality of units," which we can ascertain mediately by counting.

These four relations are very important because they show us how different Hume's distinction is from the analytic–synthetic distinctions of latter-day analytic philosophers. The distinctions are similar in tracing the certainty of an *a priori* proposition to (roughly speaking) meanings rather than objective facts, but they are very different in points of detail. In Hume the focus is on mental contents, or ideas, and on a person's ability to discern – to recognize either immediately or by a number of distinct steps – certain relations between them. In some cases what is known in this way would not count as analytically true by a recent account. Consider two color-ideas whose "objects" (or contents) are reddish expanses, one redder than the other. Although this relation between the ideas is knowable intuitively on Hume's view, the corresponding assertion would be logically synthetic on a view like Gottlob Frege's because the words "occurrently redder than" are not explicitly definable and the assertion cannot (as a consequence) be reduced to a logical truth.[6]

When Hume contrasted the possible objects of inquiry, he did say "the contrary of every matter of fact is still possible because it can never imply a contradiction" – thus implying that the contrary of propositions expressing mere relations of ideas do imply contradictions. How can we account for this if what I have just said is true? One possibility is that Hume, not having a subsequent conception of analyticity to worry about, did not appreciate the significance of the case I mentioned involving *redder than* (it did not arise for him). Another possibility is that he thought of a contradiction in a much more informal way than we do today. I think the latter is more likely than the former. His general view, as I see it, was that the denial of an assertion expressing a mere relation of ideas explicitly asserts something that can be seen to be false (directly or indirectly) by anyone who understands it. What it asserts "cannot," as Hume put it, "be distinctly conceived by the mind" because it is, in a way, incoherent. It is not explicitly contradictory – any more than an assertion of "I cannot speak" or "I do not exist" is explicitly contradictory.[7] Rather, the states of affairs or idea-relations it immediately or mediately brings to mind are "contradicted" by what it explicitly says. As a result, the total message it conveys cannot be conceived by the mind as a distinct possibility.

In the *Treatise* Hume said that propositions truly expressing the relations of ideas are objects of knowledge and certainty, the certainty depending, he said, on relations that are "unalterable so long as the ideas remain the same." [8] By contrast, propositions expressing matters of fact and existence are objects of probability and uncertainty. This classification is virtually the same as Locke's; it differs only in the status it assigns to certain propositions that Locke put in the "known to be true" class even though they did not, strictly speaking, satisfy his definition – I mean those affirming the existence of one's self, God, and objects affecting our senses.[9] Hume altered his twofold classification when he spoke of probability, however. In his *Enquiry* he said that "to conform our language more to common use, we ought to divide arguments into *demon-strations, proofs,* and *probabilities.*" [10] The conclusion of a proof is a statement like "All men must die." Such statements are not commonly described as merely probable; ordinarily understood, they "leave no room for doubt or opposition." A proof, as Hume understood it, is not a demonstration; it is "an argument from experience" whose evidential basis is so strong that a reasonable person would have no doubt about (or "opposition" to) its conclusion.

How, all things considered, are matters of fact and existence ascertained, according to Hume? His loaded answer is short and sweet: By "the present testimony of our senses," the "records of our memory," proofs, and probabilities. This answer is loaded because his views on the testimony of our senses, the records of our memory, and the forms of experimental inference that he allowed in proofs and probabilities can be adequately understood only after some careful discussion. Assuming that we have a general idea of what he probably meant by the present testimony of our senses and the records of our memory, we can form a useful picture of his general position on matters of fact by noting his summary claim that all our reasoning concerning matters of fact is founded on "a species of analogy," which leads us to expect from any cause the same sort of effect that we have observed to result from similar causes. Hume's subsequent remarks show that this summary claim applies to proofs as well as probabilities:

> Where the causes are entirely similar, the analogy is perfect, and the inference drawn from it is regarded as certain and conclusive. . . . But where the objects have not so exact a similarity, the analogy is less perfect and the inference is less conclusive – though it still has some force in proportion to the degree of similarity and resemblance. [11]

Although Hume's epistemic principles are fairly stated by the remarks I have made in this section, he has a special critical principle, which I should also mention here. This principle concerns meaning or significance rather than truth or probability. I mentioned earlier that, for Hume, the meaning of a word is the idea "annexed" to it, the idea it expresses. It often happens, Hume thought, that words appearing in abstract discourse (particularly that of philosophers) are not really annexed to ideas: strictly speaking, such words are meaningless, though they are not generally believed to be so. Since these words are abstract and abstruse, it is commonly difficult to decide whether they are annexed to an idea or not. A principle is needed here, and Hume supplied one. In his view any term not satisfying his principle can safely be regarded as meaningless.

Hume's principle of meaning is derived from his view of the human mind and the origin of its ideas. As he could tell from his own experience, the perceptions of the human mind (all its occurrent furniture) can be divided into two classes, depending on their "force and vivacity." For lack of a better term, he called the liveliest perceptions "impressions," taking them to be "original occurrences" produced in the mind by (he believed) objects affecting his senses and by the mind's own objects and activities. (In the *Treatise* he divided impressions into many subclasses, the most general being impressions of sense and impressions of reflection.) He called the less lively perceptions, the fainter and duller ones, "ideas": these, he believed, are "copies" of the lively ones, or they are made up of such copies. Ideas naturally come to mind when an experience is recalled to memory or something is anticipated by the imagination. They are, he added, the basic materials of our thought: the creative power of the mind amounts to no more than the faculty of compounding, transposing, augmenting, or diminishing them.[12]

As these last remarks indicate, a genuine idea is either simple or complex. If it is simple, it is a "copy" (a natural trace) of an original impression. If it is complex, it is built up from simple ideas. Hume supported this view by empirical considerations. In the first place, when we analyze our ideas or thoughts, we always find that, however "compounded or sublime" they may be, we always find that they resolve themselves into simple ideas that have been copied from a preceding feeling or sentiment. Anyone who disagrees with this claim has only to find an idea that cannot be so resolved. For his part, Hume has not found any, and he challenged his opponents to bring one forth.[13] In the second place, if we examine a person who lacks some sense, we find that he lacks the corresponding ideas. "A blind man can form no notion of colors; a deaf man of sounds." But restore to either the sense he is lacking, and you will "open a new inlet for sensations" and find that he has no difficulty forming the appropriate ideas. There is, he admitted, one possible exception to this that he could think of. If a man who has enjoyed his sight for thirty years and been acquainted with all colors except a certain shade of blue is presented with a chart containing the other shades of blue in an order descending from the deepest to the lightest, he will no doubt be able to form an idea of the shade that is missing. But this exception is so "singular," Hume said, that it does not require him to alter his maxim.

If a word is meaningful, it is annexed to a definite idea. How can we tell if something is a definite idea? Hume's answer is: "Find the impression from which it is derived! " If no such impression can be found, the impression that a word is being used without meaning or idea will be confirmed.[14] Actually, Hume's answer is oversimplified. Important ideas, ideas annexed to words of philosophical importance, are generally complex, built up from simpler ideas. Hume's injunction thus applies only to simple ideas, the elements of complex ones. To discover whether a word is associated with a definite idea, we really have to ascertain several things: Is it associated with any simple ideas? If so, which ones? And how are these simple ideas arranged in the complex? This last question is very important because, although Hume did not mention any principles of coherent idea formation, such principles must exist for a theory like his. I doubt if an idea such as *damp souls of housemaids sprouting at area gates* [15] or *the square root of Mary's smile* could make a word meaningful.

As I have described them in this section, Hume's epistemic principles can be summarized as follows. If words are meaningful and express (when suitably arranged in sentences) a definite "object of inquiry," then those words are annexed to definite ideas that can be traced back to original impressions. An object of inquiry is either a mere relation of ideas or a matter of fact and existence. If it is the former, it is independent of anything that is "anywhere existent in the universe" and can be ascertained *a priori* by "the mere operation of thought" – that is, by intuition or demonstration. If it is a matter of fact and existence, it can be ascertained by the present testimony of our senses, the records of our memories, or by experimental inference, the latter being arguments from experience that are either proofs or probabilities. In the famous concluding paragraph of his *Enquiry Concerning the Human Understanding*, Hume emphasized the power of these principles by considering the havoc we should make if we used them to evaluate the contents of a library:

If we take in hand any volume – of divinity or school metaphysics, for instance – let us ask, *Does it contain any abstract reasoning concerning quantity or number?* No. *Does it contain any experimental reasoning concerning matters of fact and existence?* No. Commit it then to the flames, for it can contain nothing but sophistry and illusion.[16]

2. Hume on experimental inference

Critical principles of such potency deserve careful examination, and Hume, curiously, was the first to provide it. In fact, his title for the chapter in the *Enquiry* where he introduced his principles is "Sceptical Doubts Concerning the Operations of the Understanding." In the present section I shall discuss his skeptical doubts about experimental inference. In a later section I shall discuss his skeptical doubts about the testimony of our senses and our memory, and shall also comment critically on his claims about meaning and comprehensible objects of inquiry.

Hume began his discussion of experimental inference with the observation:

All reasonings concerning matter of fact seem to be founded on the relation of *Cause and Effect*. By means of that relation alone we can go beyond the evidence of our memory and senses.[17]

He supported this observation with examples in which the existence or presence of some thing is inferred from an observed phenomenon: the author of a letter is inferred from the handwriting on the letter, the existence of a human being on an island is inferred from a watch that is found there, and the presence of a person is inferred from a voice heard in the dark. This kind of evidence does not prove that all reasoning by which matters of fact are ascertained is causal, but it does make us realize that, at least in a good share of such reasoning, causation is "either near or remote, direct or collateral." [18]

Since Hume is commonly said to have been concerned with inductive reasoning here, it is worth observing that he was very casual about identifying the logical structure of what he called "experimental inferences." His actual words accord with the view, which it would probably be anachronistic to ascribe to him, that experimental conclusions are obtained by arguments of widely varying logical forms. In some cases he clearly seemed to suppose that a matter of fact is inferred from a causal principle and an observed phenomenon. If, explicitly using the principle "Bread is nourishing," a man were to conclude that the bread he is holding is nourishing, his experimental reasoning could be reconstructed as a syllogism:

All bread is nourishing
All this is bread.
Therefore, all this is nourishing.

In other cases (for example, when he wrote about reasoning in animals) [19] Hume seemed to suppose that the reasoning merely accords with a causal principle, as in:

This is bread.
So, this is nourishing.

In this last sort of case Hume supposed that the reasoner's knowledge of the effects of a thing disposes her to expect similar effects in similar things. The inference is "founded on" the relation of cause and effect in the sense that the reasoner's knowledge of certain causes and effects creates a "general habit" of expecting (or inferring) certain sorts of effects from certain sorts of objects, and vice versa.

Having identified the relation on which experimental inference is founded, Hume proceeded to consider how we arrive at the "knowledge of this relation."[20] His initial claim was that the knowledge of this relation (he meant the knowledge of a causal principle) is not, in any instance, attained by *a priori* reasoning; it invariably arises from the experience of the "objects" involved. He supported this claim by two basic observations. The first is that every effect is a distinct event from its cause and cannot, therefore, be discovered in the cause: any *a priori* conception of either cause or effect would be "entirely arbitrary." The second is that even if we were supplied *a priori* with the conceptions we term cause and effect, we would not thereby be supplied with the connection between them.

When I see . . . a Billiard-ball moving in a straight line
towards another – even suppose motion in the second ball
should be suggested to me as the result of their contact or
impulse – may I not conceive that a hundred different events
might as well follow from that cause? May not both balls
remain at absolute rest? May not the first ball return in a
straight line, or leap off from the second in any line or
direction? All these suppositions are consistent and
conceivable.[21]

That a certain sort of event has a particular cause or effect is a
matter (not of reason but) of fact and existence; to ascertain such a
thing, we must appeal to *experience*.

A contemporary objection to Hume's appeal to experience here is
that a principle is analytic (or knowable *a priori*) not by virtue of
the objects it refers to but by virtue of its means of referring to
them. A bug's act of biting something is "distinct" from the effect it
brings about; yet the principle "Bugbites are the effects of a bug's
bite" is true by definition. The reply Hume would have made to this
is easy to imagine. Since "bugbites" means "the effects of a bug's
bite," the suggested "principle" is mere shorthand for "Any effect of
a bug's bite is an effect of a bug's bite" – and this is no more a causal
principle than "mass times acceleration = mass times acceleration"
is a law of nature. If one wants to insist (in what Hume called "a
spirit of pugnacious captiousness") that the tautological sentence *is*
a causal principle, then the claim Hume was really concerned to
make can be saved by a minor amendment: empirically informative
causal principles are not true *a priori*; they are ascertained only by
experience.

How does experience yield the knowledge in question? What is
the foundation (as Hume put it) of these conclusions from experience? Hume's first response was a negative answer: even after we
experience the operations of cause and effect, the conclusions we
form "are *not* founded on reasoning, or any process of the
understanding." [22]

Hume's defense of this negative answer began with a description
of the experience on which the relevant conclusions (about causes
and effects) are based. This experience is invariably of certain
objects "attended" with certain effects. This is all we actually
experience. This experience includes no "necessary connection"

between the objects and their effects; the most it discloses is a constant conjunction between object and effect: whenever an object of kind A is experienced, an effect of kind B is experienced with it. That is all there is. One billiard ball is observed to hit another; the other is observed immediately to move (and a noise is heard). This sort of experience is repeated again and again. The observer soon forms the belief that when (in such circumstances) one billiard ball strikes another, it causes the latter to move.

Hume concluded his defense of his negative answer by arguing that the sort of experience on which causal principles are founded provides no *rational basis* for the conclusion that these principles are true. His argument is short and clear. Causal principles tell us what effects objects *will* have as well as what effects they have had or have right now. Yet the experience supporting these principles is restricted to the past and present; it does not (because it cannot) include future objects. Since there is no contradiction in the idea that the effects of future objects will be different from those we have experienced or are now experiencing, our experiential evidence provides no intuitive or demonstrative basis for any causal principle. As far as our *reason* is concerned, we therefore have no basis for accepting a causal principle. Demonstrative reasoning (and intuition) concerns the mere relations of ideas, and these relations are incapable of identifying true principles that concern matters of fact and existence.

Demonstrative reasoning is not the only kind we are capable of, however. Can't we support causal principles by probable arguments – arguments concerned with matters of fact rather than relations of ideas? Well, we do use such arguments, but their rational credentials are what is in question here. For our present purposes, a probable argument would be useless. As Hume put it:

> We have said that all arguments concerning existence are founded on the relation of cause and effect; that our knowledge of that relation is derived entirely from experience; and that all our experimental conclusions proceed upon the supposition that the future [or future objects] will be conformable to the past [or present and past objects]. To endeavor, therefore, the proof of this last supposition by probable arguments, or arguments regarding existence, must be

evidently going in a circle, and taking that for granted, which is the very point in question.[23]

I noted earlier that Hume introduced his epistemic principles in a chapter whose title is "Sceptical Doubts Concerning the Operations of the Understanding." His claim that our conclusions from experience cannot be rationally supported expressed his principal skeptical doubt about the human understanding. In the following chapter he offered a "skeptical solution" to this doubt, arguing that conclusions from experience do have a firm basis – even though their basis is not reason or some operation of the understanding. The basis is "custom or habit," a mental mechanism that determines our expectations, our beliefs, and the inferences we make. This "solution" to a legitimate skeptical doubt has brought little comfort to the minds of many of Hume's readers, but it is very important and I want to say something about it.

When Hume said that all "inferences from experience" are the effects of custom or habit, he actually understated his case, for every inference is an effect of the reasoner's habits. Philosophers who deal with very simple logical paradigms often fail to see this point, imagining that reason of itself can select the conclusion to be drawn from a set of premises. The error they make leaps to mind when it is pointed out that infinitely many conclusions can be drawn with equal validity from any set of premises: no single conclusion is distinguished by logic. If one is presented with the premises P and *If P then Q*, one will naturally think of Q as a proper conclusion rather than P, $P \& Q$, $P v P$, and countless others that are validly drawn, but one will think this way only because of one's custom or habit of using *modus ponens*. This is a particularly simple inference pattern, but it is not distinguished by the general notion of validity. It is not even needed to get Q from P and *If P then Q*: this can be validly done in literally countless ways.[24]

The claim that custom rather than reason selects our experiential conclusions can be understood two ways, both of which accord with Hume's position. One is that reason in the guise of intuition and demonstration cannot select a particular causal principle that is to be inferred from the testimony of our senses and our memory. As I have noted, this claim has a counterpart in the case of the consequences warranted by logic or demonstration. The other way of understanding Hume's claim is that reason in the guise of

67

intuition and deduction cannot determine, on the basis of the stated evidence, which causal principles (if any) are true. This last claim does not have a counterpart in the case of demonstration. Reason may not be able to select the conclusion we are to draw from certain premises, but it is capable of determining whether the conclusion *we* select is demonstrated (shown to be true) by those premises.

Hume's skeptical doubts about experimental inference are focused on the fact that the truth of an experimental conclusion is not insured by the truth of the relevant premises. It is obvious that the *truth* of the conclusion is not insured by the premises of an experimental inference because such conclusions are sometimes false. If, on the basis of scratching a lot of matches and seeing them light, I conclude that the next one I scratch will also light, I shall be making an experimental inference whose conclusion might well be false. Good, reasonably drawn experimental conclusions are not, therefore, guaranteed to be true if their premises are true. Is there any sort of guarantee that they do provide? Hume did not deal with this question himself, but his skeptical doubt applies to an answer that might reasonably be given. This answer is that the experimental conclusions drawn from true premises must be true *more often than not* if the inference is of an acceptable kind. Hume's doubt applies to this answer because there is no way of proving that the conclusions drawn from past, present, and future experimental inferences actually have this property. They may have been true more often than not in the past, but there is no way of knowing what the future will bring.

But what about probability? Can't we say that the conclusions of good experimental inferences are probable? The answer to this question depends on what we mean by "probable" or, to use the noun, "probability." If we conceive of probability as frequency of truth, we might regard a conclusion of kind C as probable to degree n in relation to premises of kind E if conclusions of this kind are true n per cent of the time when premises E are true. Hume's doubt applies to probable conclusions so understood, for we cannot demonstrate anything about the frequency of true experimental conclusions in the future. If we conceive of probability in a different way, the situation is different. As it happens, Hume introduced a notion of probability that we *can* justifiably apply (given his arguments) to our experimental conclusions. This notion of probability is an appendage to Hume's skeptical solution of his doubts.

Hume's conception of probability conforms to what is now called a "subjectivist" or "personalist" conception.[25] Hume was a little unclear about what probability is, but he associated it with the degree to which something is believed or expected. In his section "Of Probability" in the first *Enquiry*, he remarked that there are two sorts of probability, or two bases for it; he called them "the probability of chances" and "the probability of causes." Hume used the example of a die to illustrate this first sort of probability. If a die has six spots on each of four sides and a single spot on the remaining two sides, a normal person considering the possible outcomes of a roll will be more confident (believe more strongly) that a six will turn up than that a one will. Although Hume was not entirely explicit about it, he seemed to identify the relevant probabilities – the probability of the relevant "chances" – with the degrees of expectation or belief that are naturally formed here. These probabilities can be considered objective because they are founded on an objective property of the human mind, a mental mechanism of belief-formation. They can also be considered subjective because they are associated with a property of the observing subject rather than the objects the subject observes.

Hume's "probability of causes" is intimately connected with his views on experimental inference. Custom determines us, he said, to transfer the past to the future: to expect similar effects from similar causes. Where our experience of certain objects has been "entirely regular and uniform," we expect similar effects from similar objects "with the greatest assurance and leave no room for any contrary supposition." But when different effects have been found to follow causes that appear similar to us, we expect such effects from similar causes in proportion to their relative frequency in our experience, and we believe they will occur with corresponding degrees of firmness. Thus, if 80 per cent of the matches we have scratched on a rough surface have lighted, we will strongly expect (be 80 per cent confident) that the next match we strike on a similar surface will light as well. Since a conclusion of this kind is, for Hume, a probable one, we can say that the evidence regarding matches makes it 80 per cent probable, for us, that the next one we scratch will in fact light.

Is what is probable for us probable for the next person, or do probabilities vary with each investigator? The answer Hume would have given, I think, is that investigators with different evidence will disagree about the probability of a conclusion, but they will agree about it if they agree about the evidence – and the latter will depend entirely on the experience they have. Assuming that normal observers receive similar experiences from the same natural objects and also that they can (as he emphasized) modify each others' beliefs by rational discussion, Hume could have said that a community of rational investigators will tend to move toward a consensus on the probability of causes. Such probabilities will thus be objective in a important sense: experienced investigators can agree about them.

I introduced Hume's conception of probability in connection with the question whether the conclusions of good experimental inferences can be said to be probably true. Hume clearly agreed that they are probable, for observers with the relevant experience will believe them with the required degree of firmness – and believing a conclusion is equivalent to believing that it is true. This was Hume's "solution" to his skeptical doubt. The solution remains skeptical because he admitted (indeed, insisted) that the beliefs in question are *rationally* unfounded: there is (there can be) no proof that they are true even more often than not. As far as we *know*, they may be false as often as they are true.

Philosophers unhappy with Hume's skeptical solution to his doubts about experimental inference often agree with this last claim; they agree, that is, that we do not actually *know* that our experimental conclusions will turn out to be true more often than not. They are unhappy with Hume's solution because they think it is *reasonable* to trust these conclusions – to believe that they will be true more often than not. To say, as Hume did, that normal people who are reasonable in the sense of being serious about evidence do in fact have this belief *because of the way their minds happen to work* does not show, these philosophers say, that such people are reasonable in a commendable sense, or that the belief deserves to be accepted. To make this charge stick, one must explain what the desired sort of reasonableness – the "commendable" sort – is supposed to be. I shall have a lot to say about this matter in the chapters to follow.

One final point. The experimental conclusions I have been talking about thus far have been restricted in generality: they concern objects declared to be similar to certain others that have been observed. Such conclusions are significantly unlike the ones usually identified in discussions of induction. According to the discussions I have in mind, if the objects of a large and varied class, A, have been observed to have some property P, the inductive conclusion to draw in the absence of conflicting evidence is "All A's are P" rather than "The next A will be P." Hume's discussion of experimental inference makes it clear that he thinks our experience makes us form both kinds of belief, but his discussion of probability is focused (in the way I have explained) on the latter sort. It is, however, easy to unify his view. If just 80 per cent of the many matches we have struck on a rough surface have lighted, then we will be 80 per cent confident that the next match we scratch on such a surface will light and a 100 per cent confident that 80 per cent of all matches so struck will light. As we shall see, this sort of view is a bit crude, but it is an important step on the way to an adequate conception of experimental inference.

3. Hume and the road to solipsism

According to Hume, our beliefs about matters of fact are naturally formed in three basic ways: by observation, memory, and experimental (or causal) inference. Having argued that the conclusions we form by causal inference are not rationally defensible, he devoted the last parts or chapters of his great works on the human understanding, the *Treatise* and the *Enquiry*, to a discussion of skepticism. In these concluding discussions he investigated the rational credentials of observation. As in the case of our experimental conclusions, the result of his investigation was negative: even our most confidently held observational beliefs are rationally unfounded.

In the *Enquiry* Hume opened his discussion of these beliefs with a general remark about their natural basis:

> It seems evident that men are carried by a natural instinct or prepossession to repose faith in their senses and that, without any reasoning or even almost before the use of reason, we always suppose an external universe which depends not on perception but would exist though we or every sensible creature were absent or annihilated.[26]

When people follow this blind and powerful instinct, he added, they "always suppose the very images presented by the senses to be the external objects" and "never entertain any suspicion that the one are nothing but representations of the other." The very table we see to be white and feel to be hard is believed to exist independent of our perception and to be something external to our mind, which perceives it. It is also believed to preserve its existence "uniform and entire, independent of the situation of intelligent beings, who perceive or contemplate it." But this universal and primary opinion "of all men" is "destroyed by the slightest philosophy, which teaches us that nothing can ever be present to a mind but an image or perception, and that the senses are only inlets through which these images are conveyed" – not means of "immediate intercourse" between the mind and an external object.[27]

The supposition Hume claimed we are naturally induced to make here has seemed purely imaginary to many contemporary philosophers. No one, they say, ever supposes such a thing. People do suppose that a table they see to be white and feel to be hard exists independent of their perception and external to their mind; but an object of this kind is certainly not a mind-independent image, and it certainly does not represent something external to the mind. Our senses disclose perceptual objects to us; they are not inlets through which mysterious representations are conveyed. In contrasting an imaginary and bizarre instinctive supposition with the object of an erroneous (or confused) philosophical lesson, Hume opened his discussion with a serious blunder that started him off in the wrong direction. No wonder he ended up struggling with solipsism!

The most that can be said in defense of this captious objection is that Hume's language is unusual and also slightly misleading; his discussion contains no blunder and shows no confusion on his part. We ordinarily speak of seeing such things as desks, and we commonly suppose (at least if we are not philosophers) that the things we see exist external to and independent of our consciousness. When we think of a white thing, we ordinarily think of a visible thing – something with an occurrent whiteness spread out over its surface and perhaps permeating its interior as whiteness permeates the interior of an apple. The whiteness we have in mind, like the beautiful red and purple Berkeley saw in the clouds, is not a mere power whose existence must be inferred but something that can be immediately apprehended. When we are immediately aware of such an expanse, we generally suppose that the white thing we are thus aware of is a physical thing that exists external to, and independent of, our consciousness. Yet the occurrently white expanse we apprehend is really not (we are told) in the external world; it somehow belongs to our consciousness. In Hume's terminology, some of the things belonging thus vividly to our consciousness are mere images. This usage is not usual or wholly ordinary, but it is easy to understand.

When Hume spoke of the referents of terms such as "this house" and "that tree" as being images, perceptions in the mind, and fleeting copies or representations of other existences, he was making Berkeley's assumption that the normally intended referents of such terms are sensible objects, not inferred objects with inferred powers. Although the expanses we are immediately aware of when (as we say) we perceive a white desk from several angles differ in the attributes we associate with the words "size" and "shape," we believe we are perceiving the same colored thing. This remark is open to criticism so long as we think of color "naively," as Berkeley did and as Hume thinks we ordinarily do: either there is more than one object of visual apprehension or the object of apprehension is something other than an image – perhaps it is a complex of images. But Hume never implied that all is well with the object of our instinctive belief.[28] He claimed that "we are necessitated by reasoning to contradict or depart from the primary instincts of nature and to embrace a new system with regard to our senses." [29]

The new system that Hume thought philosophy requires us to embrace is presumably Locke's, but he did not dwell on details when he emphasized its importance. Its distinctive feature, for him, is the distinction it draws between external objects and the sensory effects they produce in our consciousness. Light from the clouds stimulates our eyes, our nerves, and our brain; as a result, we have sensory experiences that represent those clouds and their features to us. If Locke was right, these sensory experiences vary significantly in representational fidelity, but they constitute our evidential basis for believing in objects of perception. The vital point to grasp initially is that the natural, instinctive system cannot be right; we must (for theoretical purposes) adopt a new one in which the distinction between external objects and sensory effects is carefully drawn.

Unfortunately, the new system cannot be justified, Hume added. The difficulty concerns the available means of proving that the perceptions of the mind are caused by external objects that are "entirely different from them, though resembling them (if that be possible)." Since it is a question of fact whether these external objects exist, the only possible means of settling it is by appealing to experience. But here, Hume said, experience is and must be entirely silent:

> The mind has never anything present to it but the perceptions and cannot possibly reach any experience of their connection with objects. The supposition of such a connection is, therefore, without any foundation in reasoning.[30]

The force of this argument flows directly from Hume's analysis of arguments from experience. According to that analysis, all arguments of this kind are based on the relation of cause and effect – a relation knowable only by experiencing a constant conjunction between events of the relevant kinds. Since it is conceded that the causes in question here are never actually observed, a constant conjunction of the appropriate kind is *never* experienced. An argument from experience is, therefore, totally unfounded in this case.

The difficulties are compounded, Hume said, if the new system includes the fashionable view that secondary qualities exist only in the mind. Hume's arguments for this claim are highly compressed and follow Berkeley's line that primary qualities cannot be separated from secondary qualities even in thought. Without either kind of quality, Hume said, external physical things are in a manner annihilated, leaving only an "unknown, inexplicable *something*" (Locke's *substratum*) as the cause of our perceptions – a notion so imperfect that no skeptic will think it worth arguing against. Since in his *Treatise* he referred to a *substratum* as an unintelligible chimera, he can be read as claiming that the new system reduces the non-mental cause of our perceptions to unintelligible chimeras.[31]

What is the upshot of these difficulties? What should we conclude from them? Should we reject the new system and return to the instinctive view? To this last question Hume's answer is no. As he put it in the *Enquiry*:

> the first philosophical objection to the evidence of sense or to the opinion of external existence consists in this: that such an opinion, if rested on natural instinct, is contrary to reason, and if referred to reason, is contrary to natural instinct, and at the

same time carries no rational evidence with it to convince an impartial inquirer. The second objection goes farther and represents this opinion as contrary to reason: at least, if it be a principle of reason that all sensible qualities are in the mind, not in the object.[32]

This statement seems to imply that no opinion is tenable: no opinion can be shown to be true or recommended on some stable practical ground. Faced with this outcome in the *Treatise*, Hume in effect made no recommendation, saying that different opinions appealed to him at different times and that when the conflict between them became intolerable, he got relief by thinking of something else.[33] His response was different in the *Enquiry*, where he represented his criticism of the two systems as the work of a skeptic whose purpose is a bit elusive.

I shall comment on Hume's attitude toward skepticism a little later. I now wish to consider how far one can push the line of criticism that Hume began. This line of criticism is based on what have become distinctively empiricist principles: one, the division of meaningful assertions into two basic classes, those involving mere relations of ideas and those involving matters of fact and existence; two, the restriction of demonstrative or *a priori* reasoning to relations of ideas; and three, the possibility of ascertaining matters of fact and existence only by experience – in the first instance, by direct observation and memory; in the second instance, by experimental inference as Hume understood it. It is easy to see that, as delimited by these three principles, the sphere of acceptable opinion is very small indeed.

The application of these principles as I have formulated them depends largely on what is to count as observation. Hume conceded that in common life external objects are considered observable; and he even admitted that many things often taken to undermine the acceptability of such observations do not succeed. Such things include the imperfection of our senses, the crooked appearance of an oar in water, the different appearances objects present under different perceptual conditions, and the double images that appear when an eye is pressed. These things merely prove, Hume said, that the senses alone are not implicitly to be depended on; we must "correct their evidence by reason and by considerations derived from the nature of the medium, the distance of the object and the disposition of the organ." When these corrections are made, he added, the senses will be rendered "within their sphere . . . the proper *criteria* of truth and falsehood." [34] In his remarkable discussion, in his famous section "Of Miracles," of how human testimony should be evaluated, he described further corrections that can be made. The sphere within which these corrected observations are acceptable is "common life"; but what is acceptable here is rationally dubious for deeper reasons involving the basic mechanisms of perception.

When these mechanisms are rationally considered, the "new system with regard to the senses" is forced upon us, and the door to skepticism is opened. As I have explained, the first thing one sees then is that what is actually before the mind in sensation are images or perceptions – impressions, as Hume officially called them. These items are the ultimate input for experimental inference: they are what we really observe (in the technical sense in question); and they are what (critically speaking) we really remember having occurred or existed. Since experimental inference (assuming that it is rationally acceptable) can assure us of causal relations only between objects that we can experience, we have no rational basis for any opinion that extends beyond the sphere of what we can experience. In particular, we have no rational basis for any opinion about mind-independent external objects.

Can we adopt Descartes' strategy here and attempt to increase our sphere of rationally founded opinion by appealing to the goodness of God? Hume said no:

> To have recourse to the veracity of the supreme Being in worder to prove the veracity of our senses is surely making a very unexpected circuit. If his veracity were at all concerned in this matter, our senses would be entirely infallible; because it is not possible that he can ever deceive. Not to mention that if the external world be once in question, we shall be at a loss to find arguments by which we may prove the existence of that Being or any of his attributes. [35]

It might seem that Hume was being unfair to Descartes here, for Descartes had an explanation of how the fallibility of our senses is compatible with God's veracity. Yet Descartes' explanation was not acceptable to Hume. It is worth mentioning why.

As the reader may recall, Descartes' explanation of the compatibility Hume denied was based on the presumption that the proper source of knowledge (or acceptable information) about matters of fact is rational demonstrations based on indubitable premisses, and also that the errors we make in such matters can be traced to our misuse of our free will. We freely assent to matters where we should suspend our judgment, Descartes said, and the fault is ours, not God's. Hume rejected both presumptions: the first because he thought it is plainly a mistake to seek demonstrations for matters of fact; the second because our beliefs (and therefore our judgments) are not under our control. Our beliefs, he thought, are automatically formed by our experience; we can control what we say but not what we believe.

It seems to me that Hume was clearly right on this matter. I often prove his point to students by offering five dollars to anyone who can make him or herself believe – even for a minute – that the moon is made of green cheese or that I am holding a frog in my open hand. It is easy for them to *say* that they believe such a thing, but they know full well that if they say it, they will not be telling the truth. On the other hand, I can quickly get them to believe I am holding a frog by taking one in my hand and letting them see it. (Actually, I fake this last experiment: I hold up a ceramic frog rather than a real one.)

As for the existence of God, Descartes thought he could prove this *a priori*, by reflecting on his idea of a perfect being.[36] Since the existence of God, if it is actual, is a matter of fact, it could not in Hume's view be proved *a priori*; it could be proved only by an argument from experience. Hume implied that no argument of this kind could be given if the existence of the external world is called in question, but it is obvious that no argument of this kind would be available unless one had experience of a divine action constantly conjoined with some effect. Of course, if one had this kind of experience, one would not need an argument from experience: one would have direct experience of God himself.

If we cannot prove or render probable any opinion that extends beyond the sphere of our immediate perceptions, we are left with a view that (at least in its reasonably founded respects) is solipsistic. Solipsism, as I am using the term here,[37] is the view that the reasonably held factual opinions of each conscious subject or self are limited to two targets: that subject and its (his or her) conscious states. The empiricist principles I have been discussing lead to an even more limited version of solipsism, however. Consider the alleged self or subject of experiences. What basis is there for believing in such a thing? No such self seems to be observed among the data at hand. When in common life I think of myself, I think of a short but stocky man of middle age; one who, in addition to eating, drinking, and taking exercise every day, spends much of his time reading, writing, and listening to music. If I cannot reasonably suppose that physical bodies actually exist, I cannot suppose that a self of this kind exists either. What is left if I subtract everything physical from the self I think I am? Hume in effect asked himself this question, and the famous answer he gave was, in essence, this:

> when I enter most intimately into what I call *myself*, I always stumble on some particular perception or other, of heat or cold, light or shade, love or hatred, pain or pleasure. I never can catch *myself* at any time without a perception and never can observe anything but the perception.

Finding no unitary or spiritual self among his available data, Hume felt compelled to say:

> I may venture to affirm of the rest of mankind [if any such actually exist!] that they are nothing but a bundle or collection of different perceptions, which succeed each other with an inconceivable rapidity and are in a perpetual flux and movement. . . . The mind is a kind of theater where several perceptions successively make their appearance, pass, repass, glide away, and mingle in an infinite variety of postures and situations. There is properly no *simplicity* in it at one time nor *identity* in [all its successive] differences – whatever natural propension we may have to imagine that simplicity and identity. The comparison of the theater must not mislead us. They are the successive perceptions only, which constitute the mind; nor have we the most distant notion of the place where these scenes are represented or of the materials of which it is composed.[38]

This is Hume's famous "bundle theory" of the self. It is a consequence of the principles he accepted that one's well-founded factual opinions are the opinions of a certain bundle and that the objects of those opinions (the things they are about) are elements of that bundle or constructs out of them.

This bundle-solipsism is an extremely limited view, but it is not the most limited (or most extreme) form that solipsism can take. The most extreme form can be called "bundle-solipsism of the present moment." Moderate bundle-solipsism is compatible with well-founded beliefs about past and future elements of the bundle to which those beliefs belong, but beliefs about the past and future can be put in doubt by highly stringent empiricist principles. Take the future, for instance. Beliefs about the future can be regarded as acceptably probable if the sort of experimental inference (or argument from experience) that Hume described is considered acceptable. Yet if (as empiricists almost universally allow) Hume's skeptical doubts about this form of inference are sound, it provides no good reason for accepting experimental conclusions. The toughest-minded empiricist would not endorse conclusions for which no good reason can be given, and this negative attitude would extend to all beliefs about the future.

What about the past? Hume accepted the "records of our memory" as acceptable sources of knowledge or reasoned opinion, but his deeper principles put memory in a very dubious light. An occurrence that we merely remember is, when we remember it, over and done with. Our act or state of ostensibly remembering it is, therefore, distinct from it and cannot (as a mental occurrence) insure its occurrence by a mere relation of ideas.[39] If an event or state M is a reliable indicator of a distinct past occurrence O, this can be known only by experience. The fact that we call M a "memory record," a "memory trace," or even a "memory impression" cannot assure us that it is a reliable indicator of a past occurrence any more than the fact that we call a certain arm-swing a knockout punch can assure us that someone was, in fact, knocked out by it. In both cases the terminology (with its nominal implications) is rationally justified only if one event is appropriately related to the other. Yet how can experience possibly assure us of a relation between a present occurrent and a past event? The answer, strictly speaking, is that it cannot: what was is not here to be observed. There is, therefore, no way of verifying that any memory impression, memory record, or memory event actually corresponds to anything that existed before it. The hard data of our here and now experience are compatible, as Bertrand Russell once observed, with the hypothesis that the world came into existence just five minutes ago with all its apparent paleolithic traces.[40]

A bundle-solipsist of the most tough-minded sort would be moved by Russell's observation and the reasoning I have cited to restrict her well-considered claims to the present contents of "her" bundle. Any beliefs she might happen to have (and however strong they may happen to be) about the past and future contents of her bundle would be too badly founded to have a place in such a philosopher's considered views. It is possible to push this epistemic retreat even further – to what Hume called "the destruction of all assurance and conviction" – but bundle-solipsism of the present moment is as extreme an empiricist view as we need contemplate here.[41] Other questions about Hume are more deserving of our attention.

I have been neglecting one of Hume's most distinctive critical principles, the one concerning meaning or significance. According to this principle, a word is meaningful only if it is associated with an idea that is either a copy of an original impression or made up of such ideas. Since we have no impressions from which an idea of a *substratum* can be copied or constructed, the word "*substratum*" should no doubt be declared meaningless and Locke's principal claims about mind-independent material bodies be dismissed as strictly meaningless as well. Hume did contend that the idea of a *substratum* is an unintelligible chimera, and he insisted that because he could experience shapes independently of secondary qualities, he could not conceive of such things or frame an appropriate abstract idea. He did not, on the other hand, use the principle to attack other putative ideas – for example, *external body* and *necessary connection between events* – that do not appear to be copies of impressions or built up from such copies. Instead, he made these dubious ideas conform to his principle by inventing an appropriate origin for them in impressions produced by the mind's own activities. As a result, these specially constructed ideas are really not what they seem to be.[42]

One application of Hume's principle of significance is particularly important for the subject of experimental inference. When he explained the basis for a skeptical doubt about the existence of external bodies, he emphasized that we cannot conclude that our perceptions result from such bodies because we cannot experience a constant conjunction between them (anything we experience will inevitably be an idea or perception rather than a mind-independent cause of such a thing). One might hope to remove this doubt by altering the rules for acceptable experimental inferences, but Hume's principle of significance will impose a very powerful constraint on one's effort. The reason is that, according to his principle, it is, in his words, "impossible for us so much as to conceive or form an idea of any thing specifically different from ideas and impressions." [43] If the idea of an object that is genuinely external to our consciousness cannot really be formed or conceived, then no tinkering with rules of experimental inference can possibly remove the skeptical doubt that Hume was officially concerned with in the *Enquiry*: it cannot really be entertained. If we accept his principle of significance, we shall have to allow that when we suppose we are thinking about external objects, we are really thinking about some cohering system of ideas.

4. *Hume's attitude to skepticism*

When Hume argued that our opinions about external things are objectionable whether they are founded on natural instinct or on reason and philosophy, he seemed to be expressing a thoroughly skeptical attitude toward the external world. His attitude is certainly skeptical, but its nature is not easy to make out. I want to discuss it briefly because I think its complexity is very instructive.

In the *Treatise* Hume agonized over the conflict between the instinctive, popular system and the new, philosophical system, and the difficulties with each. As I mentioned earlier, he thought the former system was based on a gross illusion; he said that the latter system is "the monstrous offspring of two principles, which are contrary to each other"; and he observed that the skeptical doubts arising from the defects of the two systems and their mutual incompatibility is a "malady which can never be radically cured but must return upon us every moment, however we may chase it away." [44] Observing that the malady is increased by "intense reflection," he noted that "carelessness and ill-attention alone can afford us any remedy." [45] This remedy is not really satisfactory, he admitted in his concluding section, for " 'tis almost impossible for the mind of man to rest, like those of beasts, in that narrow circle of objects which are the subject of daily conversation and action." [46] But what is to be done? What course of reasoning is to be followed if no view of the world is satisfactory and experimental inferences (arguments from experience) are not rationally justifiable?

This last question is the most acute that can be asked here, for if arguments from experience are not rationally justifiable, no kind of reasoning is rationally justifiable. This outcome is not troublesome merely because it seems to call *our* reasoning about matters of fact into question – the reasoning of, we believe, the wisest and most enlightened people. Worse than this, the outcome puts our reasoning about such matters on the same level with the reasoning of superstitious fanatics, astrologers, and, as Hume liked to say, ignorant and stupid barbarians who are ready to swallow even the grossest delusion. Having devoted much of his *Treatise* to criticizing the arguments of philosophical opponents, Hume would be in a very embarrassing position if he had to admit that his reasoning is really no better, no more acceptable, than the reasoning he criticized.

Hume tackled this last question in the *Treatise*. After observing that, unlike animals, human beings cannot restrict their attention to "that narrow circle of objects which are the subject of daily conversation and action," he said that it is pointless to deliberate about *whether* we should think about objects outside this narrow circle. The thing we can reasonably deliberate about is what guide to follow in this thinking, and "we ought to prefer that which is safest and most agreeable."[47] Since we cannot claim to know which guide will lead us to the truth more often than not, we must choose our guide on practical grounds. In the passage where he identified the choice we ought to make here he was specifically concerned about whether we should follow the guide of philosophy or of superstition in thinking about objects in the wider sphere. By "superstition" he evidently meant dogmatic or "revealed" religion. He himself found philosophy much more agreeable than superstition, but he thought any reasonable person would concede that it is also much more safe: "Generally speaking," he said, "the errors in religion are dangerous; those in philosophy only ridiculous." [48]

A choice between philosophy and superstition would be philosophically significant if there were only one kind philosophy and one kind of superstition, but the available alternatives are vastly more varied than this. Hume had, in fact, recognized the point in an earlier section, when he finished his criticism of "the antient philosophy," which amounted to some key Aristotelian doctrines. Denying that he was unfair in criticizing the Aristotelians for making use of principles that (like his) are not rationally justifiable, Hume said that a distinction must be drawn between two sorts of principles:

[those] which are permanent, irresistable, and universal, such as the customary transition from causes to effects and from effects to causes; and . . . [those] which are changeable, weak, and irregular, such as [the ones he has been criticizing]. . . . The former are the foundations of all our thoughts and actions, so that upon their removal human nature must immediately perish and go to ruin. The latter are neither unavoidable to mankind nor necessary, or so much as useful in the conduct of life; but on the contrary are observ'd to take place in weak minds and, being opposite to the other principles of custom and reasoning, may easily be subverted by a due contrast and opposition.

He appended two examples and an important observation to this crucial distinction:

One who concludes somebody to be near him, when he hears an articulate voice in the dark, reasons justly and naturally – though that conclusion be derived from nothing but custom. . . . But one who is tormented, he knows not why, with the apprehension of spectres in the dark may, perhaps, be said to reason, and to reason naturally too. But then it must be [natural] in the same sense that a malady is said to be natural: as arising from natural causes, though it be contrary to health, the most agreable and natural situation of man.[49]

These important remarks make it possible to provide a plausible practical justification for experimental inference (as Hume understood it) and for beliefs about the existence of external objects. The basic consideration is that, owing to the evident nature of the human mind, people invariably employ arguments from experience in everyday life, and they agree about their cogency in that domain. The principles they assume in these arguments (where they infer like effects from like causes, and like causes from like effects) are "permanent, irresistible, and universal." No one but a philosopher ever disputes them, and philosophers actually employ them even if they dispute them. Objectionable principles are those "opposite to" or, as we should say, *inconsistent with* the permanent, irresistible, and universal ones. They are objectionable for the simple reason that *no person can consistently employ them.* Idiosyncratic principles that are consistent with the universal principles are not, on this view, objectionable *per se*, but one might insist that something (consistent with the universal principles) should be said in their favor.

This sort of practical justification places a great value on consistency, and one might wonder what can be said in favor of it. Hume did not explicitly discuss this value, but reflective people are perhaps invariably committed to it – so that it might amount to another permanent, irresistible, and universal principle. Like Walt Whitman, people occasionally make gestures against consistency, but those gestures are rarely (if ever) well considered. However this may be, recent work on non-demonstrative inference also places great weight on consistency, so this is a topic that I shall discuss in a chapter to come – Chapter VII, specifically.

One final point: I said that Hume's remarks provide a plausible means of justifying beliefs about external objects. From Hume's perspective, at least, this is no doubt an important matter, though he does not dwell upon it. A belief is not justifiable merely because it is instinctive; yet if everyone accepts it by (as it were) a necessity of nature and its acceptance has no harmful consequences, there can be no objection to accepting it. Does the belief in external objects have any harmful consequences? The question is not pointless because harmful consequences can be purely intellectual: the acceptance of a given belief can be harmful to the development of good theories. It seems to me that if the belief in external objects is fairly empty, theoretically, not including a substantive commitment to the nature of such things and the mechanism of their interaction with us, then Hume must concede that it is harmless to accept it. Doing so is rationally justifiable in the attenuated sense of being rationally permissible.

CHAPTER IV

Kant and Phenomenalism

Kant claimed that Hume's skeptical writings awoke him from his dogmatic slumbers.[1] Before reading them, he had uncritically assumed that it is possible to have *a priori* knowledge about the basic matters of fact covered by general metaphysics; after reading them, he realized that the possibility of such knowledge was highly problematic and needed justification.[2] The justification he eventually discovered was, in his view, momentous, for it required a "Copernican revolution" in philosophy. Just as Copernicus had argued that the movements of heavenly bodies could be explained by the radically new hypothesis that the spectators moved and the stars remained at rest, so Kant argued that the possibility of metaphysical knowledge could be explained by the radically new hypothesis that objects in the world had to conform to our means of knowing things. His idea was that anything thus conforming to our cognitive requirements would have basic features that must be possessed by any object of our knowledge. Such features could, in his view, be identified and known *a priori* even though the relevant propositions stated matters of fact rather than mere relations of ideas.[3]

Kant's writings are famous for their extreme difficulty: his prose is difficult to follow, and his ideas are difficult to comprehend. Although even experts on his philosophy disagree about the content of central doctrines,[4] his general approach to the epistemological problems of concern in this book is relatively easy to understand and to assess. His views on our knowledge of the external world are, I shall argue, unacceptable in important respects, but his Copernican revolution in philosophy is, to a significant extent, still in effect: it changed the course of epistemology.

1. Kant's classification of knowledge

To clarify the epistemological problem that Hume raised for him, Kant introduced his famous distinction between analytic and synthetic judgments. A judgment, for Kant, is the sort of mental affirmation or thought expressed in language by a declarative sentence. Although judgments can be false as well as true, Kant's distinction is applied to true ones; thus, the predicate "analytic" is equivalent to "analytically true," and a corresponding equivalence holds for "synthetic." Later philosophers have departed from Kant's usage, saying that certain judgments are analytically false and synthetically false; but this terminological variation is unimportant. An analytically true judgment, as Kant understood it, is one that can be seen to be true "by analysis"; an analytically false judgment, as later philosophers understand it, is one that can be seen to be false "by analysis." The crucial concept here is that of *analysis*. Compared to this, the terminological differences are insignificant.

Kant first introduced his distinction by reference to simple affirmative judgments, but he noted that it can easily be extended to negative judgments. In affirmative judgments of this simple kind, the subject is related to the predicate in two ways, Kant said:

> Either the predicate B belongs to the subject A as something which is (covertly) contained in the concept A, or B lies outside the concept A, although it does indeed stand in connection with it.

In the first case the judgment is analytic; in the second case it is synthetic. Affirmative analytic judgments are therefore, he added, those in which the connection of the predicate to the subject is "thought through identity"; those in which this connection is thought without identity are synthetic. The point of this last claim can be seen by reference to the judgment, "Red skies are red." The predicate *red* is explicitly contained in the subject concept *red skies*; this predicate (the property explicitly predicated of the subject, red skies) is connected in thought to the concept of the subject by identity: it is identical with something in that concept and it adds nothing to it. Its conceptual redundancy is what accounts for the judgment's *a priori* certainty.

Since the predicate of an analytic judgment adds nothing to the concept of its subject but merely makes explicit something perhaps confusedly thought in it, Kant said that an analytic judgment can be called *explicative*. By contrast, a synthetic judgment may be called *ampliative*, for its predicate adds something to what is thought in its subject concept and cannot be extracted from the latter by some kind of analysis.[5] What sort of analysis can be used in extracting predicates from the relatively opaque subject concepts of some analytic judgments? The sort Kant mentioned in his first *Critique* is based on the principle of contradiction. Claiming that *A body is extended* holds *a priori* and is not empirical, Kant explained that the concept *body* contains all the conditions required to determine its truth: "I have only to extract from it, in accordance with the principle of contradiction, the required predicate, and in so doing can at the same time become conscious of the necessity of the judgment." [6] This suggests that a predicate P is properly extracted from a concept S (and thus shown to be implicit in it) when S and -P yield a contradictory judgment.

Kant emphasized the relation between analyticity and the principle of contradiction in his *Prolegomena to Any Future Metaphysics*. In this later work he said that "the common principle of all analytic judgments is that of contradiction." [7] This general characterization of analytic judgments is not very clear by contemporary standards, but it has the merit of applying to all analytic judgments, even those lacking affirmative subject–predicate form. Kant himself recognized that some judgments are hypothetical or disjunctive in form, and he explicitly repudiated the view, common in his day, that such judgments are "different clothings of categorical judgments and . . . may be altogether reduced to the latter."[8] If an analytic judgment is irreducibly hypothetical or disjunctive in form, its analyticity cannot then be owing to the relation between its subject and its predicate, for it has neither. The common principle Kant identified in his *Prolegomena* fills the needed gap: the judgment is analytic if (and presumably only if) its denial is self-contradictory. Although Kant offered no examples of analytic judgments of hypothetical and disjunctive form, the following are obviously true by analysis: "If it rains tomorrow, it rains tomorrow" and "Either it will rain tomorrow or it won't." According to elementary logic, the denials of both these sentences are equivalent to "It will rain tomorrow and it will not (at any time during that day)," which is explicitly self-contradictory. No doubt Kant would have classified the sentences as analytic on this basis.

I remarked that although Kant's common principle gives us the generality we want, it is not very clear by contemporary standards. The unclarity lies in the word "contradictory." If we think of a contradictory judgment as one that is, in the modern sense, explicitly contradictory, then no analytic judgment has a contradictory denial. The point is obvious because the explicit denial of a judgment J is -J, and an explicit contradiction is a conjunctive judgment of a different form, *S & -S*. To apply Kant's principle we must therefore think of a contradiction more informally – perhaps as something *equivalent* to an explicit contradiction.

This possibility raises problems, however. How are we to understand the relevant notion of equivalence? If we say "logical equivalence" (meaning "equivalent by virtue of logical form") then we have a clear criterion, but one too narrow for Kant's purposes, since the denial of "Bachelors are unmarried" is not *formally* equivalent to an explicit contradiction. (The syllogistic denial, which Kant would have had in mind, is "Some bachelors are married"; and this is not explicitly contradictory or false by virtue of its logical form.[9]) If, on the other hand, we say "equivalent in content or meaning," then we need some criterion for judging this kind of equivalence. Without it, we shall be judging the contradictoriness of a judgment's denial on some intuitive basis. I am not saying (at least here) that Kant's principle is inherently defective; my claim is merely that by contemporary standards it is not very clear. Fortunately, later philosophers have attempted to improve upon it; I will discuss their attempts in later chapters.

Kant accompanied his distinction between analytic and synthetic truth with a distinction between *a priori* and *a posteriori* knowledge. Knowledge is *a priori*, Kant said, just when it is "independent of experience and even of all impressions of the senses." It is *a posteriori*, by contrast, just when it is obtained from experience.[10] Apart from its source, *a priori* knowledge is distinguished by two features or criteria: necessity and universality. "Experience teaches us," Kant said, "that a thing is so and so, but not that it cannot be otherwise." Consequently, if we think of a proposition as necessary, that proposition is known *a priori* if it is known at all. Again, experience "never confers on its judgments true or strict, but only assumed and comparative *universality*, through induction. We can properly only say that, so far as we have hitherto observed, there is no exception to this or that rule."

If "universality is essential to a judgment," it can be known to be true only *a priori*. Necessity and strict universality are "sure criteria of *a priori* knowledge" and, Kant added, they are "inseparable from one another." [11]

Kant's two distinctions allow us to construct an illuminating classification of our knowledge. Mathematically, there are four possibilities to consider:

analytic *a priori.*
analytic *a posteriori.*
synthetic *a priori.*
synthetic *a posteriori.*

The first and fourth possibilities raise no problems. The first class has members because analytic truths, as Kant understood them, are decidable by analysis, which is an *a priori* process. The fourth class has members because empirical judgments are invariably both synthetic and *a posteriori*. The second class is obviously empty, for an analytic judgment concerns the relations between ideas (or the content of concepts) and, as such, is properly decidable by analysis rather than by observation, memory, or experimental inference (which Kant called "induction"). The third class is the problematic one. Hume would say that the class is empty, since no matter of fact (statable by a synthetic proposition) is decidable *a priori* (by considering the mere relations of ideas). Kant insisted, however, that the third class has members. He attempted to prove it in his *Critique of Pure Reason.*

The relevance of the third class of judgments to the subject of this book is obvious in view of Hume's arguments. According him, there is no rational basis for thinking that the future will be like the past, that predictions based on past experience will be true more often than not, that sensory experience is reliably correlated with external objects, that memory experience is, in fact, generally reliable, and that there is anything more to a mind than the experiences making it up. There is no rational basis for thinking these things, in Hume's view, because they all concern matters of fact and existence and yet cannot be ascertained by direct observation or by a non-circular form of experimental inference. To know that the unobserved is like the observed, or that the observed is related in a special way to something not observed (the past, external objects, a unitary self), we must have knowledge that is both synthetic and non-empirical – that is, synthetic *a priori* knowledge. The question Kant sought to answer in his *Critique* was "How is synthetic *a priori* knowledge possible?"

2. Kant's Copernican revolution

As I explained, Kant thought that the answer to his basic question about knowledge could be obtained by his Copernican revolution. In this section I want to describe some of the considerations on which Kant's proposed revolution was based, then discuss some of its principal features, and finally relate what I have been saying to the complicated answer Kant gave to his basic question.

If we attend to our reflective experience, we shall find that it provides a highly organized representation of a spatio-temporal world of objects. This represented world might conceivably be as delusive as a dream, lacking any relation to a genuinely external world, but it is certainly present to our consciousness. As a product of our reflective experience, it also involves a good deal of interpretation. The sounds it includes are the squeaks of chairs or the rustling of leaves; its odors appear as the fragrance of lilacs or the stench of garbage; its colored shapes are masses of clouds or groups of people; and so on. Athough this represented world is (all things considered) remarkably stable, it is not static. The objects it includes move about in a common space interacting with one another, altering with time, and occasionally ceasing to exist.

Inspection of this represented world shows it to be a construction, something put together by a conscious subject. Consider the experience of hearing a short fragment of a familiar tune – say, the first four notes of Beethoven's Fifth Symphony. To anyone familiar with the symphony, the notes are intimately unified: the da-da-da-daa is heard as a single musical gesture, just as a series of finger movements is seen as a single sign or signal. Yet even in this world of experience the other notes have not actually sounded when the first is heard; the first is over and done with when the second sounds; and when the last is heard, the others are things of the past. Thus, the ingredient sounds do not occur together when the measure is heard. For the notes to be heard as a unitary gesture, they must somehow be held together in consciousness: a remembered past, a perceived present, and an anticipated future must be unified in some way. Since the elements are distinct, the perceived whole must be the result of a constructive act or process.

Kant used the world "synthesis" where I have used "construction"; the common metaphor is that of things put together.[12] It is easy to see that other syntheses, other sorts of putting together, are involved in the represented world of our reflective experience. If, as I naturally believe, I move my head from side to side, patterns of color recur in my visual field, and I unthinkingly interpret the recurring patterns as (I take them to be) persisting objects that I observe, look away from, and observe again. Further reflection complicates this simple picture. I turn on my light (as I naturally believe), and the color patterns I now perceive are in certain respects different from those I remember perceiving: colors have altered, but there is continuity in contrasts and shapes. I naturally interpret the patterns as different "appearances" (appearances under different conditions) of the same objects – as it happens, the same shelves of books. Different perceptions occurring at different times are thus unified in my representation of the world as appearances of the same persisting object perceived at different times and under different conditions.

As in the case of every person, my perceptions are further unified by the phenomenon of dating. I represent events as having occurred at times (dates) that precede the present moment by some number of years, months, or minutes. This means of temporal indexing involves an extremely complicated constructive process. To measure a temporal interval, we must use some kind of clock, which we represent in our experience as a persisting object that undergoes some periodic change. A very primitive example of a clock, conceptually speaking, is the moon, which changes from new to full and back again in a series of phases. If I think of myself as using this clock, I should think of processes temporally coinciding with a single lunation (or series of phases) as lasting for one moon, and I should think of occurrences that coincided with the beginning of the most recent lunation as having occurred one moon ago.

The syntheses required to represent even this primitive kind of dating involve several distinct processes. One process is needed to delimit and unify a variety (or manifold, as Kant would say) of perceptions into appearances of the moon during its various phases. Another process is needed to relate the occurrence to be dated to a group of perceptions that are unified as appearances of some persisting object to which the occurrence belongs. (Kant thought that occurrences are invariably represented as belonging to some persisting thing.) Finally, the synthesis that represents the temporal coincidence of the occurrence with the lunar period is needed. If one is concerned with scientifically precise representations of minimal or astronomical changes, the required syntheses are enormously more complicated.

The representation of places is in many ways similar to the representation of times. We think of physical things as near or far, radiating out from us spatially; but because we think of ourselves as active beings that move around, the fixed points in relation to which we locate objects spatially are not ourselves but something we regard as stable, such as (for non-technical purposes) a town, a house, or a monument. Just as we need clocks to measure (impose a metric on) time, we need measuring rods (or something comparable) to measure distances, and compasses (or something comparable) to ascertain directions. For any but the most trivial specifications of relative position, representations of time and place go hand in hand. At time t_1, X is two miles north of Y; at time t_2, X is five miles north-west of Y (appropriate altitudes could be mentioned as well). Since monuments, measuring rods, and compasses are all represented as persisting things, the syntheses required to represent a world of objects moving about in specifiable places at specifiable times are extremely numerous and complicated almost beyond belief.

Given that our representation of the world we believe we live in is an extraordinarily complicated construction (or synthetic whole), what conclusions pertinent to the possibility of synthetic *a priori* knowledge can we draw from it? The conclusions Kant drew were built on the idea that anything we can have genuine knowledge of must be capable of being represented in a complex construction of this kind. *Anything* thus represented *must*, he thought, have certain features: without them, it could not belong to a coherent, comprehensible representation of the world of experience. The relevant features are, he added, spatial, temporal, and categorial. Since his claim here is not analytic and yet can (in his opinion) be known to be true, and since it is both universal (holding for anything representable) and necessary (anything . . . *must* have the features), it follows that synthetic *a priori* knowledge must be possible. Such knowledge will concern the spatial, temporal, and categorial features of representable objects.

3. More on objects of experience

It will be useful to introduce a little detail about the features Kant thought objects of experience must possess. The most basic features in his view are temporal and spatial. Our representation of the world not only includes ourselves but the experiences — the aches and pains — that we are conscious of having. Every occurrence, even these subjective experiences, must be represented as having a location in time, Kant thought. Although he called time a universal "form" of experience, he thought of it as an infinite dimension, a unitary thing that we can "intuit" or be conscious of. This thing is not a mind-independent reality; it is something that we contribute to our experience. Because we contribute it – because we synthesize (or organize) our primitive sensory data in relation to it – we can have *a priori* knowledge of it. The possibility of this kind of knowledge accords with a leading claim of Kant's Copernican revolution – namely, "we can know *a priori* of things only what we put into them." [13]

Like time, space is another "form" of our experience: this time our "outer experience." Some objects of our experience are invariably represented spatially; we call them "physical bodies." Although our sensory experiences are obtained serially – the glimpse of a nose appearing before the glimpse of an eye and the sensation of touching a hand – they contribute to our awareness of complex objects spread out three-dimensionally in space. Our consciousness of space is not something we abstract from foreign, incoming data, for those data are not three-dimensional: what we experience as three-dimensional is the result of our pre-conscious synthesizing activity, and our *a priori* contribution to experience is exhibited there. If we mentally subtract from our experiential representation of a body the features our understanding contributes to it (its substantial unity and divisibility) and the features contributed by sensation (color and hardness, for example) we will be left with its "extension and figure" – the portion of three-dimensional space that it occupies. Our awareness of this three-dimensional reality is "pure," not empirical; it is present in our experience as our own formal contribution.

In describing our experiential representation of a material body I spoke of the features our understanding contributes to it. One of Kant's most important contentions was that our thought has a peculiar conceptual structure that is fundamentally different from anything temporal, spatial, or sensory, and that this conceptual structure is reflected in (rather than contributed by) our experience of objects. The structure so reflected provides a further source of synthetic *a priori* knowledge, Kant thought. Where the forms of sense (time and space) made synthetic *a priori* knowledge in arithmetic and geometry possible,[14] the conceptual structure of thought makes synthetic *a priori* knowledge in general metaphysics possible.[15] Although the term is rarely used today, "general metaphysics" was used in Kant's time to refer to the traditional philosophical subject concerned with the necessary features of substances, attributes, causes, and effects. The term was distinguished from "special metaphysics," which Kant applied primarily to the subjects of God, freedom, and immortality.[16] Kant denied that synthetic *a priori* knowledge is possible in special metaphysics, but he argued (for reasons that I shall mention) that certain beliefs about these subjects can be defended on practical grounds.

The clue to what we might call the conceptual structure of experience can be found, Kant thought, in the logical structure of a judgment. The possible variety in this sort of structure is represented, in his view, by the classification of judgments that was accepted then. According to this classification, judgments have the generic features of *quantity*, *quality*, *relation*, and *modality*. Kant listed the specific forms that these generic features can take in the following *Table of Judgments*:

I
Quantity

Universal
Particular
Singular

II		III
Quality		*Relation*
Affirmative		Categorical
Negative		Hypothetical
Infinite		Disjunctive

IV
Modality

Problematic
Assertoric
Apodeictic

For a modern reader, the basic significance of the table can be indicated by the following display, which lists some of the possible additions that can be made to a subject term S and a predicate term P in a conceptually allowable judgment:

Quantity		*Quality*		*Modality*		*Relation*
$\begin{bmatrix} \text{All} \\ \text{Some} \\ \text{This} \end{bmatrix}$	S	$\begin{bmatrix} \text{is} \\ \text{is not} \end{bmatrix}$		$\begin{bmatrix} \text{possibly} \\ \text{in fact} \\ \text{necessarily} \end{bmatrix}$	P	$\begin{bmatrix} \text{period.} \\ \text{only if} \ldots \\ \text{or.} \ldots \end{bmatrix}$

Kant's *Table of Judgments* would not be news to Locke, Hume, or Berkeley, for it is the sort of table that was taught to every student of traditional, Aristotelian logic – a subject they certainly studied. Yet the variety of these possible forms of judgment seems to have had little effect on their conception of human consciousness. All three thought that words and sentences owe their meaning to the ideas they are associated with, but none had much to say about the ideas associated with words like "all," "some," "or," or "if," which are crucially important to the logical structure of meaningful sentences. Kant held that these words represent "functions of unity" in judgment. A judgment is a discursive means of representing the world, and the logical words included in the traditional table of judgment forms stand for different ways of representing the world by judgments containing common subject and predicate terms, S and P.

Kant related "the functions of unity" in judgment to corresponding abstract concepts which he called "categories." Although his account of the relation between judgment function and category is in some respects very difficult to follow,[17] it is easy to see that the contributions made to a judgment by logical words such as "all," "some," "not," "if," and "or" are closely tied to concepts represented in his *Table of Categories*:

I

Of Quantity

Unity
Plurality
Totality

II	III
Of Quality	*Of Relation*
Reality	Of Inherence and Subsistence
Negation	Of Causation and Dependence
Limitation	Of Community (reciprocity . . .)

IV

Of Modality

Possibility–Impossibility
Existence–Non-existence
Necessity–Contingency

Consider the concepts listed under the first heading, *Quantity*. Corresponding to the judgmental function of universality (expressed by "all") is the category of unity. The connection is obvious here because in judging all S's to be P, one mentally unifies the S's as P's or places them all in a single class. Corresponding to the judgmental function of particularity (expressed by "some") is the category of plurality. Again, the connection is obvious: in judging some S's to be P, one mentally places (according to syllogistic doctrine) at least one S in the class of P's and leaves open the possibility that there are S's not in that class, thus thinking of S's as comprising a possible plurality. Corresponding, finally, to the function of singularity (expressed by "this") is the category of totality. The connection is perhaps not obvious this time, but Kant's idea seems to be that in judging *this* S to be P, one places a given thing totally (without remainder) in the class of P's.

The concepts listed under *Relation* are particularly interesting. A categorial judgment is one in which a property is predicated (according to some quantity, quality, and modality) of a subject: the simplest case is that in which *this* S is judged to be P. In making this judgment one applies the category of Inherence and Subsistence, in effect judging the predicate P to inhere in the subsistent subject S. In a hypothetical judgment one judges that if *p* then *q*. The corresponding category is given as Causation and Dependence in Kant's *Table of Categories*, but his subsequent discussion makes it clear that this designation is inexact and misleading. A much better designation would be *Of Ground and Consequent*, for Kant's view is that when, generally speaking, one judges that if *p*, then q, one is judging the propositions *p* and *q* to be standing in a ground–consequent relation, *p* the ground and *q* the consequent. In the special case in which *p* is judged to provide a *temporal ground* for *q*, they are judged to stand in the relation of causation and dependence, *p* stating a causal condition for what is asserted by *q*.

4. *Kant's transcendental deduction*

The categories, according to Kant, are *a priori* concepts which apply to objects in a purely *a priori* manner. To show that they are so applicable, he offered a "transcendental deduction" of them. His exposition of this deduction occurred in two versions, for he restated it in the second edition of his *Critique*. Since both versions comprise some of the most difficult pages in all modern philosophy, I cannot analyze their contents here, important as they are. The most I can do is reconstruct what I take to be the main thrust of Kant's reasoning. My reconstruction will be as fair as I can make it and as detailed as my purposes require.[18]

When Kant introduced the term "transcendental deduction," he intimated that he was using "deduction" somewhat as jurists do when they speak of the deduction of a legal right or claim. Such a deduction is, he said, a proof that someone has a right or legal claim to something. The aim of his transcendental deduction was to prove, he implied, that we have a right (of some epistemic kind) to use the categories in application to our experience. The philosophical importance of this aim is easily illustrated by the categories of Inherence and Subsistence (or substance) and Causality and Dependence (or causation).

Recall Locke's remarks about *substrata*. Like most philosophers, Locke assumed that when we make a categorical judgment of the form *this S is P*, we ascribe a property or attribute to a subject. This apparently innocent assumption leads to trouble because the subject we have in mind is evidently distinct from the attributes we ascribe to it; yet apart from these attributes, we seem to have no distinct idea of what this subject is. Locke described a *substratum* as "a thing I know not what" that supports the attributes inhering in it. Berkeley denied having any such idea, and Hume's principle of significance for ideas casts serious doubt upon it. The claim that the category of substance (or Inherence and Subsistence) actually applies to something is highly questionable in view of this dispute, and it obviously needs justification – or some kind of clarification.

A similar difficulty arises in connection with the category of cause (or Causation and Dependence). Although Hume conceded that the idea of causation is the idea of a necessary connection between events, he denied that this idea is what it appears to be. Since there are no necessary connections in nature or in our experience, we have no experience of a necessary connection and therefore, in a strict sense, no idea of a necessary connection either. On the other hand, if we have observed a constant conjunction between events of kind C and kind E, we will expect to observe one of kind E when we observe one of kind C, and the experience (or "impression") of expecting this will yield a corresponding idea, which will be joined to the idea of the constant conjunction between C and E. This resulting idea will be our non-strict idea of necessary connection between C and E.[19] Clearly, it will not apply to an actual necessary connection. Kant did not agree with Hume that the necessity here is only apparent; as he saw it, the concept of a cause is applicable to x only if something y follows from x necessarily and in accordance with an absolutely universal rule.[20] Since, like Hume, he thought it is impossible to prove empirically that something is a cause in this sense, he had to agree that the application of the concept *cause* to experience requires justification.

Although Kant, in the process of giving his transcendental deduction, specifically mentioned the need for justifying the application of *cause* to experience,[21] he did not, in fact, proceed to show in his deduction that any particular categories are applicable to experience. What he did proceed to show (or attempt to show) is something vaguer and more general – namely, that reflective human experience (the kind we actually have) is possible only if "the categories" (specified in very general terms) are applicable to it. He came to terms with specific categories and offered arguments showing their application to our experience in a subsequent section of the *Critique*, which he called "the Analytic of Principles." I will say something about these arguments after I have commented on his general argument or deduction.

I anticipated part of Kant's general argument when I described his Copernican revolution. According to this argument, our reflective experience provides a representation – a conceptual picture, one might say – of a world of spatio-temporal objects. The world thus represented is, as I put it, a construction: it is a put-together (or synthetic) unity. Anything apprehended in space and time is apprehended as spatially and temporally extensive – as having spatial and temporal parts. The spatial parts are apprehended together; and closely related temporal ones seem to be so apprehended, though the earlier ones (having already occurred) must actually be recollected and imaginatively fused with what the perceiver is currently aware of. Heterogeneous appearances apprehended at scattered times are also sometimes unified as appearances of a single thing – for example, a bookcase viewed from different angles when the light is on, when it is off, when it is day, when it is night, and so on.

A distinctive feature of the world represented in our experience is that it contains us as central figures. Past and future occurrences are represented as minutes, moons, or years before or after our *now*, and spatial *there's* are represented as feet, miles, or even light-years from our *here*. As objects in the picture, we are appearances ourselves. To whom are we appearances? To ourselves – to the selves that, working behind the scenes as it were, construct the represented world by the unifying acts that I have described. Kant called this behind-the-scenes I the "transcendental" I. It is not an object of perception, for perceived objects are unities that the I constructs from a manifold (a many) of appearances. What can we know about this transcendental I? Very little, Kant said. We are conscious of our experience as ours, and *I think* (or *I am conscious of*) can accompany any of our thoughts, experiences, or (as Kant put it) our representations. But the *I* in this *I think* does not represent anything we are immediately aware of. Reflection shows that it represents an intelligence that combines (or unifies) experiential elements into complex representations. We know it, Kant said, solely by its power of combination.[22]

The claim that we are (or always can be)[23] conscious of our experience as ours may be understood collectively as well as distributively. Kant intends it to be understood in the stronger, collective sense. It is not just that we can be conscious of any given experience (or representation) as ours; we can be conscious of all

our experiences (the totality) as ours. This latter sort of consciousness involves a synthesis, an act of combination, because a manifold
of representations is here brought together as the object of a single *I
think* or *I am conscious of.* As Kant put it:

> The thought that the representations given in intuition one and
> all belong to me is therefore equivalent to the thought that I
> unite them in one self-consciousness, or at least can so unite
> them. . . . In other words, only in so far as I can grasp the
> manifold of representations in one consciousness do I call
> them one and all *mine.* For otherwise I should have as many-
> colored and diverse a self as I have representations of which I
> am conscious to myself.[24]

The manifold of representations Kant spoke of here corresponds to
the elements of Hume's mind-bundle. Although each element in the
bundle may be said to be a conscious experience, Kant was in effect
insisting that the bundle will not have the self-consciousness of a
mind if its elements cannot be unified as a collective object of
consciousness. For this unification to occur, a unifying subject of
experience – an I or self distinct from the bundle – must in his view
exist.

In part because he assumed that we, as transcendental subjects of
experience, *have knowledge* – we know, at least, that the elements
of our bundles belong to us – Kant confidently spoke of us (in this
role) as minds or intelligences.[25] An obvious question to ask, then,
is "How can a mind or intelligence combine a manifold or unify a
bundle of impressions and ideas?" The obvious answer, for Kant, is
"By some mental act – specifically, by an act of judgment." Since we
know what the possible forms of judgment are and also know what
categories are applied when judgments of these forms are made, we
therefore know that some categories must be applicable to the
contents of our bundles: they must, that is, be applicable to *our
experience.* Kant expressed this conclusion a bit carelessly by
saying that the manifold of our intuition is "necessarily subject to
the categories." [26] His formulation is careless because the most that
he had shown in his deduction is that our experience (the manifold
of our intuition) is subject to at least some category. This carelessness is in effect remedied by the arguments supporting his "Principles of Pure Understanding," on which I shall comment shortly.

5. *Some categories and principles*

Much of the interest of Kant's transcendental deduction lies in material that is logically incidental to the reasoning I have just described. Some of this material, which Kant virtually eliminated from the version in his second edition, concerns the relation of appearances to an object. Since objects may be collective as well as single, Kant's discussion of this relation has important consequences for his view of our entire experiential world. I shall begin with his view of a single object of experience and then gradually work my way to his conception of a world of causally interacting substances.

As I mentioned earlier, when we construct a conceptual representation of a persisting thing, we unify a variety of sensory data as appearances of an object. Kant made a special point of explaining what this unification amounts to. Offhand, one might suppose that X,Y,Z are appearances of an object O when they are somehow correlated with it – when, say, they are effects of O in our consciousness. O, on this view, is an extra-mental object of representation. Although there is, Kant conceded, a germ of truth in this idea,[27] it is disallowed by our knowledge of objects, which is restricted to the field of our experience: "outside our [experiential] knowledge we have nothing," he said, to "set over against this knowledge as corresponding to it."[28] Thus, the relation of appearances to an object must consist in their "agreement" with one another, with the kind of unity they possess. This is an imposed or constructed unity based on a concept. The object is "no more than" an ideal "something" the concept of which specifies the required unity among the appearances.[29]

Kant's thought on this matter can be clarified by reference to a very simple example. Consider the appearances characteristic of a basketball. These appearances include round russet expanses, tactile experiences of a leatherish surface on a light bouncy object, and auditory experiences of thumps as a circular expanse seems to move up and down in one's visual field. Now compare these appearances with those that would constitute an illusion or hallucination of a basketball. In this last case certain appearances are conspicuously missing.[30] A special unity of size-, weight-, and color-appearances is therefore distinctive of basketball, and this unity is not possessed by a mere hallucination. On the basis of these considerations it seems reasonable to say that a group of appearances represents a basketball if and only if its members are unified in a way appropriate to the concept of a basketball – if and only if they measure up to the specifications (Kant said the "rule") implicitly contained in the concept. A single appearance would refer to a basketball (be an actual appearance of one) if and only if it belonged to a family of appearances that are unified in accordance with the concept. A hallucinatory experience would not refer to a real object because the family of appearances to which it belongs (if, indeed, an attainable family actually exists) does not possess the required unity. Typically, it has too many gaps.

Kant's account of the relation of appearances to their immanent or experiential object throws some light on the application of the category of substance to experience. If a certain experienced quality Q is a stable appearance of a sensible object O, we can truly say that O has Q. The subject here is not a *substratum* in Locke's sense; it is a unified system of appearances.[31] Q inheres in O in the sense that it is one of the appearances belonging to O, or unified with certain other appearances under the concept of O. A substance is, Kant agreed, something that is relatively permanent in time: it persists, remaining one and the same, while its qualities change. But this persistence does not require the presence of a mysterious *substratum*; it is a property (for lack of a better word) of a unitary system. The concept specifying the subject of change specifies the unity that must endure. As in the case of the first measure of Beethoven's Fifth Symphony, a substantial unity is in some cases the unity of a pattern.

I mentioned earlier that our reflective experiences provide a highly organized representation of a spatio-temporal world of objects. This highly organized representation seems to possess the collective unity that makes transcendental self-consciousness possible, for all the items of one's mental bundle can be unified within it. The world represented in this total system contains representations of spatio-temporal objects in the sense that the system imposes large-scale unity on a manifold of unified sub-systems, each sub-system specifying a spatio-temporal object of which some class of appearances is distinctive. In his "Analogies of Experience" Kant attempted to prove not only that the permanent in this system of systems is substance (whose "quantum in nature is neither increased nor diminished") but that "all alterations take place in accordance with the laws of the connection of cause and effect" and "all substances that can be perceived to coexist in space are in thoroughgoing reciprocity" (or mutual interaction).

Kant did not attempt to prove these analogies by induction from experience or by the analysis of concepts. On the contrary, his proof had the structure of what he called a "transcendental argument." The basic idea of his very complicated proof can be seen in this passage:

> Taken together, the analogies declare that all appearances lie, and must lie, in *one* nature, because without this *a priori* unity no unity of experience, and therefore no determination of objects in it, would be possible.[32]

The basic premiss of Kant's proof is that one's experience has an *a priori* unity – a unity not just discoverable in it but one that can be known to be there *a priori*. (Without the unity there could be no self-consciousness; and without self-consciousness there could be no subject of experience and therefore no such thing as *one's* experience.) This unity of experience is possible, Kant argued, only if the items making it up are unified into one system. In our case (the case of human beings), at least,[33] the system is spatio-temporal and subject to the categories. The changes in such a system must be identifiable by reference to persisting things, or substances; the substances must be located in a common space; their genuine alterations must (unlike mere associations of ideas) be irreversible, subject to rules of succession, and, therefore, causally related; and the things existing at any one time must be in a state of reciprocal interaction.

6. Kant's transcendental idealism

Before making any critical observations about Kant's analogies or the arguments by which he supported them, I want to say something about his notion of a self or subject of experience. I mentioned earlier that Kant viewed our represented world of objects as a system of appearances – a system unified by the behind-the-scenes activities of an unperceived, transcendental self. Although this self is not perceived or even known as it is in itself, an image corresponding to it is featured at the center of the represented world. This image, which is a unified sub-system of appearances, constitutes one's empirical self. It is the central subject of experience *represented* in the constructed world of one's experience.

To avoid serious confusion about Kant's philosophy, it is important to distinguish two different relations, which appearances bear to objects. One may be called the relation of *immanent* appearing or representing: this is the relation that holds between an appearance and a unified group of appearances to which it belongs. The round expanse I mentioned is an appearance in this sense of a basketball, which, as a complex object of experience, belongs to the world of appearance. So understood or conceived of, the basketball belongs to the represented world that we construct from the elements of sensation. Every object of this constructed world is (or arguably may be) an appearance in a *transcendental* sense: it is (or arguably may be) the appearance of a non-empirical, transcendental object.

The notion of a transcendental appearance is easiest to understand in relation to one's self. One's empirical self is a collective appearance in the immanent sense: it has the unity required by the concept of an object. But it is also, Kant thought, an appearance to one's transcendental self *of that self*. Apart from the knowledge that, as a transcendental subject of experience, I have certain powers of "combination," I have, Kant said, "no knowledge of myself as I am but merely as I appear to myself." [34] My empirical self (the organized system of appearances) is the appearance to my self of my self; it is how I appear to myself as the result of experiential input and conceptual processing.

Although every element in my constructed world of mental representation is an item of the bundle unified by my transcendental self, not every element in that world is, Kant thought, an appearance (in the transcendental sense) of that self. My empirical self has a human form, and the hand of mine that I see is visibly in touch with a basketball. Both hand and basketball are transcendental appearances, but only the hand is part of my transcendental appearance: the basketball is an appearance (to my transcendental self) of a transcendental object that somehow presents that appearance (or bundle of appearances). Since Kant held that things-in-themselves are unknowable for us, he could not claim to know that there is a distinct thing-in-itself corresponding to the observable basketball. I say "distinct thing-in-itself" because he did claim to know that empirical objects are, in whole or part, transcendental appearances of something existing in itself.[35] The concept of a thing-in-itself is too "indeterminate," as Kant described it, to justify us in claiming to know that there is a discrete pairing of appearances and transcendental objects.

If the objects of empirical knowledge – if such things as round, bouncy basketballs – are, for Kant, nothing but unified systems or "sums" of appearances,[36] then Hume's skeptical doubts about the external world are avoided by a strategy akin to Berkeley's: objects such as basketballs are not mind-independent objects but experiential constructs. As far as sensible objects are concerned, we have no need to bridge a gap between sensory data and mysterious reality. Sensible objects as Kant understood them are not, of course, wholly presented to our consciousness; so we do, at least ideally, have to infer their existence from our sensory data. But these inference do not carry us across a significant gap: they take us, by secure inductive strategies, from some appearances to others. In denying us knowledge of things-in-themselves, Kant did, it is true, admit to a kind of skepticism. But the objects he denied us knowledge of are inconceivable to us and thus not the sort of thing we think we know anyway.

The claim that Kant avoided skepticism about sensible objects by a strategy akin to Berkeley's is often rejected on the basis of the "Refutation of Idealism," which Kant inserted into the second edition of his *Critique*. In his opening remarks, Kant explicitly criticized Berkeley's "dogmatic idealism," and he proceeded to prove a thesis which certainly appears to be contrary to Berkeley's considered views – namely, that the "mere, but empirically determined, consciousness of my own existence proves the existence of objects in space outside me." [37] Yet Kant not only misdescribed Berkeley's view, saying that Berkeley regarded "things in space as merely imaginary entities," but he added that Berkeley's dogmatic idealism "is unavoidable if space be interpreted as a property that must belong to things in themselves." [38] Although Berkeley insisted that sensible things exist only "in the mind" and not in an extramental space, he claimed that their geometrical qualities are inseparable from them and thus exist "in the mind" as well. Kant, in insisting that space is not a property of things in themselves, substantially agreed with Berkeley on this point. If there is a difference between them here, it concerns the sort of "appearance" they took space to be. Kant, thinking we can conceive of an empty space, rejected the view that space can be understood as a system of relations.[39] Berkeley, rejecting Newton's absolute conception, evidently held a relational view.[40] Obviously, this difference has no bearing on the truth of an idealist interpretation of the spatio-temporal world.

Kant's claim that Berkeley's idealism is "unavoidable if space be interpreted as a property that must belong to things in themselves" actually made it obvious that he held some form of idealism himself. In fact, he did; he called it "transcendental idealism." [41] If, as he said in his opening remarks, space is not a property of things in themselves, the phrase occurring in the thesis, "the existence of objects in space outside me," must be taken to refer to the existence of appearances. And if objects do exist in space outside me, I must exist in space as well; for "outside" is a spatial predicate. Yet if "I" exist in space, "I" must be an appearance as well. Thus, Kant's thesis must pertain to the empirical I, the one constructed from the data received by the transcendental I. The content of Kant's thesis, then, is that I can be conscious of my existence as an empirical self (a unified, conscious object in space and time) only if proof is available to me that empirical objects objectively appear to exist in space outside me. I use the verb "objectively appear" here because the assertion that an empirical object exists in space is true, for a transcendental idealist, just in case certain bundles of spatio-temporal appearances are objectively available or appropriately "bound up" (as Kant put it) "with the material conditions of experience." [42]

7. Remarks on Kant's epistemology

There are indications that, toward the end of his life, Kant was in the process of working his way out of his transcendental idealism.[43] To succeed in this, he would have had to abandon the view that space, time, and the objects of experience are mere appearances. The thought of him abandoning this view prompts one to ask why he accepted it in the first place. The answer is complex. Basically, he inherited a mass of problems – metaphysical and epistemological – from his predecessors, and his transcendental idealism provided a means of resolving them in a systematic way.

One of the epistemological problems he hoped to resolve is

central to my concern here: if natural objects are independent of our conscious experience and exist in a separate spatio-temporal domain, how can we possibly have knowledge of them? Another problem is posed by the question, "How is synthetic *a priori* knowledge in geometry, mathematics, and general metaphysics possible?" Kant was convinced that we have this sort of knowledge and that transcendental idealism is the only way of accounting for it. His conviction on this last point was reinforced by his belief that a non-idealist view "cannot be thought without contradiction." [44] He defended this belief in his "Antinomy of Pure Reason," where he argued that his transcendental idealism provides a uniquely satisfactory means of avoiding four basic contradictions, which inevitably arise in speculative thought. These alleged contradictions concern the beginning of time, the limits of space, the parts of composite entities, natural causation and personal freedom, and the existence of a God or necessary being.

The problem about synthetic *a priori* knowledge no longer adds much credibility to Kant's transcendental idealism. For one thing, few philosophers, if any, would now agree that we have synthetic *a priori* knowledge in general metaphysics; and those who would insist that we have such knowledge in mathematics would seriously doubt that it is adequately accounted for by Kant's brand of idealism. The ability of his idealism to avoid the contradictions (or resolve the antinomies) that he mentioned also adds little credibility to his system today, for few contemporary philosophers would agree that those contradictions actually arise and need to be avoided by a system like Kant's.[45] The remaining grounds on which his system might be defended lie in its intrinsic credibility and its ability to deal with the epistemological problems I have been discussing in this book. In what follows I shall comment on both.

As far as the intrinsic credibility of his system is concerned, Kant's claims about the domain of unknowable things in themselves deserve a low mark. The question one naturally asks in response to those claims is: "How can we possibly know (or have good evidence) that something exists if we have no idea what the something is?" In the preface to his second edition Kant said that "though we cannot *know* these objects as things in themselves, we must yet be in a position to *think them* . . . otherwise we should be landed in the absurd conclusion that there can be appearance without anything that appears." [46] His observation is reasonable, but in the absence of *any* information about the nature of things in themselves, the language of appearance is dubiously applied to objects of experience. I happen to believe (and will argue in later chapters) that Kant's language is aptly applied to objects of experience, but my conviction on this point requires me to reject Kant's view that things in themselves are theoretically unknowable and not causally related to observers *via* ambient media such as light and air. Kant did, it is true, say something about a transcendental self, but his claim that it is a distinct bundle-unifier is hardly daunting to a critic like Hume. If the alleged unifier does the job (as Kant claims) by making judgments, these judgments are simply further items requiring unification, and an attachment to an unknown and unknowable subject does not do the needed work.

Since Kant's arguments in his analogies and "Refutation of Idealism" explicitly concern the structure of the represented world of appearance, the objects and selves of which we have knowledge are unifications or (as he put it) "sums" of appearances. The world described by these arguments has a coherent spatial-temporal-causal structure, and, if its relation to the unknowable domain of which it is a transcendental appearance is ignored, it amounts to a version of what we now call "phenomenalism." Such a view was defended by John Stuart Mill in the nineteenth century and was revived in the early years of our century, reaching its most sophisticated development in such works as Bertrand Russell's *Our Knowledge of the External World* [47] and Rudolf Carnap's *Der Logische Aufbau der Welt*.[48] A primary motivation of phenomenalism is to avoid a gap (or abyss) between evidential data and natural object. Such theories are now generally rejected, but they deserve some discussion because they exemplify a persistently adopted strategy for resolving a particularly stubborn problem. I propose to end this chapter with some critical observations about them.

8. Phenomenalism

Fundamentally, there have been two kinds of explicitly phenomenalist theory. The earliest kind is metaphysical in a traditional sense: it includes theories that concern the ultimate nature of the world. The latter kind is avowedly anti-metaphysical; the theories it includes are concerned with the meaning of empirical statements or assertions. Although the difference between these kinds of theory is significant, it is not decisive for the problem that concerns me in this book. Both kinds of theory arose from the same basic stimulus – the wish to avoid solipsism or skepticism about the external world – and both fail for a common reason: as endeavors to satisfy the wish that prompted them, they require a fund of knowledge which, if the wish is reasonable, cannot be obtained.

The view J. S. Mill expounded in his *Examination of Sir William Hamilton's Philosophy* is best understood as a view of the first kind. According to Mill, the relatively permanent objects of nature are distinct from the sensations we experience, but they are not unknowable things-in-themselves: they are "permanent possibilities of sensation." I see a white piece of paper on the table, Mill said. Although I cease to see the paper when I go into another room, I am persuaded that the paper is still there. My conviction here does not concern an unknowable non-white thing or even a *substratum* with a Lockean power to produce "ideas" of whiteness; it concerns an objective possibility – the possibility of getting paper-sensations of the sort I had earlier *if* I return to the room. Mill generalized the point this way:

> The conception I form of the world existing at any moment comprises, along with the sensations I am feeling, a countless variety of possibilities of sensation; namely, the whole of those which past observation tells me that I could, under any supposable circumstances, experience at this moment together with an indefinite and illimitable multitude of others which though I do not know that I could, yet it is possible that I might, experience in circumstances not known to me. These various possibilities are the important thing to me in the world. My present sensations are generally of little importance, and are moreover fugitive: the possibilities, on the contrary, are permanent, which is the character that mainly distinguishes our idea of Substance or Matter from our notion of sensation. These possibilities are . . . *conditional certainties*, [not] . . . mere vague possibilities, which experience gives us no warrant for reckoning upon.[49]

An important feature of these "certified or guaranteed possibilities of sensation" is that they concern not single sensations but sensations joined together in groups:

> When we think of anything as a material substance, or body,

109

we either have had, or think that on some given supposition we should have, not some *one* sensation, but a great and even an indefinite number and variety of sensations, generally belonging to different senses, but so linked together that the presence of one announces the possible presence at the very same instant of any or all of the rest.

In addition to recognizing such fixed groups of sensations as distinctive of the permanent possibilities making up our world, we also recognize a fixed order among the groups. This fixed order is the basis of our ideas of natural law – of cause and effect. The possibilities and the connections between them belong as much, Mill said, to other human or sentient beings as to ourselves:

> Other people do not have our sensations exactly when and where we have them; but they have our permanent possibilities of sensation; whatever indicates a present possibility of sensation to ourselves indicates a present possibility of sensation to them, except insofar as their organs of sensation may vary from the type of ours. This puts the final seal to our conception of the groups of possibilities as the fundamental reality in nature. The permanent possibilities are common to us and to our fellow creatures; the actual sensations are not.[50]

To round out his phenomenalism, Mill had to come to terms with minds or subjects of sensation. He did so by following the basic strategy he used in accommodating physical objects: apart from their current contents, minds are nothing more, he said, than permanent possibilities of feeling, thinking, and the like. Minds differ from one another, moreover, just as bodies differ: they are permanent possibilities that involve different "fixed groups." [51] My mind is a permanent possibility that involves this and that sensation or thought; other minds are permanent possibilities that involve other (but generically) similar items.

The existence of minds other than his own raises a serious problem for Mill's phenomenalism. How does he know that such things actually exist? The answer is: "by an analogical argument." In his words:

> I conclude that other people have feelings like me, because, first, they have bodies like me, which I know, in my own case,

110

to be the antecedent conditions of feelings; and because, secondly, they exhibit the acts, and other outward signs, which in my own case I know by experience to be caused by feelings.

He expanded upon this answer as follows:

> I am conscious in myself of a series of facts connected by a uniform sequence, of which the beginning is modifications of my own body, the middle is feelings, the end is outward demeanour. In the case of other human beings I have the evidence of my senses for the first and last links of the series, but not for the intermediate link. . . . In my own case I know that the first link produces the last through the intermediate link and could not produce it without. Experience, therefore, obliges me to conclude that there must be an intermediate link which must either be the same in others as in myself or a different one. . . . By supposing the link to be of the same nature [in both cases] . . . I bring other human beings, as phenomena, under the same generalizations which I know by experience to be the true theory of my own existence. And in doing so I conform to the legitimate rules of experimental inquiry.[52]

Although Mill's reasoning may seem reasonable and straightforward here, it involves a difficulty that is a direct consequence of his phenomenalism. Consider the sequences of supposed facts on which Mill bases his inference. According to the first sequence, a modification of (or change in) Mill's body is followed by a feeling he has, and the feeling is succeeded by a change in his body's outward demeanor. Mill claims that he knows of this by experience, but his phenomenalism makes this claim extremely dubious. To know that a real body exists, he must know that a suitable possibility (a very complicated one) is permanent. According to the "final seal" of his own statement, the relevant possibility must include feelings that are "common to us and to our fellow creatures." These common feelings are needed because a physical body is a publicly accessible object – not a complex subjective phenomenon, like an illusion or hallucination. Since Mill is concerned, in his argument, to prove that other minds or mind-bundles exist, he cannot assume that the required possibilities involving common feelings exist: to be rationally assured of their existence,

111

he would need to know what he is trying to prove. His analogical argument does not, therefore, succeed.

In view of the importance of Mill's argument and the brevity of my criticism, it is advisable to formulate the difficulty in another way. Consider the following. To avoid any circularity in his analogical reasoning, Mill cannot assume that the permanent possibilities corresponding to his body include sensory data available to any mind other than his own. The first series of facts he mentions in his argument can amount, therefore, to no more than this: there is a uniform sequence among *his sensations*, of which the beginning is sensations of a type *P*, the middle is sensations of a type *F*, and the end is sensations of a type *D*. He associates sensations of type *P* with something that is, to him, a permanent possibility of such (*P*-like) sensations; he associates sensations of type *F* with another permanent possibility (to him) of *F*-like and other sensations; and he associates sensations of type *D* with another permanent possibility – the same one, presumably, as that with which he associates *P*-like sensations. The second series of facts that he mentions is similarly restricted to his own sensations. The fact that the second series lacks intermediate sensations of type *F* does not, considered in conjunction with the first series, provide a plausible basis for concluding that sensations of that type exist in some other series – one to which Mill has no access. In relation to the facts cited in the argument, this conclusion has no plausibility at all.

If a phenomenalist theory is to provide a means of avoiding skepticism or a version of solipsism, it cannot identify a physical body or another mind with a construct based entirely on the data (the sensations, thoughts, and so forth) of a *single* consciousness. This would make it solipsistic. If, on the other hand, it identifies bodies and minds with constructs based on data belonging to different centers of consciousness, it makes crucial assumptions that it cannot justify – or, to put it another way, it takes for granted things that a phenomenalist cannot pretend to know. If I cannot claim knowledge of a domain of physical things external to my consciousness, how can I reasonably presume that I have knowledge of a domain of mental things external to my consciousness? The obvious answer is that I cannot.

This difficulty with metaphysical phenomenalism, the first kind that I mentioned, is shared by the linguistic phenomenalism that

112

was elaborated in the early years of our century. According to this second kind of phenomenalism, it is an error to say that physical objects are composed or constituted (in some way) by phenomenal items, or that physical objects are fictions and phenomenal items are real. The thesis, rather, is that statements (thoughts, sentences, or propositions) about physical objects are equivalent or "reducible to" statements about phenomenal data. This is a conceptual thesis, and it is properly evaluated by logico-analytic rather than scientific considerations.

Much of the argumentation concerning linguistic phenomenalism was focused on the basic objects of the theory and on difficulties pertaining to the translation of sentences in one idiom into sentences of another.[53] The basic objects, which I have referred to as phenomenal items, were called "sense data," and a good share of the critical writing on phenomenalism was concerned with the nature of sense data and the manner in which they are to be identified. One of the difficulties regarding translation that phenomenalists struggled to overcome can be indicated by an example. Take the physical object statement: "Tom's cat is yellow and weighs ten pounds." A first stab at translating this into phenomenal terms might be, "If you were to have sense data (or appropriate experiences) of Tom's cat, your data would be yellowish (of something yellow) and of something weighing ten pounds." Obviously, this translation is seriously inadequate because, for one thing, you might be color-blind and incapable of experiencing anything yellowish and, for another, no class of sense data is uniquely correlated with something weighing ten pounds. A modified translation could avoid these specific defects, but as past work on phenomenalism has shown, a new translation will generate new problems of its own. By the late 1940s even philosophers sympathetic to phenomenalism began to believe that the desired translations could not achieved.[54]

Although the point seems not to have been appreciated by linguistic phenomenalists, the fundamental defect of the whole program concerned the required knowledge of phenomenal regularities that phenomenalists could not reasonably claim to possess. The phenomenal (or sense datum) counterpart to a physical object statement must concern the actual and possible experiences of *all* (actual, normal, or standard) observers; yet no phenomenalist could reasonably claim to know, given his or her epistemic standards, what experiences any other observer would possess under any range of experiential conditions. I include the proviso "given his or her epistemic standards" because a philosopher who is attracted to phenomenalism possesses epistemic standards that render knowledge of "other minds" doubtful. As I shall argue in subsequent chapters, philosophers who believe they can achieve well-founded opinions about objects external to their consciousness can consistently claim to have well-founded opinions about those external-to-their-consciousness "objects" that are mental states of others. But these philosophers are not attracted to phenomenalism, metaphysical or linguistic. Philosophers attracted to phenomenalism are normally (if not invariably) trying to avoid skepticism or solipsism, and they have serious trouble justifying any claims that concern a domain (mental or physical) to which they lack immediate (or direct) access.

The objection to phenomenalism that I have been emphasizing here does not prove that phenomenalism is an erroneous doctrine; what it proves, if it is sound, is that phenomenalism does not provide a means of avoiding solipsism. If the world is constructed from a single phenomenal domain, one having the unity of a single consciousness, as Kant would have said, then the world is essentially solipsistic. We may feel, as I do, that a solipsist's world is seriously objectionable; but nothing I have said in this chapter proves it to be so.

CHAPTER V

A New Start

Although phenomenalism was a dominant view in the early years of the twentieth century, it began to lose ground in the 1930s and was generally abandoned twenty years later. Different groups of philosophers abandoned the view for different reasons. Some, like Bertrand Russell and Rudolf Carnap, came to believe that the quest for certainty is a delusion, that solipsism is as impossible to believe as it is impossible to refute, and that the claims of physical science should be accepted as approximately true even though they cannot be verified by standard empiricist methods.[1] Others, finding their inspiration in the later work of Ludwig Wittgenstein, became convinced that the subjective basis of classical empiricism is demonstrably incoherent and that "theories" such as solipsism and phenomenalism actually do not make sense. I shall devote the bulk of this chapter to the claims of the second group; I shall comment on the others' view in Chapters VI and VII.

1. Prelude to the "private language" argument

The conviction that the subjective basis of classical empiricism is demonstrably incoherent was largely created by the "private language" argument recorded in Wittgenstein's posthumous *Philosophical Investigations*.[2] This argument is rambling and discontinuous – a cluster of arguments, really – and sufficiently difficult to expound that individual commentators have devoted more than a hundred pages to the task.[3] Instead of proceeding directly to my own exposition of its principal contentions, I shall begin with a discussion of some of the background assumptions that relate the argument to the claims of actual empiricists. After giving my own exposition and evaluation of Wittgenstein's argument, I shall then undertake a general reconsideration of the traditional problems concerning our knowledge of the external world.

Sympathetic readers of Wittgenstein have insisted that the basic factual knowledge claimed by classical empiricists and accepted by solipsists and phenomenalists requires a basic, absolutely private language.[4] The language is supposed to be basic in the sense that its primitive expressions are not derivative from, and understandable only in relation to, the expressions of some further language; it is supposed to be private in the sense that no one but its possessor (a single mind, consciousness, or person) can possibly understand it. The conviction that a phenomenalist or solipsist must have such a language is a little surprising, because Locke, Berkeley, and Hume did not (as one can tell from my previous chapters) actually presume such a thing, and neither did Kant or Mill. On what ground, then, do Wittgenstein's sympathetic readers accept it? How can it be maintained in view of the actual claims of traditional empiricists?

Since it is useless to speculate about the views of Wittgenstein's readers, the latter question is the one I propose to answer. The obvious thing to say here is that, if Wittgenstein's argument is to apply to the empiricists I have mentioned, they must have made claims that committed them (whether they realized it or not) to the possibility of a private language – or central claims they made must be false if they could not possess such a language. The question is: Did their claims require such a possibility? Would the impossibility of a private language undermine the epistemic position they were concerned to hold?

Since the idea of a private language is complex, it is wise to begin with one of its elements. Take the bare idea of a language. Is there any reason to assume that a classical empiricist – one tempted by, or struggling with, phenomenalism or outright solipsism – is committed to having any language at all? One answer is that, without some language, an empiricist view could not be written down and communicated to anyone else. This answer would not trouble a philosopher who feels compelled to take solipsism seriously: he or she would have to insist on the possible futility of any communicative act. A better answer, one that Wittgenstein himself might have given, is that a basic representational system (a language, in an important sense of the term) is needed to accommodate a double-barreled assumption that every classical empiricist tacitly accepted – namely, that sensory impressions are present to a center of consciousness and that the center of consciousness can explicitly register the presence of those impressions and classify them as instances of appropriate kinds.

This better answer can be supported by the following considerations. As even Descartes recognized, explicit knowledge that something is the case requires more than mere sensation: it requires judgment, which is exercised in mental affirmations to the effect (in simple cases) that *something is such-and-such.* Kant made it clear that a mental affirmation not only has logical form but includes representational elements (intuitions, concepts) that apply to the objects it concerns. These representational elements play the role of subjects and predicates, and they are associated with elements playing the role of quantifiers, connectives, and copulas. Abstractly speaking, these semantic roles can be described as linguistic in a logical sense of the term; and the system to which the elements playing them belong can be described as a language in a logical sense of that term – even though the system may lack any communicative function. Philosophers are nowadays accustomed (as they were in Wittgenstein's time) to speaking of semantic systems as "languages."

It is true, as I mentioned earlier, that the early empiricists – Locke, Berkeley, and Hume – did not acknowledge a basic language in which to represent primitive convictions about their ideas or impressions. Their failure to do so was in certain respects just a symptom of their inadequate conception of mental representation. This inadequacy stands out sharply in Hume's account of the distinction between impressions and ideas. As he explained on the second page of his *Treatise*, the distinction he intended to draw is illustrated by the contrast between feeling and thinking. Although he placed ideas in the context of thinking and reasoning, he proceeded to assimilate thinking to imaging:

> When I shut my eyes and think of my chamber, the ideas I form are exact representations of the impressions I felt; nor is there any circumstance of the one, which is not to be found in the other.[5]

In describing ideas as "exact representations" of impressions, he implied, or at least suggested, that ideas represent certain impressions because they are faint copies of them. This is an inadequate account of mental representation and an impossible account of thinking. When I identify an impression as a passion or physical sensation, I not only refer to (or represent) that impression without producing a faint copy of it, but I classify it in a certain way. My thought that the impression is a physical sensation has judgmental form, as Kant would say; and it is too complicated to be identified with a Humean idea or even a complex of such ideas. At the very least, it must somehow involve or exemplify an assertoric function – one by which a subject is classified as an instance of a kind.

If mental representation requires, at the very least, a system of elements that play referring, classifying, quantifying, and connecting roles, then the claim that a classical empiricist requires a basic sensation language is not unreasonable. But need such a language be private? When Wittgenstein introduced the notion of a private language, he was thinking of the supposed referents of words in a language specially designed to give verbal expression to a person's "inner experiences":

> The individual words of this language are to refer to what can only be known to the person speaking; to his immediate private sensations. So another person cannot understand the language.[6]

The idea is that if words merely refer to immediate sensations, they are referring to items knowable only to the speaker (or thinker) and not anyone else. Such items are private to the person experiencing them.

This view of "immediate sensations" was not actually expressed by the classical empiricists, and it is not forced on them by the requirement that a domain of such sensations can be mentally represented and classified only by a representational system that can be described as a language. Not only did Hume raise skeptical doubts about a subject of experience, claiming that a mind is evidently nothing more than a bundle of impressions and ideas that conform to certain psychological laws (of idea formation, association, and the like); he did not explicitly rule out the possibility that a given idea or impression could belong to more than one bundle. To rule out such a possibility Hume would have needed more information about conscious subjects, or mind-bundles, than he claimed to possess; and he would have needed even more such information to support the claim that a language referring to immediate sensations could not be understood by anyone other than a certain subject. Wittgenstein's description of a private language thus presumes things that classical empiricists did not hold and, I would say, could not defend. The philosophers he argued against, in his critical reflections on a private sensation language, are theoretically less austere than a skeptic like Hume.

Hume's inability to defend the assumptions Wittgenstein made about a sensation language may, of course, be a symptom of a deeper inadequacy in his system. Although he did not acknowledge a distinct subject of experience, might he not have to do so if he is to deal coherently with mental representation and classification? An affirmative answer is certainly not obvious here, but the point is arguable and very important. A key consideration, brought out in Wittgenstein's argument, concerns the notion of reference, either verbal or mental. It is possible, I claimed earlier, to single out an object of experience (an impression, perhaps) without producing a faint replica or Humean idea of it. If I am right about this, there is more to mental reference than Hume evidently allowed. In his private language argument Wittgenstein claimed in effect that a thing S (a word or symbol) can refer to a thing O only if S is associated with a practice that governs the behavior of a community of conscious subjects. If this sort of claim is correct, Hume's empiricism is incoherent on account of its theoretical austerity. To be coherent, a basic epistemological theory must do something Hume failed to do: it must acknowledge the referential and classificatory practices of some community.

This last claim may or may not be correct. If it is, the relevance of Wittgenstein's argument to classical empiricism (and to the subject of this book) is shown by the contentions it includes. I shall consider them now.

2. Wittgenstein's argument

After introducing the idea of a private sensation language, Wittgenstein asked how the words of such a language could stand for sensations.[7] Since the language is intended to be private and not dependent on the language of some community, the words could not stand for sensations in what Wittgenstein took to be the customary way – by being tied up with the natural behavioral expression of sensations. The answer he initially considered is that names are "mentally associated" with sensations and used in descriptions of them. Yet a mental association between name and sensation could make the former *stand for* the latter only if it brings it about that, in future uses of the word, the language-user uses it correctly – that is, applies it to the *right* sensation.[8] Unfortunately, a solitary language-user (one cut off from a linguistic community and concerned with a domain of private sensations) can have no criterion of correctness here. Although she may later have the impression that a certain sensation is the one with which she associated a name *S*, she will have no way of knowing whether this impression is correct or not. Yet if she has no way of knowing this – no way of distinguishing *seeming to be right* from *being right* – she cannot reasonably maintain that such a distinction exists and that the name *S* really stands for that sensation, or any other.

The expression "mental association" is a little misleading in the context of Wittgenstein's argument, for if a word *S* is genuinely associated with a sensation (or kind of sensation)[9] *E*, it would be perfectly reasonable to take an occurrence of *S* as indicating the presence of *E*. Wittgenstein clarified matters in his next paragraph, however, replacing his reference to a mental association with a reference to a private ostensive process – one of repeating a word and concentrating one's attention on the relevant sensation (once, twice, or many times). This sort of process is supposed to *result* in a stable association between word and sensation – one sufficient to make the word represent the sensation. Wittgenstein argued that an ostensive process of this kind cannot yield such a result. One may have the impression, after carrying out the process, that one reliably associates the word *S* with a particular sensation, but this impression cannot be *assumed* to be correct. Instead of having become stably associated with a determinate sensation (or kind of sensation), *E*, the word *S* may have become associated with "anything or nothing" – in which case *S* will not represent the desired private object.

To see the point of the "anything or nothing" association, suppose that the sensations in the presence of which *S* is uttered actually comprise what we or God would identify as a highly heterogeneous class – one consisting of a twinge of pain, a sinking feeling in the stomach, a feeling of elation, and other dissimilar elements. If we describe the members of the class as "just anything," the association between S and those members will be insufficient to render S the name of a conceptually distinct (or unified) sensation. If, on the other hand, we describe the correlate of S as "nothing" – finding nothing plausibly common to the members of the class – a naming relation between S and a sensation will not be set up either. Since a *mere impression of sameness* is compatible with both these possibilities, the ostensive process producing it cannot single out or identify a suitable referent for S. To single out such a referent, one must appeal to something *independent* of one's mere impression.[10] But the creator of a private language has nothing of this sort available.

It has been objected that the creator of a private language can certainly appeal to one thing that is independent of his mere impression here: he can appeal to a rule that he has freely created. The idea is this.[11] Suppose the alleged creator of the private language (call him "Privatus") is under the impression that he has associated the word S with a sensation of kind E and that he is now experiencing a sensation of this kind. To corroborate this impression, he may appeal to a rule that he has freely created to govern his use of S. The rule is, "Sensations of kind E are distinguished by the features A, B, and C." Noticing that the sensation he is now experiencing has the features A, B, and C, Privatus appeals to his rule specifying the kind E and concludes that his sensation is indeed of this kind. In proceeding this way he has found something independent of his mere impression to confirm his belief that the sensation in question is of kind E. This possibility undermines the force of Wittgenstein's argument.

Even if we concede that Privatus has the sort of rule that he is supposed to have here, we can deny that the objection is adequate to its purpose. Wittgenstein's argument is focused on the ultimate relation between words and their referents, and the objection is not focused on that relation. If Privatus has rules relating a classifying expression E to predicates $A, B,$ and C, then he can confirm his impression that a sensory occurrence is correctly classifiable as an E by appealing to these rules, which are independent of that impression. But to apply these rules in the case at hand, Privatus will have to be assured that the predicates $A, B,$ and C are truly applicable in that case. Thus, the problem Wittgenstein raised for him is not resolved but redirected. Wittgenstein raised the problem by querying the relation between an expression *E* and certain sensory objects, but he did not present *E* as a special expression raising special problems: he presented it as a representative example of a private word. An attempt to resolve Wittgenstein's problem about the correct application of *a* private word to *a* private domain by appealing to a rule whose use requires the application of private words to a private domain is a blatant example of question begging. By itself, it cannot succeed.

I said that the objection cannot succeed "by itself" because it is arguable that the objection is successful when joined to other considerations. But what might these other considerations be? A philosopher opposed to Wittgenstein might attempt to identify them by the following line of reasoning: Any attempt to assure oneself that a word *W* is correctly applied to an object O must of necessity appeal to a conviction whose acceptability requires that some other word is correctly applied to an object. This is not special to a private language. If I attempt to assure myself that I have applied a word *X* to an object y by appealing to another person, I can succeed only by assuming that some words (or possibly some gestures) that she uses are correctly used. I need not make this assumption uncritically, for I could become convinced that she spoke inconsistently, incoherently, or maliciously. Yet if I do accept her words as supporting or correcting mine, I must in the end accept at least some of them as correctly used. In fact, I must in the end accept more than this: I must accept some impressions I have of what she is saying – of what words she is uttering and what she is referring to when she is using them. In doing this I shall be evaluating (confirming or correcting) one impression of what a word applies to by other impressions of what words apply to. This will always be true, ultimately, no matter how many people are brought into the picture.

In his interesting book, *Wittgenstein on Rules and Private Language*,[12] Saul Kripke argued that the basic problem Wittgenstein addressed in his discussion of a private sensation language was focused on the general notion of following a rule. This basic problem was a skeptical one, he said, like Hume's problem of causal inference; and the solution Wittgenstein offered was, like Hume's, a skeptical one as well. Wittgenstein's skeptical problem about rule-following arose from the fact that nothing true of a person's previous use of a word – nothing in her mind when she used it, and nothing in the "instructions she may have given herself" concerning its use – determines how it is rightly applied in subsequent cases. Kripke discussed the problem at great length, but the upshot of his discussion can be indicated very simply by saying that everything true of the person's previous use of a word is compatible with "indefinitely many" different hypotheses about how that word is correctly interpreted. The skeptical solution he read Wittgenstein as providing is that social practice (rather than anything true of an individual speaker) will determine what is correct in future cases. This solution is not applicable to a private language, and that is Wittgenstein's fundamental objection to such a thing.

Kripke's description of Wittgenstein's skeptical problem is closely related to the gist of my reply to the claim that Privatus could confirm his questionable impression by appealing to a rule that he has adopted. I said that this claim merely redirected Wittgenstein's question about the relation between a private word E and the objects of a private domain to a question about the relation between predicates in the rule and objects in that domain. If a particular interpretation of those predicates is not assumed (a matter falling within the scope of the question Wittgenstein is asking) the rule is useless as a means of confirming the impression about E. In posing what he took to be Wittgenstein's skeptical problem, Kripke said that the correct application of a word cannot be determined by anything in the speaker's mind when the word is uttered because anything in her mind at that time can be interpreted in countless ways. Thus, if she follows the rule "E applies to green color-sensations," the future applications of her word E are still open to question because the same is true of the words in her rule: as far as her total state of mind and mental history is concerned, her word "green" could mean "grue" – that is, "green if experienced before time t and blue otherwise."[13]

Is the skeptical solution Kripke attributes to Wittgenstein really satisfactory? Does the appeal to social practice provide a better solution than an appeal to an individual's practice? I am doubtful in both cases. If an individual must be able to appeal *without relevant circularity* to something independent of his mere impression that he is using a word correctly, it is hard to see how the verdict of some community can provide the assurance he needs. To take account of that verdict, he must employ words that he can understand; and if the words he thus employs are, in their own terms, subject to countless rival interpretations, the same should be true of that social verdict. As for the relation between an individual's practice and a social practice, Wittgenstein's view seems to have been that an individual's future practice (or behavior) in applying a word is too indeterminate to provide an acceptable means of settling a question (or resolving a skeptical doubt?) about its correct application in a given case. Yet I cannot see that the behavior of a community is any more determinate than that of an individual. Social agreement is logically compatible with tandem randomness, where a whole group of people utter the same words in the presence of objects belonging to what I called highly heterogeneous classes. Thus, the possibility of individual randomness in the application of a word or, indeed, an entire vocabulary should be no more significant, for the interpretation of language, than the possibility of a tandem randomness in the same thing.

3. On the common-sense basis of Wittgenstein's argument

Whether one agrees with Kripke's interpretation or not, one must acknowledge that there are two principal parts to Wittgenstein's private language argument. There is a part in which a problem of interpretation is described and attributed to a private language, and there is a part in which the problem is said to be avoided by a language subject to social control. To be successful, both parts of the argument must succeed. I have just expressed some general doubts about the second part – some doubts relating to the contrast between social and individual practices or semantic regularities. I now want to discuss some possible doubts of another kind. These latter doubts are based on epistemic considerations pertinent to the subject of this book.

To show that a public or community language does not involve the problems that, in his view, undermine the possibility of a genuinely private language, Wittgenstein made numerous claims about social practices and what he called "forms of life." When, for example, he asked "How is the connection between a name and the thing named set up?", he replied:

This question is the same as: how does a human being learn
the meaning of the names of sensations? – of the word "pain"
for example. Here is one possibility: words are connected with

the primitive, the natural, expressions of the sensation and used in their place. A child has hurt himself and he cries; and then adults talk to him and teach him exclamations and, later, sentences. They teach the child new pain-behavior.[14]

Put in the context of a philosophical investigation in which the existence of an external world and a human community is in question, the credentials of such claims are highly dubious. If we are to refute solipsism or phenomenalism by an argument concerning the requirements of mental representation or reference, we cannot simply assume that there is an external world inhabited by adults and children who learn a community language, talk to one another, and express their feelings by laughter and cries.

During the Wittgensteinian revolution in the 1960s many philosophers seemed to move directly from the conviction that private languages are impossible to the conclusion that common beliefs about a publicly observable world are beyond serious question and that the only natural objects, events, or states whose existence is worth serious philosophical discussion are publicly unobservable – such things as the pains and thoughts of others and the micro-objects postulated in the physical sciences. The traditional problem concerning the external world and constructive programs such as phenomenalism were quickly abandoned in this transition, and the problem of other minds and the acceptability of scientific realism moved to the top of the agenda in analytic epistemology.[15] The agenda of the 1960s is now seriously dated, and the weakness of the transition should be painfully obvious to anyone who seriously considers the arguments of Locke, Berkeley, and Hume with a philosophically unbiased, open mind. Bias, unfortunately, is extremely difficult to avoid in philosophy, and the transition in question is aided and abetted by a philosophical picture that has, in my opinion, long outlived its usefulness. The picture concerns the structure of our knowledge or justifiable opinion.

As I explained in Chapter I, Descartes inherited from his medieval forebears and, ultimately, from Aristotle a distinctive conception of "science," or organized knowledge.[16] According to this conception, genuine knowledge involves rational certainty, which is either intrinsic or inferential. Intuition is crucial to both kinds of certainty: intrinsic certainties are intuitively obvious; and inferential certainties are obtained from intrinsic ones by a form of certainty-preserving inference, each step of which, for Descartes and, to some extent, even for Aristotle, must be intuitively acceptable.[17] This picture of knowledge – this scientific ideal – was also officially accepted by Locke, who emphasized the limitations of our knowledge and the importance of well-founded uncertainty (or probability) for rational opinion.[18] Hume decisively abandoned the ideal, not only denying that demonstration is appropriate for matters of fact, but declaring (in an optimistic moment) that a non-demonstrative "argument from experience" may sometimes provide such compelling evidence for a conclusion as to deserve the name of "proof."[19]

In spite of their increased respect for rational uncertainty, Locke, Hume, and even Mill retained the conviction that beliefs obtained by inference are ultimately supported by a foundation of privileged data. As Hume put it:

> If I ask you why you believe any particular matter of fact
> which you relate, you must tell me some reason; and the
> reason will be some other fact connected with it. But as you
> cannot proceed after this manner *in infinitum*, you must at last
> terminate in some fact, which is present to your memory or
> senses; or must allow that your belief is entirely without
> foundation.[20]

The foundational facts Hume speaks of here must be present to one's memory or senses – and not, in his opinion, ascertained by *a priori* intuition – because the conclusions concern matters of fact and existence. As I explained in Chapter III, Hume held that *a priori* truths were independent of anything "anywhere existent in the universe."[21]

Philosophers convinced that rationally well-founded opinions must ultimately rest on a foundation not supported by further facts will be faced by a dilemma if they are convinced by Wittgenstein's argument against private languages. Assuming they agree that well-founded opinion or belief requires a conceptual system that is, in the logical sense, a language, one can express the dilemma very simply: either no well-founded opinion is possible in matters respecting the actual world, or foundational opinions must be attainable in a non-private or publicly accessible domain. To accept the first horn is to accept utter skepticism in empirical matters; if skepticism is unacceptable, or if one cannot accept it, the alternative is evidently a common-sense view of the world – just the thing that Wittgenstein appeared to accept.

Anyone accepting the foundations picture and convinced by Wittgenstein's objections to private languages will find it easy to reject radical skepticism. Wittgenstein portrayed the skeptic as a confused and unreasonable person whose intelligence, like that of others in philosophical trouble, has been "bewitched" by means of language; and his sympathetic reader will presume that a skeptical doctrine must involve some kind of mistake. A common-sense alternative to skepticism will thus be very attractive to such a reader. Her inability to defend the alternative will not be discouraging if she accepts the foundations picture, for foundationalists are never in a position (really) to defend the foundation they favor: foundational truths are supposed to be ultimate justifiers, and foundationalists are committed to denying that there is anything more basic that could possibly justify them.[22]

Although a foundationalist accepting a commonsensical view of the world will naturally suppose that classical empiricism must rest on impossible foundations, it is important for impartial investigators to keep the actual arguments of Locke, Berkeley, and Hume in clear perspective. It is particularly important to realize that, in spite of their evident attraction to the foundationalist ideal of rational opinion, these empiricists did not put themselves on the road to solipsism by a naive and unreasoning commitment to a private or subjective foundation for empirical knowledge. In fact, each of them began with a commonsensical view of himself and the world around him, and then, as the result of difficulties forced upon him by critical reflections on that view, each drew conclusions that led to a theoretical outcome which only in Hume's case was admittedly skeptical. The difficulties they found in a commonsensical view were plausible and serious, and the problems raised with Locke's alternatives by Berkeley and Hume cannot reasonably be dismissed by Wittgenstein's critical observations on supposed private languages.

4. Reinventing the problem

Although Wittgenstein's private language argument raised important and interesting issues, I want to spend a few pages supporting my conviction that it did not effectively solve, dissolve, or otherwise dispose of the problem that I am concerned with in this book. To provide this support I shall reconstruct the problem without making the assumptions that Wittgenstein attributed to a defender of private language. Perhaps such a defender can be forced to accept such assumptions as a condition of raising my problem, but this will have to be shown by an argument Wittgenstein did not explicitly supply. To get my ball rolling, I shall begin with some reminders about Locke's view of the physical world, which is still initially attractive to anyone who takes physical science seriously.

One of Locke's principal contentions was that an object's secondary qualities – its color, smell, taste, and the sounds it makes – are mere powers to produce "ideas" in suitably situated perceivers. As Berkeley rightly insisted, however, mere powers cannot be seen, smelled, tasted, or heard: their presence in objects must be inferred from (ultimately) things that are immediately sensed but not inferred. These "things" are, he added, mind-dependent qualities that ordinary people regard as colors, odors, tastes, and sounds. In spite of its paradoxical implications (that colors cannot be seen, etc.)[23] Locke's conception of colors, odors, tastes, and sounds is now almost universally accepted by scientifically informed people. Nevertheless, Berkeley made a profoundly true observation when he said that the beautiful red and purple we see in the clouds are not really in those clouds, though they appear to be there. Sophisticated people may insist that the words "red" and "purple" properly apply to clouds, flags, and fire engines rather than items existing in a mind, but they cannot deny that the qualities ordinary people (and even themselves in careless moments) associate with these words not only exist but do so in some perceiver-dependent way.

If, looking out on what we take to be the world, we accept Locke's claim that the sensible qualities we immediately perceive – the colors we see, the bangs and rumbles we hear, the odors we smell, and the flavors we taste – are not observer-independent qualities of external objects but effects (or manifestations) of powers that we call "secondary qualities," we might ask ourselves what we take the subjects (or possessors) of these powers to be. Locke's corpuscularian view comes to mind as a rough approximation to the truth. The objects affecting our senses are aggregates of miniscule particles that reflect light, produce vibrations in the ambient air, and thereby bring about changes in the cells of our sense-organs, which are themselves aggregates of miniscule particles. These miniscule particles, which, at higher levels of analysis, compose what we call physical bodies, have "primary qualities" as Locke said they do: roughly speaking, they have position and extension in space and time; they are in rapid motion; and they interact with one another, causing changes in one another's position, velocity, and the like. I speak of "higher levels of analysis" here because the atoms composing molar objects are now regarded as aggregates themselves. The fundamental objects composing physical aggregates are now believed to have few if any qualities Locke would have considered primary: they do not even possess a determinate spatio-temporal position.[24]

The belief that the molar objects of our world are systems of ultimately exotic micro-entities whose collective sensible qualities are really powers to produce sensory effects in our consciousness has dramatic consequences. One is that the individual objects thus believed to make up our world are not observable and have no sensible qualities at all: their existence is merely postulated by basic physical theory. The colored expanses present in our experience, which also exemplify what Berkeley called primary qualities, do not actually belong, therefore, to external objects. Saying this is compatible, again, with the linguistic fact that words like "red" and "round" are ostensibly applied to physical things (believed to be aggregates) rather than private (or subjective) entities. Another consequence is that, if we direct our attention to ourselves, looking down at our torsos or peering into mirrors, we merely encounter sensory effects of what we believe to be additional physical bodies – that is, further systems of micro-objects. From this perspective, our own bodies are just as theoretical and exotic as other so-called molar objects. But what about our minds, our "centers of consciousness"? If we "look inwardly", as Hume did, we find no spiritual subject that holds our experiences together. What we are immediately aware of, apart from various thoughts and feelings, is what we have hitherto taken to be our bodies and the world around us. If this object of awareness is actually a unified system of sensory effects, it amounts to a subjective world of appearance.

Such an object of awareness not only exists in my experience but, I am convinced, would exist there even if I lacked the ability to identify and classify its constituents. Its existence does not therefore require me to have a language or conceptual scheme. What is not obvious is what the object actually is and what exists in addition to it. Perhaps it is the temporally extended, internally unified system of largely sensory effects that I believe it to be. But what can justify this belief? What can justify the belief that the object is associated with a self and indicates the presence of an external world? To take matters a step further, what justifies my belief that countless systems of micro-objects and other centers of consciousness also exist? These questions reasonably arise in spite of Wittgenstein's private language argument, and they pose a problem regarding our knowledge of ourselves and the external world to which Hume could offer only a skeptical solution.

5. A problem about the self

To ask how certain beliefs that I have can be justified is not to project myself illegitimately into a context where my existence is being questioned. The query concerns *what* I believe, a certain proposition; and evidence pertinent to this proposition can be considered without presuming that I exist as a believing subject. This disclaimer is idle if R. M. Chisholm is right, however. In his view the sensory experience I have described is "self-presenting" and, in consequence, "necessarily such" that it acquaints me with my self.[25] Claims as potent as these should be considered right away.

Unfortunately, Chisholm presents his views in a series of definitions constructed on the basis of a minimum philosophical vocabulary that presupposes a controversial ontology of "eternal objects." To understand what he wishes to convey by most of his definitions, one has to consult further definitions, working one's way back to those containing expressions from his minimum vocabulary. And then, to relate the views expressed in his minimum vocabulary to the subject in which one is interested, one has to relate that subject to his special ontology. Since I do not wish to spend time working through his definitions and relating them to the alleged direct awareness of the self, I shall informally explain his leading ideas on this subject and then comment on just a couple of his definitions.

Chisholm believes that certain states of affairs, including what Hume called impressions and ideas, are self-presenting to a person and known directly by that person. Chisholm also believes that "whenever a person thus knows something directly he may be said to have *direct knowledge of himself*"; in Russell's terms, "he may be said to be *directly acquainted* with himself." Self-presenting states involving impressions and ideas are, Chisholm adds, "states of the knower himself"; and "in knowing them directly, he knows himself directly."[26] Chisholm also expresses his view in slightly different words, speaking of properties rather than states of a knower or states of affairs. "If you are now awake and conscious", he says, "then you have certain properties such that you are now known directly by yourself to have those properties. Thus you may now be such that you seem to hear a voice, or believe yourself to be in North America or in Great Britain. . . . If you do have such properties as these, then you have direct knowledge of yourself."[27]

A self-presenting state of affairs (or proposition)[28] is one that occurs to a person at a certain time and that "is necessarily such" that, whenever it occurs, it is certain for that person.[29] When accepting it at that time is more reasonable for that person than withholding it, and when there is nothing more reasonable for her to accept at that time. Chisholm says that the first clause of this last sentence can be re-expressed by saying that the relevant proposition is "beyond reasonable doubt" for the person at the time. His idea, then, is that if, say, a person feels pain at a given moment, then a certain proposition or belief is *necessarily beyond reasonable doubt for* that person at that time and no proposition is more reasonable for her to accept then.

Chisholm defines the sense of "direct acquaintance" whose target is, or may be, a self as follows:

> s is acquainted with x at t = Df. There is a p such that (i) p is self-presenting for s at t and (ii) there is a property that p implies x to have.

To appreciate the significance of this definition, it is helpful to consider an example. Take the state of affairs *my feeling depressed*. According to Chisholm, this state of affairs implies the property *feeling depressed*. Chisholm's notion of implication (or entailment) is very unusual: not only can states of affairs or propositions imply properties (they do so when the truth of a proposition, or the occurring of a state of affairs, ensures that something has the property), but they do so only when it is necessary that anyone who accepts the proposition believes that something has the property.[30]

How does this apparatus apply to a philosopher like Hume?

131

Suppose that a certain impression occurs at a time t. Is this sensory item self-presenting in Chisholm's sense? As I have expressed it, the question is not easy to answer. According to Chisholm's definition D.I, a state of affairs is self-presenting to a person s at a time t only if it is necessarily such that, whenever it occurs, it is certain for s. For the impression I mentioned to satisfy this definition, it must necessarily be such that *it* is certain for some person whenever it occurs. But can a particular impression occur at more than one time? And can a particular impression (a sensory one) be certain? I should say no in both cases. Chisholm, obviously, is thinking not of particular sensory (or mental) occurrences but of occurrence-types (as they may be called), which may be exemplified, or "occur", at various times. Moreover, what he takes to be certain are not these types but corresponding beliefs (or propositions) to the effect that an impression-of-this-type is exemplified here.[31] Does the impression I mentioned satisfy this condition? How are we to know? Chisholm would probably claim that the answer is obvious, but no empiricist would agree. Why? Because the certainty of a contingent belief is not "necessarily" assured by the occurrence of any distinct matter of fact: there is no contradiction (as Hume would say) in the idea that the impression occurs and no contingent belief is certain.

Since the point here is very important, it is worth putting it in another way. As Chisholm defines "self-presenting," the entity that is self-presenting at a time is also the entity that is certain for the subject to whom it is presented. But a headache or even a headache-type (supposing there to be such a thing) is not the sort of thing one may be *certain* about or "accept." As Chisholm himself seems to recognize in his gloss on his definition, if *my feeling depressed* is a self-presenting state, then (as he believes) people are necessarily such that, if they are depressed, then they are certain that they are depressed.[32] The self-presenting state that he says *occurs* here is a feeling, the feeling of being depressed; but what he implies is *certain for people* is a proposition to the effect that *they have this feeling.*[33] A classical empiricist (like Hume) would reject the claim that people are necessarily such that, if they have a certain feeling, then a particular proposition concerning that feeling is certain for them because the occurrence of a mere feeling cannot guarantee that anyone has any conception of what that feeling is or has the ability to classify it as a feeling rather than as a horse or a bolt of lightning.

The claim, with or without the word "necessarily," is not an analytic truth expressing a mere relation between ideas.

When Chisholm identifies his representative state with the words "my feeling depressed," he gives a specious plausibility to the idea that the occurrence of this feeling makes him acquainted with his self. This acquaintance is implied by his definition if there is a proposition p that is self-presenting and a property that p implies him to have. Assuming that the state of his feeling depressed is self-presenting, we can easily identify the required value of the variable "p" as the proposition that he is depressed – a proposition clearly implying that *he* has the property of being depressed. Chisholm's idea here has a specious plausibility because the words he uses to identify the feeling in question gratuitously supply a subject for a self-presenting proposition that has the implication he desires. But a mere feeling of depression does not itself identify a subject or provide a description: *it* identifies or describes nothing. Since "percepts," as Kant rightly said, are blind without concepts, mere feelings can possibly (or in principle) occur without any contingent proposition being certain or reasonably believed by anyone.[34]

After presenting his definitions relating feelings to the direct awareness of the self, Chisholm offered some critical remarks about the Humean tradition on the subject of experience. Some of his remarks were directed against an argument that he attributed to Hume, an argument supporting the conclusion, "I cannot be directly aware of myself." I want to say something about this argument because Chisholm's remarks about it not only misrepresent Hume's philosophy but instructively misrepresent the problem that led Hume to his skeptical view of his self.

According to Chisholm, the "essence" of Hume's argument concerning the self can be represented as follows:

1 I cannot be directly aware of any object unless that object is an impression.
2 I am not an impression.
3 Therefore, I cannot be directly aware of myself.

Chisholm observed that "oddly enough, Hume did not explicitly defend the first premiss," but the oddness is misplaced: not only did Hume not offer the argument, but its first premiss and conclusion are at odds with his empiricist doctrine. Note that the first premiss

133

and the conclusion contain the modal word "cannot," which connotes some kind of impossibility. According to Hume's doctrine,[35] impossibilities are either *a priori* or *a posteriori*: the former are genuine and concern mere relations between ideas; the latter are feigned and represent the mind's acquired tendency to expect one thing when another thing is experienced, the tendency resulting from the experience of a constant conjunction between things of appropriate kinds. Hume did not suppose that the first premiss and the conclusion express mere relations between ideas (and are what we might call analytic), nor did he suppose they express an invariant constant conjunction between objects of experience. Neither statement would therefore be acceptable to him.

Did Hume offer any argument for his view that no self is observable when one "looks inwardly"? I can find no argument, though one might contend that a tacit inductive generalization is present: roughly, "No self was apparent; no self is apparent; so, no self will be apparent." Hume was led to his view by a search for the impression that, according to his account of idea formation, must be available if the idea of a single, simple, indivisible self is properly formed. The question he asked was: "From what impression cou'd this idea be deriv'd?" And in raising it he observed:

> This question is impossible to answer without a manifest contradiction and absurdity; and yet 'tis a question which must necessarily be answer'd if we would have the idea of self pass for clear and intelligible.[36]

In his appendix to the *Treatise* he noted that "upon a more strict review of the section concerning *personal identity*, I find myself in such a labyrinth that, I must confess, I neither know how to correct my former opinions, nor how to render them consistent." If this is not a good "general" reason for skepticism, he added, it is at least a sufficent one for him to entertain a "diffidence and modesty" in all his decisions.[37]

After criticizing the argument above, Chisholm made some interesting critical remarks about Hume's bundle theory of the mind. Our idea of a mind – "if by 'a mind' we mean, as Hume usually does, a person or self" – is not, Chisholm says, the idea of mere particular impressions:

> It is an idea of that which loves or hates, and of that which

134

feels cold or warm (and, of course, of much more besides). That is to say, it is an idea of an x such that x loves or x hates and such that x feels cold or x feels warm, and so forth.[38]

Hume's considered response to this claim would be complicated. It is true, he would say, that our idea of a mind (or conscious being) purports to be the idea of a subject, a thing, that loves, hates, feels warm, and the like. But an alleged idea of this sort, lacking a discernible basis in experience, is not "clear and intelligible." Given the experience we actually have, the clearest and most intelligible idea of a self we can reasonably claim to have is that of a certain bundle of impressions and ideas – that is, the bundle containing *this* and *that* (the *this* and *that* denoting certain occurrent ideas or impressions).

Hume's view of idea formation is, I concede, defective, and so is his distinctive principle for criticizing alleged ideas.[39] But the basic problem he set regarding the self still remains if we are careful to reconstruct the epistemic context in which it arises. I described this context in the last section of this chapter. We begin by thinking of ourselves as psycho-physical beings that we can see, pinch, or observe in mirrors, but theoretical reflections convince us that the colored, bulgy expanses that vision presents us with are, like the phenomena we receive from our other senses, "mere appearances," not independent realities. When we "look inwardly," attending to what we regard as our own subjective reality, we encounter more phenomena, not a unitary thing that has them. We continue to think "*I* see this," "*I* feel that," but the referent of our first-person singular pronouns, is now obscure: we do not know what, if anything, it attaches to. So we have a problem.

Chisholm acknowledges no such problem. He "knows" that he is an x that thinks, feels, loves, hates, and the like. Does he also "know" that he is a large man at least six feet in height who breathes, eats, sleeps, and works at a desk? Does he "know" that he is an animal? I am not sure how he would answer this last question. But if (for the sake of argument) we accept Hume's skeptical doubts about physical bodies, we cannot suppose that the x Chisholm speaks of is an animal of the species *Homo sapiens*. What, then, can we suppose about this x he speaks of? Can we suppose that it is a Cartesian spirit – an unextended, indivisible, spiritual entity? Well, is such an entity ever observed or introspected? Is the existence of such a thing reasonably inferable from the twinges and color-expanses whose existence is patent? Possibly so, but the required inference is not supplied merely by Chisholm's definitions. When the referent of the possessive pronoun in "my feeling depressed" is not apparent in experience (even if that experience is, for some reasons unknown to me, *mine* in some elusive sense) it is highly questionable whether I am "necessarily such" that I am certain *I* am depressed if, in fact, I am depressed.

6. Is reference to a self inevitable?

At the end of his remarks on Hume, Chisholm offered a brief argument for the claim that, when Hume looked inwardly in search of a unitary self, he could not have reported his findings in a "selfless" way – that is, without relating them to himself. Chisholm's argument calls attention to two sorts of findings, which are vitally important for Hume's purposes. One sort is positive, indicating what items or entities Hume encounters: these findings are restricted, he says, to impressions and ideas. The other sort is negative; findings of this sort disclose what Hume does not encounter. The crucial finding of this negative sort is that no unitary self is apparent. Logically, there is a very important difference between these two sorts of findings: a single positive finding, "impressions are found here," entails the general conclusion that "impressions are found," but a single negative finding, "a self is not found here," does not entail the general conclusion "a self is not found at all" (for one might turn up "elsewhere," in another bundle). The conclusion Chisholm drew from this is:

What Hume found, then, was not merely the particular impressions, but also the fact that *he* found those impressions as well as the fact that *he* failed to find certain other things. And these are findings with respect to himself.[40]

Although it is true that Hume merely wished to make a modest claim that a non-skeptic would express by saying that, for his part, no unitary self is observed, Chisholm's argument does not locate a defect that Hume would deplore. Instead of saying, "For my part, no unitary self is observed," he could have said, "No self is observed in this bundle." An opponent of Hume might reply, "How rash! How does he know that some spirit, perhaps God or a wandering angel, does not observe a self in that very bundle?" But Hume would not wince at this sort of reply. He made no pretence of attaining certainty. The best he could do is "proportion his belief to the [available] evidence," and this is what he did. His negative finding may, in view of Chisholm's argument, deserve weaker credibility than his positive ones. But they are not thereby unimportant or insignificant. If a unitary self is apparent somewhere, perhaps someone will know what the x Chisholm talks about is – whether it is a spirit, an aggregate of neural cells, or what.

Although the fact that *he* failed to find certain things when he looked inwardly is not, if I am right, crucial to Hume's position, I must concede that Hume constantly referred to himself in the course of his investigations. He admitted that he found himself in a "labyrinth" about personal identity; yet if a definite problem rather than mere incoherence is to emerge from his investigations, this self-reference evidently must be eliminable from the line of thought he pursued. I remarked that, instead of saying, "I observed no self" or "For my part, no self was observed," Hume could have said, "No self was observed." It is arguable, however, that the verb "observed" actually connotes a successful activity on the part of some conscious subject. If this is right, it is a verbal truth that, if something is observed, *someone* observed it. Consequently, if Hume or anyone else seriously doubts that a conscious subject exists and wishes to speak of the world without mentioning any such subject, he or she must not use verbs like "observes" – or even "thinks", "finds", and "experiences." This is a crucially important point because if all such verbs are off limits for a skeptical philosopher, a skeptical view of the self (and possibly even the external world) may not be coherently expressible or comprehensible.

The charge that a skeptical philosophy cannot be coherently stated in common language has been argued in several ways since Wittgenstein's *Philosophical Investigations* was published. P. F. Strawson argued the point in part in his book, *Individuals*. As against a skeptic about other minds who doubts that a state like depression is a unitary thing that is felt but not observed by its possessor and observed but not felt by others, Strawson replied:

> To refuse to accept this is to refuse to accept the *structure* of the language in which we talk about depression. That is, in a sense, all right. One might give up talking or devise, perhaps, a

different structure in terms of which to soliloquize. What is not all right is simultaneously to [use] . . . that structure and to refuse to accept it; i.e. to couch one's rejection in the language of the structure.[41]

If we recall Kant's claims about the structure of the conceptual system in which we locate things in space and time, we can see that an explicitly skeptical view of spatio-temporal objects cannot be expressed straightforwardly in familiar language. To specify something as occurring at a certain time, we must tacitly accept some system of dating things, and a system of this kind presupposes objective periodicities such as the successive phases of the moon, the regular movements of a standard clock's hands, or, as in contemporary physics, the regular vibrations of a cesium atom. If we question all presuppositions of this kind, we cannot single out in language or thought the occurrences whose existence the skeptic is concerned to question.

Although it is true that the coherent use of common language requires us to assume things the skeptic is concerned to doubt and that we cannot ourselves simultaneously assume and doubt such things, the epistemological problems leading to a skeptical philosophy are not thereby resolved. These skeptical problems concern the rational credibility (the truth or approximate truth) of propositions about objective, spatio-temporal objects and distinct, continuing subjects of experience. The impossibility of consistently using certain words (or concepts) and rejecting certain assumptions does not show that these propositions have that credibility. The fact (if it is a fact) that we cannot consistently reject these propositions is one thing; our knowledge that they are true or probably true is quite another. For reasons of his own, Hume held that we cannot (except for brief, unnatural moments) dispense with our common beliefs; our confidence in them is wholly natural, and almost entirely irrational – produced in us as an instinctive response to experience. Yet, philosophically, their credentials are dubious: we have no good reason to conclude that they are true.

Very recently, Donald Davidson has identified some new reasons for accepting "most of our beliefs" as true. His reasons are related to the task of "interpretation" – of making sense of the words of others. The only way of succeeding at this task is to construct a theory of meaning for another's words, and in constructing such a

138

theory we must assume that her utterances are, in general or for the most part, appropriate to her surroundings. For sentential utterances, which are the utterances expressing beliefs, appropriateness to the surroundings amounts to truth. Since the beliefs of a language-user are, at least for the most part, identifiable by reference to words expressing them, the task of interpretation is based on the presumption that most people's beliefs are true: evidently, this applies to me as well as to others because I am the target of their interpretive efforts as they are of mine. It is, Davidson adds, "meaningless to suggest" that we might "fall into massive error" in thus assuming the truth of most of our beliefs, for until we have successfully interpreted someone's beliefs "there are no mistakes to make."[42] The decisive defect of this argument is the same as that of Strawson's: what we may have to accept or believe for certain practical purposes is not the same as what we have epistemically decisive grounds for accepting as true or approximately true.[43]

Even if we assume that these replies to the arguments of Strawson and Davidson are entirely satisfactory, Hume and other skeptics are still faced with a fundamental difficulty: they cannot describe in common language the view of conscious subjects and the world that they are skeptical about, and they also cannot so describe what they take to be their basic sensory data. To describe the latter, they must speak of impressions, experiences, or ideas, which imply that they exist as a subject of these data; and to describe the world associated with their doubts, they must make the assumptions they are attempting to question. Is there any way out of this difficulty other than trying to invent a new "language" that no one can understand?

I think there is a way out of this particular difficulty. A philosopher concerned about the epistemological problems in question can employ what Quine has called "semantic ascent."[44] Instead of using the language whose application to reality one is concerned to question, one can "mention" or refer to that language, and ask whether or how one can know that it does, in fact, apply to an appropriate item of reality (its intended object) and that the assumptions implied by its use are, in fact, true. One can ask these questions even if, like Hume, one accepts the latter assumptions. The questions are purely epistemic, and one could consistently reply with skeptical answers because one will not be using (but merely be referring to) the words carrying a commitment to the assumptions one is questioning.

7. On basic epistemic principles

As I explained in Chapter III, Hume's skeptical doubts about his self and the world arose from critical reflections on two "systems," one associated with the primary instincts of nature and the other tantamount to Locke's corpuscularian view of the world. The error of the instinctive system is destroyed, Hume said, by "the slightest philosophy"; but the new system, (though initially "necessitated by reasoning," leads to "the destruction of all assurance and conviction." I have expressed by agreement with Hume's rejection of the instinctive system, and I have treated with respect the problems he raised with Locke's system. Although these problems have in recent years been treated as the results of various blunders and confusions, a review of Hume's reasoning will show that they were equally (I would say substantially) the result of the empiricist principles he accepted. In addition to one questionable principle about the origin of legitimate ideas, these empiricist principles traced all *a priori* knowledge to the mere relations of ideas and identified just three basic sources of rationally acceptable opinion about matters of fact and existence: direct observation, recollection, and experimental inference.

It should have been obvious that Chisholm's anti-Humean account of self-awareness and self-knowledge (the awareness of one's self and one's mental states) is incompatible with Hume's basic empiricist principles. In fact, it must have been apparent that his view of these matters was Cartesian in two fundamental respects. First, like Descartes in elaborating his *cogito*, Chisholm claimed that a conscious thing can be known to be the subject of certain thoughts and feelings even though that thing is known only as an x that thinks, wills, and feels – not as a rational animal, a non-extended spirit, or any other specific sort of thing. As I noted, an empiricist (one rejecting Hume's principle concerning the origin of proper ideas) might well concede that the ideas of thinking, willing, and feeling are the ideas of a *subject's* activities or attributes and that "Thinking requires a thinker" is an analytic truth specifying a mere relation of ideas. Yet if no thinker, no self, is apparent, the ideas of thinking, willing, and feeling would have a questionable application for that empiricist, and some other ideas – some ideas not analytically joined to the idea of a conscious subject – would no doubt be applicable in their place. A purely *a priori*, analytic truth could provide no basis, he would insist, for a conclusion affirming the existence of a mysterious (because undetectable) subject of mental "acts" and "states."

The other respect in which Chisholm's view is Cartesian concerns the relation he alleges between the occurrence of a sensory experience and the subject's knowledge or rational certainty *that* the experience occurs. Chisholm claims that the relation here is both necessary and, as a general phenomenon, knowable *a priori*. Although Locke, Berkeley, and Hume did not have a distinct opinion on this matter, a consistent empiricist could not accept Chisholm's particular claim – and neither, incidentally, could a philosopher like Wittgenstein. The abstract possibility of being mistaken about the character of one's experience is, in effect, presupposed in Wittgenstein's private language argument; and a consistent empiricist could never allow that the certainty of a belief can be *necessitated* by a matter of fact entirely distinct from it, a non-propositional sensory experience. She or he would insist that the reliability of an introspective report or mental identification is a purely empiricial matter, which can be ascertained, if at all, only by some kind of generalization from experience.

Since Hume's epistemic principles have not only been a central factor in the creation of his skeptical doubts about his self and the world, but are regarded today as dubious in important respects, it is worth considering what a philosopher like Chisholm might say in opposition to them. When I discussed Chisholm's view of self-awareness, I commented on his criticism of Hume, but I did not identify the positive basis he evidently had for his view. I want to say something about this now.

As it happens, Chisholm offered no direct defense for his views; he simply asserted that impressions and the like are self-presenting states (or "properties") and that in knowing them directly one knows oneself directly.[45] His view that "in knowing one's self-presenting states, one knows oneself" seems to be a consequence, nevertheless, of a general principle that Descartes held and expressed by saying, "No quantities or properties pertain to nothing, and . . . where some are perceived there must necessarily be some thing or substance on which they depend." As I explained in Chapter I,[46] Descartes regarded this principle as self-evident, obvious, and "known by the natural light." A contemporary Cartesian is not apt to appeal to the dictates of the natural light, but one can expect him or her to make regular appeals to self-evidence and intuitive obviousness. Such appeals can be expected because the Cartesian system requires intrinsically acceptable first principles as axioms or unproved provers. Principles as general as the one I have just quoted seem to be of this axiomatic kind.

Synthetic *a priori* claims about necessary connections, at least when made by Cartesians, are also claimed to be intuitively obvious or inferable from intuitively obvious principles. Chisholm's second claim, which implies that any thought or sensory experience is a self-presenting state necessitating the certainty, for the subject, of the proposition that she is in that state (or of the appropriate self-attribution of a property), seems to have such an intuitive basis. Chisholm does not actually say that when a proposition is certain for a person at a particular time, she entertains or considers that proposition then; but he evidently believes that a woman having a headache will not form the erroneous belief that the sensation she has is a pang of anxiety, or will have no idea that she feels pain at all. Obviously, if a person in pain has no idea that she is feeling pain, it would be wrong to say that the proposition that she is feeling pain would be certain for her. Chisholm no doubt thinks this state of affairs is not just unlikely on empiricial grounds, but impossible. That is why he speaks of the subject as *necessarily* being such that the proposition is certain if the feeling is felt.

Since Cartesians (or "epistemological rationalists") regard basic necessities as incapable of proof, they are unable to support their claims that this or that proposition is in fact a basic necessary truth. The only thing they can say is something to the effect that a given proposition is obvious or self-evident. Saying such a thing is acceptable to other Cartesians who agree that the given proposition is true, but it is not acceptable to others. I think that *it should not be acceptable to anyone* because there are two powerful objections to it. The first is based on the fact that propositions identified as intuitively acceptable or self-evident by one person are not identifiable as such by every other careful, informed thinker. The mere conviction that something is self-evident cannot therefore be sufficient to render it self-evident; if it is really self-evident, its self-evidence must be identifiable by some other property. Yet no

CHAPTER VI

Reforming Empiricism

The traditional problem of the external world was generated by the epistemic principles of the classical empiricists. Although these principles have been subjected to serious criticism in the past thirty years,[1] they are not entirely misguided, and they deserve revision rather than outright rejection. In a revised form, which preserves their critical, undogmatic spirit, they can be used to solve the problems created by their ancestors.

1. Problems with an analytic–synthetic distinction

One of Hume's distinctive principles was that matters of fact and existence cannot be known *a priori* by the mere operation of thought. The only things so knowable are the relations of ideas or, as we might express it somewhat roughly today, matters that can be decided merely by attending to the terms (the words or concepts) of some proposition. To ascertain what exists and what a natural thing is like, we must appeal, Hume thought, to observation, memory, or experimental inference: purely *a priori* speculation is useless. As I explained in Chapter III, Hume did not himself draw a distinction between analytic and synthetic truth, but his insistence that anything knowable purely *a priori* concerns the mere relations of ideas is naturally associated with the slogan that all truths knowable *a priori* are analytically true. The relevant kind of analysis is performed, after all, on meanings or ideas; and the result is knowledge of how ideas are related.

The most influential document critical of modern empiricism is Quine's "Two Dogmas of Empiricism."[2] I say modern empiricism because one of the dogmas Quine attacked – the reductionist dogma that "each meaningful statement is equivalent to some

144

logical construct upon terms which refer to immediate experience" – was not held by Locke or Berkeley, and was only implicit in Hume's claim that every "clear and intelligible" idea can be traced back to original impressions. The other dogma, which does capture the spirit of a principle fundamental to the empiricism of Locke, Berkeley, and Hume, is the belief that there is "a fundamental cleavage between truths which are *analytic*, or grounded in meanings independently of matters of fact, and truths which are *synthetic*, or grounded in fact." Quine argued that both dogmas are ill-founded and that the distinction between analytic and synthetic truths has not, "for all its *a priori* reasonableness," been satisfactorily drawn.[3]

The difficulties Quine identified with attempts to draw an analytic–synthetic distinction do not provide a proof that an analytic–synthetic distinction cannot be drawn. Their effects are really twofold: one is to disclose serious problems with empiricist attempts to specify an acceptable conception of truth that, depending merely on the relations of ideas or the meaning of words, is attainable purely *a priori*; and the other is to create a problem for empiricists who wish to retain such a conception of truth. It is important to emphasize these consequences of Quine's criticism because, even if no exception can be taken to it, a fundamental tenet of Hume's empiricism remains intact – the tenet, namely, that no matter of fact and existence can be ascertained *a priori* by the mere operation of thought. As far as Quine's criticism is concerned, the fact may be that nothing can be ascertained purely *a priori*. Quine himself seems to hold this opinion, actually. No statement, he says, is "immune to revision," even the laws of logic: "The totality of our so-called knowledge or beliefs, from the most casual matters of geography and history to the profoundest laws of atomic physics or even of pure mathematics and logic, is a man-made fabric" whose constituent threads "face the tribune of sense-experience not individually but only as a corporate body."[4]

Although Quine's criticism of the analytic–synthetic distinction is actually in line with an empiricist approach to matters of fact, it has had the effect, in recent years, of supporting a Cartesian approach to *a priori* truth and basic epistemic principles. Instead of concluding from Quine's criticism that all our beliefs must face the tribune of sense-experience, many philosophers have simply concluded that *a priori* knowledge cannot be obtained by mere analysis: it requires, and gets, the support of intuition.[5] Since neo-Cartesians like R. M. Chisholm contend that even empirical knowledge rests on intuitively ascertained epistemic principles,[6] a discussion of analyticity that comes to terms with Quine's criticism is vitally important for my purposes in this book: it is needed to develop the properly reformed empiricism that solves the problems I am concerned with.

As I explained in Chapter IV, Kant's best, most inclusive definition of analyticity is focused on the negation of a judgment: J is analytically true just when -J is self-contradictory. The fundamental defect with this definition, I said, is that it is objectionably unclear by contemporary standards. The difficulty lies in the word "self-contradictory." If it means "explicitly self-contradictory," no statement is then analytically true, for the denial of no statement is an explicit contradiction. The point is easy to see: an explicit contradiction has the form of "P and -P"; the explicit denial of a statement has the form "-S"; the form of the latter is patently different from that of the former. If Kant's definition of analytic truth is applicable to anything, the word "self-contradictory" must be understood as meaning "implicitly contradictory." But what is an implicit contradiction? How is such a thing recognized? These questions are very difficult to answer. If, as I suggested, we answer the first one by saying that an implicit contradiction is a statement equivalent to an explicit contradiction, we are immediately confronted with a problem about how such an equivalent is recognized. If we weaken our answer, saying that an implicit contradiction is one implying an explicit contradiction, we are faced with a problem about implication. We cannot understand this in a purely formal sense because an explicit contradiction cannot be obtained from "A sister is not a sibling" by purely formal means.

Using the notion of a definition, Gottlob Frege attempted to "state accurately" what he thought Kant meant by an analytic truth. According to his account, a proposition is analytically true when and only when a proof that it is true can be obtained merely from general logical laws and definitions.[7] Since a proof, as we know from Lewis Carroll, requires rules of inference as well as logical laws,[8] Frege's conception of analytic truth amounts to this:

S is analytically true iff S is formally deducible (or deducible by valid logical rules) from a set of formulas consisting of nothing but general logical laws and definitions.[9]

This conception can be applied in the following way. Suppose we have the definition, "x is a sibling of y = df x is a brother of y or x is a sister of y." Assuming rules permitting the valid substitution of predicates for schematic variables in logical laws and of definiens for definienda in appropriate contexts,[10] we can infer "(x)(y)(x is a brother of y or x is a sister of y → x is sibling of y)" from the logical law "(x)(y)(Rxy → Rxy)." Substituting appropriate formulas for the schematic letters in the law "(x)(y)(((Fxy v Gxy) → Hxy) → (Gxy → Hxy))" and using *modus ponens*, we may then conclude: "(x)(y)(x is a sister of y → x is a sibling of y)." Since this conclusion has been obtained in accordance with Frege's specifications, we can say that it and its vernacular counterpart, "A sister is a sibling," is an analytic truth.

If we can identify valid logical rules, general logical laws, and appropriate definitions, we can then, as in this last example, identify analytic truths. But how, Quine asked, can we identify appropriate definitions? His reply is that, except for "the explicitly conventional introduction of novel notations for purposes of sheer abbreviation," definitions always rest on the synonymy of various expressions. In the case of what might be called reportive definitions, the synonymy of definiens and definiendum are necessary and sufficient for the correctness of the definition; in the case of what Carnap called "explications," the appropriateness of explicans and explicandum rests, he says, on the synonymy of other expressions.[11] How are synonyms to be understood and identified? Can we understand the relevant notion of synonymy without understanding what an analytic truth is? Quine says no.

Note that if "synonymy" means "complete identity in psychological associations or poetic quality," no distinct words are synonymous: even "sister" and "female sibling" fail this test. The desired weaker notion may be called *cognitive* synonymy. The problem is to understand this weaker notion. The terms "bachelor" and "unmarried man" are synonymous in this sense just in case the statement "All and only bachelors are unmarried men" is analytically true – but the analyticity of a general statement cannot be used to define "cognitive synonymy" if the latter is to clarify the notion of analytic truth. What we need is an account of cognitive synonymy not presupposing analyticity, but no such account seems available. Quine, at any rate, was unable to find one, and no one has subsequently offered an account that has been received as generally acceptable.

Quine did consider an approach to analyticity that differs from Frege's, but instead of moving directly to that account, I want to point out a further difficulty with Frege's view. This difficulty concerns the notion of a law of logic. What is the status of these laws? How do we know that they are true? A good empiricist would want to avoid an appeal to Cartesian intuition, for the ultimate acceptability of these "intuitions" is just what a good empiricist wants to avoid admitting. (If they are acceptable in connection with logical laws, there is no evident reason why they are not acceptable generally – and there is good reason, as I have shown, to deny their general acceptability.) Thus, an empiricist would like to say that logical laws are themselves analytic or true "by analysis." Yet it is absurd to say that they are true *because* they are derivable from logical laws. Derivative laws may be true because they are derivable, by truth-preserving rules, from axioms or primitive logical laws, but this tells us nothing about the status of the primitive ones. Why should we accept them as true?

Quine, like what I have called a good empiricist, rejects the rationalist's view that primitive logical laws can be known to be true by immediate intuition; as I noted, he claims that their acceptability should be judged along with "the totality of our so-called knowledge and beliefs" ultimately by the tribunal of experience. Since the acceptability of a logical principle is not the same thing as its truth, the epistemic status Quine assigns to logical truth is not necessarily incompatible with the status it receives according to an alternative conception of analytic truth – a conception that differs significantly from Frege's. The conception I have in mind here was suggested by C. S. Peirce in 1903 and fits in nicely with Rudolf Carnap's last words on the subject. Quine explicitly attacked some earlier words by Carnap in "Two Dogmas . . .," but he was less critical (or more appreciative) of the later words.[12] I shall present the alternative conception in the section to follow. In my judgment it is truer to the views of Locke and Hume than the conception Frege developed.

2. *A pragmatic approach to analyticity*

When Hume said that propositions expressing mere relations of ideas are "discoverable by the mere operation of thought, without dependence on what is anywhere existent in the universe," he was not (like Frege) advancing a conception of *a priori* truth that requires a distinction between logical and non-logical truth and a criterion for synonymy. His thought was much simpler. By considering one's ideas, or what one means by certain words, one can discover certain implications (or "relations") of those ideas – implications that do not depend on anything (any non-idea) that is anywhere existent in the universe. "A centaur is half man and half horse" gives expression to such an implication. The proposition (or sentence as Hume interprets it) is true but independent of extramental facts about men, horses, and centaurs.

It is not always easy to say what we mean by various words, or what others must mean by words they utter. Yet in speaking to others or in the course of writing, we can take steps to be "masters of our own meaning":[13] we can clarify it, making it determinate in this or that respect. We do this, Peirce said, when we fix things that are implied and not implied by our words.[14] Determinateness of meaning is in his view a matter of degree: in so far as certain implications of our words are left open, our meaning is indeterminate in a corresponding respect.[15] The implications Peirce has in mind here are *immediate* implications – things inferable without the need of further premises. Things so inferable are, he adds, "necessary consequences" of the words (the verbal formulas) in question.[16] When we identify such consequences, we identify what Quine would call the "conceptual meaning" of those words. This meaning represents our cognitive commitments in using them as we do.

Not every speaker is skilled at fixing implications, and not every speaker speaks (or thinks) with precision. But intelligent speakers, if they work at it and, perhaps, are prompted by Socratic interrogation of a friendly kind, can make some implications along some dimensions clear. Thus, although it may be very difficult for me to say what I mean (on a particular occasion) by the pronoun "on" or the connective "while," I can at least identify certain patterns of "necessary reasoning" involving them. For example, when I say that the cat is on the mat, you can understand me as implying that the mat is under the cat; and when I say that Nero fiddled while Rome burned, you can understand me as implying that Rome burned while Nero fiddled. In so far as these implications fix the meaning, in certain respects, of the words I am using, two conditional statements (one about cats and mats, the other about Nero and Rome) are analytically true in my idiolect at the time I uttered those words.

If we look for patterns of immediate inference that sophisticated users of our language will agree are obviously valid in the generic sense of having no instances with true premisses and false conclusions, we can identify a large number of ostensibly meaning-fixing implications. Consider the following examples:

1. Jones buttered the toast in the bathroom at midnight with a knife while standing on his head. Therefore, Jones buttered some toast.
2. That is a fake duck. Therefore, that is not really a duck.
3. John stabbed Harry with the intention of killing him. Therefore, John intended to kill Harry.
4. Lacking an umbrella, she hit him with a shoe. Therefore, at least on one occasion she was not holding an umbrella when she hit him.
5. Mary laughed after John left. Therefore, John may have left before Mary laughed.

Anyone skilled at logical analysis will agree, I think, that these arguments are valid in the generic sense I mentioned, but it is arguable that none is formally valid. This last point is "arguable" because none of the arguments has the surface structure of a formally valid inference. Donald Davidson has claimed that arguments like 1 and 3 can be interpreted in a way that renders them formally valid,[17] and he may or may not be right. If he is, his theory can *account* for the perceived generic validity of two of the five forms. But the other forms are no less valid. The best explanation of their validity is found, I believe, in the meaning of such words as "fake" and "real," "before" and "after," which are determinate in relevant respects. The validity of 4 depends largely on the position and function of the participle in the premiss.

Although most sophisticated speakers of English may attach a similar, fairly determinate significance to the key expressions in the arguments above, the speech of most people (even sophisticated people interested in philosophy) seems to be on the whole significantly indeterminate in meaning. This is not something for them to be ashamed of: their purposes do not require greater precision of meaning, and they often do not want to be pinned down to precise assertions. I certainly do not want to be pinned down to a precise assertion whenever I use the indicative "if" in speaking to a general audience. I intend to conform to *modus ponens* and *modus tollens* on such occasions, but in other respects my use is pretty indeterminate – particularly in respect to the value of if-statements with false antecedents.

The fact that the speech of most people is (as I believe and as Carnap insisted)[18] significantly indeterminate in meaning shows Quine to be right in one important respect: a sharp analytic–synthetic distinction cannot be drawn for the speech of most people. Since I am confident that no one's unguarded speech is wholly determinate, I think an even stronger concession is warranted: a sharp analytic–synthetic distinction cannot be drawn for anyone's speech. This stronger concession does not rule out the idea that some statements can be recognized as analytically true in the speech of most coherent speakers, or that all speakers can (if they wish) make their speech determinate in ways or contexts that yield analytic truths. In support of this last claim one can say such things as: "When I speak of preference in this discussion, I am referring to a transitive relation." In saying this one will thereby fix the occasion-analyticity (as I might call it) of potential assertions on one's part of "Preference is transitive" or, by implication, of "(x)(y)(z)(if s prefers x to y and s prefers y to z, then s prefers x to z)."

There is no single reason for making one's speech determinate in this or that way, but one kind of reason is familiar in philosophy – namely, one's wish to resolve problems about how this or that is known, how this or that is possible, or how we can consistently believe this or that if such and such a theory is true. Many philosophical problems can be resolved only by clarifying one's thoughts, and when one speaks or thinks in a significantly indeterminate way, clarification usually involves systematization and at least partial determination of meaning.

The idea that meaning is indeterminate is a truism among many philosophers influenced by Quine's later work on what he called radical translation. One such philosopher, Davidson, has gone so far as to say that "there cannot be" determinate meanings.[19] It is worth mentioning (in view of the impact of his views on the philosophy of language) that Davidson and I are actually talking about different subjects here. He is thinking of meaning from the standpoint of an interpreter: his subject is connected with the rubric, "S's utterance U at time t means that p." In the case of sentential utterances U, the formula replacing "p" here gives a complete or partial truth-condition that sometimes amounts to a translation of the mentioned utterance.[20] The subject I have been concerned with might be called "speaker's meaning," for it covers speakers' attempts to clarify their own meaning in their own language. The indeterminacy Davidson is concerned with is closely related to what Quine has called "the indeterminacy of translation," which relates one language or idiolect to another. I am concerned with the indeterminacy of implicative relations holding between the words of a single language or idiolect.

But aren't these latter implicative relations parasitic on translational indeterminacy when they belong to a common language, one in which corresponding words of different speakers are presumed to be translational equivalents (or synonyms)? The point is a delicate one, but I do not think we have to speak of translation here to make sense of speaker-determinacy. Different speakers may make similar sounds in similar circumstances, and if their verbal interactions proceed smoothly with minimum noise, we can say they are speaking the same language and are understanding one another. Strictly, each speaker is proceeding in an idiolect of his or her own; and though one learns from another, there is no need to assume, in making sense of the implications of one person's words, that they are or are not "good translations" (in an absolute *or* relative sense) of some words of another person. Actually, when we speak of the proper use, meaning, or reference of a certain word in a certain language ("unique," say, or "elm"), we are singling out the use of certain sounds and marks by some people as *precedents* to be imitated or deferred to by others.

If a necessary inference, "P; so Q," serves as a partial unpacking of "P's" meaning in someone's idiolect, the conditional statement "If P then Q" is, for that idiolect, an analytic truth. Having this status, it is not falsifiable by objects and events in the world. The latter may, however, induce a speaker to speak differently – to change the implications of his or her words. Such a speaker may thus reject the sentence "If P then Q," or, to use Quine's words, "give it up." But no falsity is thereby shown. It is easy to see this in connection with the word "lunacy." Originally, this word connoted a fancied lunar madness, an insanity caused in some way by the moon.[21] For a speaker so using the word, it is analytic that if a person suffers from lunacy, he or she suffers from lunar madness. But natural facts do not (I assume) accord with the hypothesis that there is such a thing as lunacy (so understood). As people began to believe this, they began to use "lunacy" with altered implications, and the sentence I mentioned was "given up." But it was not shown to be false. No one with lunacy *in the original sense* was found who did not suffer from lunar madness.

Some nice things about this approach to analyticity are: (a) it does not presuppose the difficult notion of synonymy; (b) it can apply to words that, owing to vagueness, are only partly determinate in meaning – words that, like "scarlet" or "warmer than" in non-iffy, Berkelean senses, cannot be explicitly defined, or given necessary and sufficient conditions. Also, this approach is easily related to (and helps us to explicate) the phenomenon of meaning-change, which may be gradual, partial, and take place in the midst of indeterminacy. In these respects – in addition to being consistent with Quine's doubts about a sharp analytic-synthetic distinction in natural languages – it is a big improvement over Frege's conception and comes closer than his does to empiricist claims about truths that depend on mere relations of ideas.

In spite of these virtues, problems remain with the conception that must be discussed. One was posed by Quine in an early article, "Truth by Convention."[22] In this article Quine argued against the view that certain truths may be merely verbal and conventional (or analytic) by saying that conventions such as definitions cannot possibly create truth; they can merely transmit it from one assertion to another. To create truth by the convention that, say, "A" is an abbreviation of "B," we need to start with at least one truth, say, "A iff A," and use the convention to conclude "A iff B." In this simple model a logical truth is presupposed in the application of any convention; and since some analytic truths are logical truths, analytic truths cannot, as a class, be mere verbal truths established or certifiable as true wholly by convention.

This problem concerning conventions and truth can be resolved by attending to the fact that not all conventions are definitional abbreviations. As far as logic is concerned, a particularly important kind of convention is a rule for the introduction and elimination of logical symbols. As I mentioned earlier, at least one rule of inference is necessary for a system of logic, and *modus ponens* (with or without a rule of substitution) is the standard choice. This rule, which permits us to infer a formula Q from a pair of premises P and *If P then Q*, is an elimination rule, for it allows the elimination of the logical symbol for conditionality – in English, for "*if* . . ., *then* . . ." Thanks to Gerhard Genzen and others, we know that all logical truths (or all the theorems of standard systems of logic) can be obtained from a set of introduction and elimination rules.[23] Since a system of this kind contains no axioms (or primitive logical truths), it is false that the conventions or rules of this system merely "transmit" truth from one logical truth to another. Here logical truths are derived from operations on mere suppositions, which are not known to be true. An extremely simple illustrative example of such a derivation is the following: Assume P; infer P *or* Q by disjunction-introduction; conclude *If P, then P or Q* by conditional proof. The conclusion thus obtained is a logical truth.

In his book *Convention*, David Lewis has explained (even to Quine's satisfaction) how verbal conventions may become established without prior conventions that specify them.[24] We can conclude from this that we do not have to assume logical conventions in order to put such conventions in effect. On the other hand, when we become self-conscious about the logic we are using and attempt to systematize it with a view to removing redundancy, achieving some kind of completeness, and dealing with troublesome cases (involving self-reference, relevance, etc.), we do use some logic to reason about logic, but we are prepared to kick away the ladder when we are done: if we are really happy about our system, we can proceed to use it.

Thinking of our logic in this Genzenized way requires a special interpretation of the ultimate uncertainty about logical laws that Quine has rightly emphasized: even these laws are subject to possible revision.[25] This ultimate uncertainty will not concern the truth of our logical axioms (we have none) but the satisfactoriness of our rules. We cannot be absolutely certain that they will never give us trouble. By assuming a higher-order logic, we can of course prove that our first-level system has desirable properties (standard systems can be proved to be consistent and complete), but a higher-order system is subject to possible revision as well: Cartesian certainty can never be reached no matter how high we fly.

These remarks about logic are easily related to Peirce's approach to analyticity. As I explained, his claim was that we can make the meanings of our words definite by fixing what (as we use them) is implied and not implied. The notion of implication pertinent to his claim is, I said, immediate implication, and what is thus implied by a premiss is, I added, a necessary consequence of that premiss. The logical rules I have been speaking of identify logically necessary consequences (immediate ones) of specifiable premisses; these consequences partially fix the meaning of formulas containing logical words. The conception of analytic truth suggested by Peirce's remarks therefore identifies logical truths by the same principles of meaning-determination that it employs in identifying analytic truths of a non-formal kind. It does not accord a basic status to elementary logical truths and a derivative status to the elementary truths of a non-logical analytic kind. The difference between a logical and a non-logical analytic truth is no greater (or no more significant) than the difference between one's logical and one's non-logical vocabulary. As is well known, a symbol like epsilon (denoting the relation of class-membership) is regarded as logical by some and non-logical by others.[26]

At the end of the last section I observed that the conception of analyticity suggested by Peirce fits in nicely with Rudolf Carnap's last words on the subject. Since the non-Fregean conception of analyticity that Quine criticized in "Two Dogmas . . ." was espoused by Carnap, a brief defense of Carnap will round out my reply to Quine's on this subject.

In earlier writings Carnap had claimed that the analytic statements of certain precise artificial languages are the statements specified by a set of explicitly formulated semantical rules. Quine had two principal objections to Carnap's claim. One was that since Carnap offered different semantical rules for different languages, he did not provide a general account, applicable to all languages, of what an analytic statement is. The other objection was that a mere list of rules (even if applicable to every language) does not explain what the term "analytic" means and thus provides no clarification of the unclear notion of analytic truth. In his later writings Carnap identified the analytic statements of various languages by a list of "meaning postulates"[27] or "A-postulates."[28] This new terminology is not itself sufficient to elude the sort of criticism Quine directed to the terminology of semantical rules.

Carnap replied to Quine that in constructing a precise list of semantical rules (or meaning postulates) for an artificial language, he was attempting to "explicate" the notion of an analytic truth for that language. Different languages require different explications, but the point of the explications is the same: to make clear which sentences in the language are to be considered true on the basis of meaning (or convention) rather than empirical fact. Carnap believed that the words and sentences of natural languages were significantly vague or unclear in meaning and that precision could be achieved only by a "rational reconstruction" of actual speech. He was realistic about the need for precision, thinking it is required only for special purposes. Since he was acutely aware of the extreme complexity of natural languages, he thought the precision required for his purposes could best be achieved by the construction of artificial mini-languages, which provided reconstructed, clarified counterparts to fragments of "the language of science" in which he was principally interested.

Considering Carnap's explicative intentions, I think his rubric "Semantical Rule," or "Meaning Postulate," could just as well be replaced by the Peircean announcement: "The following rules (or postulates) specify implications that fix the meaning in the indicated respects of formulas containing the indicated symbols."[29] His approach to analyticity can therefore be supported, I believe, by the considerations I have assembled in this section.

3. Observation

According to classical empiricist doctrine, well-founded beliefs about matters of fact and existence can be supported by nothing but observation, memory, and experimental inference. Observation is the fundamental source of the support available here because memory and experimental inference are ultimately based upon it. Anyone who remembers that p must formerly have known that p, and in the short life of a human being this prior knowledge must ultimately be based on non-remembered information obtained by some kind of direct inspection, which can be called (if only in a technical sense) observation. Experimental inference, as Hume understood it, ultimately involves a generalization from experience

– that is, from what someone observes and remembers. The idea that observation is, in this way, the ultimate source of well-founded beliefs about matters of fact is therefore classic empiricist doctrine. The idea is far more problematic than it appears, however. In fact, it does not accord with some of Hume's well-considered remarks.

Although we naturally speak of observing various objects (trees, sunsets, or colored expanses), the observational process typically results in beliefs or opinions, which may or may not amount to knowledge. When Hume discussed philosophical skepticism in the last section of his *Enquiry*, he emphasized this propositional upshot of the observational process. His occasion for doing so was his recollection of certain "trite topics" that skeptics "in all ages" dwell upon – specifically:

> the imperfection and fallaciousness of our organs on numberless occasions; the crooked appearance of an oar in water; the various aspects of objects according to their different distances; the double images which arise from pressing one eye . . . and many other appearances of a like nature.

Trite as these topics may be, they do prove, Hume admits, that "the senses alone are not implicitly to be depended on" and that we must "correct their evidence" by reason and by considerations derived from the nature of "the medium, the distance of the object, and the disposition of the organ."[30] The evidence supplied by the senses in the observational process amounts to a thought or opinion (something propositional) because it can be corrected or corroborated by various considerations.

In these astute remarks Hume unwittingly raised a serious problem, which he did not attempt to solve. The problem concerns the status of the considerations that should be appealed to in correcting or corroborating the evidence of (= the thoughts excited by) the senses. What is the basis of these considerations? How can they be rationally supported? We should expect Hume to reply that they are supported "by experience," but it is not clear how, on his view, experience could accomplish such a thing. If the thoughts excited by a sensory experience must invariably be corrected or corroborated by empirical considerations that owe their epistemic authority to experience, they too must ultimately have been excited by experience and appropriately corroborated. But what could have corroborated them? We seem to be faced with an infinite regress of empirical considerations or by some kind of corroborative circularity among them. The alternative of an intrinsically acceptable empirical consideration seems to be out of the question for a good empiricist like Hume.

I mentioned the problem that arises here in Chapter II, when I presented Locke's views on the assessment of human testimony.[31] Locke described the factors that should be considered is assessing an item of testimony as "the grounds of probability" bearing upon it, and these grounds should include the empirical considerations that Hume identified because the latter are certainly pertinent to the truth of a claim like "I saw an oar bend when it entered the water." Locke's contention was that, to be rational, we should examine all the grounds of probability bearing on a proposition and then, upon a "due balancing of the whole, reject or receive it with a more or less firm assent proportional to the preponderance of the greater grounds of probability on one side or the other."[32] In addition to wondering how a ground of probability can be identified if an observation can be assessed only by employing such grounds, one might also wonder about the principles to be followed in balancing probabilities. Neither Hume nor Locke identified these principles, and it is hard to see how they might have proceeded to do so. However that might be, we have the surprising result that, according to fairly explicit testimony present in the writings of both Locke and Hume, observational evidence should be assessed for acceptability by general considerations of an empirical kind. This is surprising because classical empiricism is generally associated with the doctrine that general beliefs about the world must be founded on a generalization from experience. This testimony seems to turn things upside down.

If we think about the considerations Hume and Locke mentioned in relation to the assessment of human testimony or observational evidence, we can identify four basic sorts of thing that should be weighed when we are evaluating an opinion created by the observational process. Suppose, for example, that our friend Tom says or forms the belief that he sees a yellow cat in a nearby room. If we are seriously concerned to ascertain whether his belief is true, we should begin by reflecting on the *perceptual process* he employed – in this case, seeing. Tom may or may not be good at this process. His vision may or may not be acute; he may or may not be able to distinguish yellows from tans; and it is even possible that he is blind and responding, in the present case, to a hypnotic suggestion.[33] Another matter is *the nature of what he ostensibly observes*. Are there such things as yellow cats? Are cats easy to see? Are they large, small, opaque, or transparent? Are there other things that look like them – things that a person like Tom might naturally (in these circumstances) take to be a cat? Then there is *the character of the circumstances* (the conditions) in which Tom's belief is formed. Was the light good enough for a person (a person like Tom) to see a cat (a yellow one) at the distance in question? And finally there is *the sort of observer* (the sort of person) Tom is. Is he intelligent, sane, critical – or gullible and demented? Is he obsessed with cats? And so on and so forth.

Many of these questions can be answered by observing Tom's behavior and recalling how he has behaved on various occasions in the past, but these answers raise further questions of the same kind about our own observations. Even if we could answer these further questions without circularity, we would be faced with general questions about observers, observable objects, observational processes, and conditions of observation whose answers are relevant to the evaluation of *anyone's* observational beliefs or reports – ours or the King of Siam's. To support these answers by reference to anyone's observations would be reasoning in a circle.

Hume did not attempt to solve the problem of how, if observational evidence must be assessed by general considerations of the kinds I have mentioned, those considerations deserve this epistemic status, because he did not think it could be solved: in mentioning these considerations he was in the process of raising doubts that could only, in his view, have a skeptical solution. The dramatic step he proceeded to make was to claim that the universal and primary opinion of all human beings regarding the external world is soon destroyed by the slightest philosophy, which teaches us that nothing is ever present to a mind but an image or perception and that the senses are only "inlets" through which these images are conveyed – inlets that cannot produce any "immediate intercourse" between mind and external object.[34] Arguing that in the absence of such immediate intercourse the new system or view of the world cannot be supported by any "convincing argument from experience," he proceeded to claim (in his *Treatise*) that he had no rational basis for the belief that he existed as a distinct subject (or observer) of ideas and impressions; he ventured to affirm, in fact, that human subjects (if they exist) are nothing but bundles of such things. The subject-less solipsism resulting from his reflections is generally believed to leave some room for rational certainty, but the very subject of rational certainty is virtually destroyed by those reflections.

If rational certainty is possible regarding any empirical object (or matter of fact), a distinction must be drawn between opinion and object, and considerations ensuring that certain instances of the former correctly represent the latter must be available. These conditions are satisfied in a relative sense by certain opinions formed in accordance with the universal and primary view of the world. Given the acceptability of that view, one can assemble considerations showing that certain opinions formed by certain observers in certain circumstances about certain natural objects are bound to be true. Yet as a reluctant supporter of subjectless solipsism, Hume could not admit that these conditions are ever satisfied. A mere bundle of impressions and ideas not only exhibits no reliable connection between opinion and object, but the conception of such a bundle leaves no basis for the distinction between opinion and object. In so far as the term "opinion" has a determinate meaning, it connotes a propositional attitude of an opining subject. If the existence of such a subject is in question, the applicability of the term is as questionable as the applicability of "lunatic" given current psychiatric opinion.

Someone will no doubt object that Hume did not question the existence of a subject or self; he merely questioned the existence of a subject distinct from a bundle of objections and ideas. In one respect the objection is sound: Hume did express himself this way. But the concept of a bundle is not the concept of a conscious subject, or self, that Hume started out with: his concept was radically redrawn. The original idea that a conscious subject is (or can become) aware of its ideas and impressions was transformed into the idea that a certain bundle contains certain ideas and impressions and can perhaps be enlarged in a certain way. The result was that it is no longer possible to express the sort of principles by which the reliability of opinions (formed in certain ways in certain circumstances by certain subjects about certain objects) can be assessed. Having kicked away the popular, instinctive principles and having introduced no substitutes in their place, Hume destroyed the basis for coherent discourse about observation (or the consciousness of objects) and about knowledge, truth, and, as he understood it, even probability.

The conclusion that should be drawn from these reflections is not that Hume's subjectless solipsism is incoherent or refutable on the basis of the very language he used. Quite the contrary, the language Hume used (as ordinarily understood) is based on assumptions that Hume, on the basis of plausible epistemic principles, has shown to be baseless and questionable. If his principles are not amended, revised, or superseded by better ones, the appropriate outcome is perhaps Wittgensteinian silence: "Wovon man nicht sprechen kann, darüber muss man schweigen."[35] To ask, as Wittgenstein did in the private language argument he included in his *Investigations*, whether sentences (one could equally say opinions) about certain sensory objects are "correct" is to assume distinctions whose credentials Hume implicitly challenged. I believe and shall argue in the next chapter that such distinctions are, in fact, defensible and that Wittgensteinian silence is not the appropriate outcome to Hume's skeptical reflections. But to defend those distinctions one must solve the problem about observation that I posed earlier in this section – the problem of how the principles or general considerations needed to assess observational beliefs can be rationally defended in a critical, anti-Cartesian way. The key to solving this problem is a satisfactory theory of experimental inference.

4. Experimental inference: some problems

As Hume described it, experimental inference is fundamentally a special case of what we should call deduction, a case distinguished by the presence of a causal principle functioning as an explicit or tacit major premiss. This basic pattern is illustrated by the schema:

(I) A's cause B's.
This is an A.
Therefore, this causes (or will cause) a B,

which can be reconstructed as a syllogism.[36] More complex experimental inferences involve premises that are analytic consequences of causal principles. In the inference:

(II) If an A occurs, a B will occur.
An A occurs (= is occurring).
Therefore, a B will occur,

the first premiss is an analytic consequence of the causal principle "A's cause B's." Like inferences conforming to pattern (I), those conforming to pattern (II) can also be reconstructed as syllogisms, the paradigm in Hume's day of a deductive inference. Other forms of experimental inference can also be reduced to syllogistic inferences, but it is not necessary to dwell upon them here.

Hume is commonly said to have written on "induction," and there is no question that he did so if a mental transition from the observation of A's constantly conjoined with B's to the belief that A's cause B's is considered an instance of induction. Hume did not regard this transition as an inference because it is not, in his opinion, "based on reason or any process of the understanding": it is merely (for him) a natural, instinctive response. A proper inference should accord with a rule of principle; and if, unlike Hume, we think that the transition he speaks of is, or amounts to, an inference, we should be able to specify the rule or principle involved. If we do not employ the modern probability calculus (as it is called), we might suggest the general principle:

> If n/m instances of a large, randomly selected class of things or occurrences of kind E are observed to have some property P (perhaps the property of being conjoined with something of another specific kind) then probably n/m instances of all Es have the property P.[37]

Obviously, this principle is extremely vague, for it does not specify how large the class of E's should be or how we are to understand a "random" selection; and it is also crude or heavy-handed, for it does not relate the degree to which the conclusion is probable or credible to the size of the evidence class. On the other hand, it does bring out the basic idea of "induction" as empiricists have generally understood it: *generalization from experience.*

Although empiricists in the classical tradition succeeding Hume regarded this sort of induction as the basic form of allowable inductive inference,[38] it has three fundamental drawbacks, which must be avoided if we are to have a satisfactory conception of experimental inference. The first is apparent from my discussion in the last section: a method of inductive generalization provides no means of assessing observational beliefs, however such beliefs are understood. The second drawback is closely related to the first one: it is that our experimental conclusions are inevitably restricted to the domain of the observable, whether this be impressions and ideas or, as Wittgenstein insisted, publicly accessible phenomena. This restriction is a drawback because it is the source of skeptical doubts about things whose existence ought to be acknowledged. Hume's doubts about the external world are clearly based upon it. As he argued:

> It is a question of fact whether the perceptions of the senses be produced by external objects . . . how shall this question be determined? By experience surely; as all other questions of a like nature. But here experience is and must be entirely silent. The mind has never anything present to it but . . . perceptions and cannot possibly reach any experience of their connection with objects. The supposition of such a connection is, therefore, without any foundation in reasoning.[39]

Empiricists who insist that, properly speaking, only publicly accessible phenomena are observable have argued analogously, claiming that beliefs about publicly inaccessible phenomena cannot be supported empirically. Where Hume, Kant, and Mill were attracted to some form of phenomenalism, later empiricists have been attracted to behaviorism and instrumentalism – the latter being the doctrine that theories ostensibly postulating things like electrons should be interpreted as sophisticated predictive devices rather than as theoretical accounts of what is literally unobservable.

The third drawback is more technical and was brought to the attention of the philosophical world only in the late 1940s, having been discovered, independently, by Bertrand Russell and Nelson Goodman.[40] Expressed generally, the drawback is that the principle of inductive generalization will allow us to draw patently objectionable conclusions from any given body of data. Russell discovered this by attending to the manner in which an evidence class and the wider class that it is taken to represent are specified; he concluded that, unless some restriction that he did not know how to make is placed on the allowable means of specifying these classes, one can use the inductive principle to draw false conclusions from true premises as often as not. His reasoning is easily adapted to the inductive principle I gave above. Suppose I am examining cattle and consider the property *being observed*. Since all the cows I observe have this property, the principle entitles me to conclude that all cows are observed – something that is clearly false. If I think of the cows I examine as members of a larger class, *physical objects I have observed*, I can legitimately draw an even more extravagant conclusion: I can conclude that all physical objects are observed by me. Cavils about whether my observations are made randomly (a possibility that Russell did not discuss) will not dispose of the problem because if my observations of cows do not count as "random," no observations that a person can make will have this status, and the principle of inductive generalization will be rendered useless for experimental purposes.

Russell's formulation of the problem was virtually ignored when it appeared, but Goodman's version was very widely discussed. Unfortunately, Goodman's point was often missed because he did not support it with "ordinary language," which Anglo-American philosophers were obsessed with at the time. Instead of describing "properties" such as *being observed, being observed by me*, or *being within ten miles of Königsberg*,[41] Goodman used the contrived predicate "grue," which is applicable to objects (he stipulated) just when they are either green and examined before a distantly future time *t* or blue and not so examined. He argued that if we are examining emeralds for color and find that they are invariably green, we can use the inductive principle to draw two incompatible conclusions, neither of which is better supported than the other. They are "All emeralds are green" and "All emeralds are grue." These conclusions are incompatible because they disagree about the color of emeralds not examined before *t*: according to one, they are green; according to the other, they are blue. The conclusions are equally well supported because every emerald we examine will inevitably be examined before *t* and thus, if it is green, count as grue. Since the time *t* may be placed arbitrarily far in the future, we cannot avoid the difficulty by waiting to see how emeralds look when *t* arrives. We have, in fact, a general problem that is merely illustrated by this case. The inductive principle, as traditionally understood, allows us to draw incompatible conclusions from the same body of data. It is, therefore, objectionable as it stands; it requires revision or significant qualification.

5. Some suggested strategies

A popular strategy for avoiding the classical empiricist's problem regarding unobservable domains is to use the so-called *hypothetico-*

deductive method. According to standard accounts of this method, some phenomenon or datum is identified as the subject of inquiry, and a hypothesis is constructed to account for it. The hypothesis is then tested by deducing consequences from it; in the standard case these consequences amount to predictions made on the basis of the hypothesis. If these consequences are verified by experience (or otherwise found to be true), the hypothesis is thereby confirmed, at least to a degree; if they are disconfirmed (or found to be false), the hypothesis is refuted and an amendment is introduced. If a hypothesis is found that, when put to the deductive test, consistently eludes refutation, it is deserving of at least provisional acceptance.

Although this description of experimental inference is plausible in some respects, it is very seriously over-simplified and will not do as it stands. For one thing, it cannot elude the Russell–Goodman problem, which applies to it as well as to inductive generalization. Instead of thinking of the rival hypotheses about emeralds as being the results of a generalization, we can think of them as hypotheses to be tested. Since any prediction about the color of an emerald that we can verify will be made prior to time *t*, we have no way of confirming one of these hypotheses at the expense of the other. An analogous point can be made about the sort of hypotheses Russell considered – for example, the hypothesis that all cows are observed or found within ten miles of Königsberg. Suitable observers will find the predictions they make on the basis of this hypothesis invariably borne out by their observations; and if they attempt to compare their predictions with evidence of other kinds (such as the testimony of others), the Goodman problem can be redirected to this other evidence. For example, the auxiliary hypothesis that the testimony of other observers is reliable can be shown to be no more likely, if we are restricted to the hypothetico-deductive method, than the alternative auxiliary hypothesis that other observers are reliable only on matters not pertaining to cows that I do not observe. Evidence pertaining to what I do not observe is always susceptible to more than one interpretation.

Defenders of the hypothetico-deductive method generally acknowledge that a body of data can always be accounted for by more than one hypothesis and that the set of rival hypotheses cannot be reduced to a single member merely by reference to the predictions about further data that these hypotheses permit one to make. We must adopt the *best* hypothesis that accounts for the data; we must make an "inference to the best explanation."[42] But how is the "best" hypothesis to be selected from a set of alternatives covering the same data? A standard reply is that, other things being equal, a hypothesis H is better than the members of a set of alternatives if it is simpler, involves more familiar explanatory principles, is more readily testable, and "coheres" better with other assumptions that we have good reason to trust.[43] Since alternative hypotheses may possess these features in different degrees, a simpler hypothesis being less readily testable, for example, than a more complicated alternative, it is not always easy to say which alternative is the best among a set of alternatives. When we cannot make up our mind on a question like this, we can proceed by keeping the best alternatives in mind, hoping that our subsequent investigations will make a reasonable choice easier to identify.

Although we commonly do make inferences to what we regard as the best explanation and also prefer explanatory hypotheses that are simpler and so forth than available alternatives, this is merely a fact about what we generally do; it provides no rationale for proceeding this way. Are simpler hypotheses more likely to be true? Do those involving more familiar explanatory principles have this status? Until we can answer these questions, or make some other positive case for the method, we should hesitate to recommend inference to the best explanation as a rationally acceptable inductive method – one by which critical thinkers can resolve the problems that arise for classical empiricists.

A striking limitation to the method of inference to the best explanation (at least as I have described it) is that it makes no provision for probabilistic considerations. I am not thinking only of the *degree* to which a hypothesis is supported or disconfirmed by certain evidence, though this is certainly important. I am also thinking of the degree to which an hypothesis is supported by antecedently unlikely evidence: If an antecedently unlikely occurrence E is predictable by an hypothesis H, then the occurrence of E will add significantly strong support to H. This sort of support is not attainable only when the evidence E is certain to occur if H is true and unlikely to occur if plausible alternatives to H are true; it is also attainable when the antecedently uncertain E is reasonably judged more likely to occur if H is true than if its plausible alternatives are true. Ordinary "experimental" reasoning – the sort we constantly employ in everyday life when we try to decide whether little Johnny is or is not telling the truth, whether Mary was joking, being sarcastic, or simply mis-speaking when she made such and such a remark, or whether a certain eruption is or is not a symptom of Lyme disease – is filled with conjectures about such likelihoods (or probabilities), and any account of inductive, ampliative, or non-demonstrative reasoning that does not accommodate them cannot be considered satisfactory.

6. *Bayesian induction*

Russell's response to the problem he raised about induction was to say that "induction as such" cannot be justified because "it can be shown to lead quite as often to falsehood as to truth." Observing that some applications of the inductive principle are rationally acceptable,[44] he wished to find some rationale for the acceptable ones. He did so by "making induction [when it is acceptable] no longer a premiss, but an application of mathematical probability to premisses arrived at independently of induction."[45] I believe that Russell's strategy here was basically correct and that the probability calculus (as it is called) provides the formal machinery needed for all forms of experimental inference – even for the acceptable forms said to be inferences to the best explanation. I shall explain my view in what follows, taking special pains to make my remarks user-friendly (as one says nowadays) to readers easily daunted by logical or mathematical symbolism.

As I see it, acceptable experimental inferences can generally be understood as applications of a simple theorem of probability theory, one known as Bayes' theorem. The version of the theorem that I shall refer to includes two elementary kinds of probability statements: *absolute* and *conditional* ones. Before stating the theorem it will be helpful to explain what these elementary statements are and how they are incorporated into the probability calculus.

An elementary absolute probability statement is one of the form "P(p) = a," where "p" is a statement such as "The next roll of the die will result in a six" and a is a fraction ≥ 0 and ≤ 1. Such a statement is read on the model of "The probability that p is a." An elementary conditional probability statement has the form "P(p given q) = a," where both "p" and "q" are non-probability statements and "a" has

167

the same significance as before. This kind of statement is read on the model of "The probability that p given q is *a*." An example may be helpful at this point. If "p" means "The next roll of the die will result in a six," we might say that $P(p) = 1/6$ if we believe the die in question to be fair: there are six possible outcomes, and a six is just as likely as the others. If we retain this interpretation of "p," we can easily answer the question, "What is the probability that p given that the outcome of the next roll will be even?" Since an even outcome must be either a two, a four, or a six, the probability of getting a six on one of these outcomes is obviously one in three, or $1/3$.

Since quantities equal to the same quantity are equal to each other, elementary probability statements (whether absolute or conditional) provide a rational basis for probability statements of a more complicated structure. If $P(p) = a$ and $P(q$ given $r) = a$, it follows that $P(p) = P(q$ given $r)$. The *Probability Calculus* provides a set of axioms from which the mathematical relations between probability statements of all kinds can be calculated. There are various versions of this "calculus," but the following is convenient for my purposes here. It consists of just four axioms:[46]

> A1: $0 \leq P(s) \leq 1$, and $0 \leq P(s$ given $t) \leq 1$.
> A2: If p is certain, $P(p) = 1$.
> A3: If p and q are mutually exclusive, then
> $\quad P(p \vee q) = P(p) + P(q)$.
> A4: $P(p \& q) = P(p)P(q$ given $p)$.

Bayes' theorem, the theorem on which a theory of valid experimental inference can be constructed, is easily derivable from these axioms. To simplify the proof and to introduce some ideas that will be useful in the discussion to follow, I shall begin with four preliminary theorems. The first is this:

> T1: $P(p) + P(-p) = 1$.

T1 is a consequence of A2, which implies that $P(p$ or $-p) = 1$, and A3, which permits us to replace $P(p$ or $-p)$ with the desired sum. The next theorem is:

> T2: $P(q$ given $p) = P(p \& q)/P(p)$,

which follows almost immediately from A4. Another basic theorem is T3:

T3: If p is equivalent to q, P(p) = P(q).[47]

This third theorem can be proved as follows. Assume that p is equivalent to q. It is then certain[48] that -(p & -q) and that -p or q. By A2, we may infer that P(-p or q) = 1 and, therefore, that P(-p) + P(q) = 1. Since, by T1, P(p) + P(-p) also = 1, we can conclude, first, that P(p) + P(-p) = P(-p) + P(q) and then, by algebra, that P(p) = P(q). The fourth theorem is:

T4: If it is certain that p only if q, then
P(q given p) = 1.

The proof of T4 depends on the fact that if it is certain that p only if q, the biconditional "p ≡ p & q" is also certain. Given the algebraic truth that P(p)/P(p) = 1, we may then infer T4 by successive applications of T3 and T2.

A simple version of Bayes' theorem (sometimes called the inverse probability law) is a trivial consequence of T2 and A4. In stating this theorem I use variables suggestive of the use to which I will be putting the theorem, "h" suggesting "hypothesis" and "e" suggesting "evidence":

$$\text{T5: } P(h \text{ given } e) = \frac{P(h)P(e \text{ given } h)}{P(e)}$$

A more complicated version of Bayes' theorem, one with an expanded denominator, is the following:

$$\text{T6: } P(h \text{ given } e) = \frac{P(h)P(e \text{ given } h)}{P(h)P(e \text{ given } h) + P(-h)P(e \text{ given } -h)}$$

This theorem is based on the logical equivalence of e and the conjunction, e & (h or -h), which is equivalent to (e & h) or (e & -h). Together with T2, these equivalences entail that P(e) = P[(e & h) v (e & -h)]. By A3, this last term = P(e & h) + P(e & -h). Elementary logic and T3 allow us to infer that P(e) = P(h & e) + P(-h & e), and A4 warrants the expansion of this last sum to:
P(h)P(e given h) + P(-h)P(e given -h). Using T3 to substitute this expanded sum for P(e) in the denominator of T5, we obtain T6.

Analogous reasoning involving mathematical induction yields a more general version of the theorem. If $h_1, \ldots, h_n$ are mutually incompatible and jointly exhaustive hypotheses, so that their disjunction is equivalent to h or -h, we can infer

T7: $$P(h \text{ given } e) = \frac{P(h)P(e \text{ given } h)}{\Sigma \, P(h_i)P(e \text{ given } h_i),}$$

the denominator being an n-termed sum involving the hypotheses h_i belonging to the alternatives in question. Since the alternative hypotheses we often consider in connection with observable data are commonly greater than two, this general version of the theorem is very useful. Usually, the versions T5 and T6 are applicable only in artificially simple cases, the sort I shall typically be using for illustrative purposes.

7. Applying Bayes' theorem

If we have a hypothesis *H* that warrants a prediction *E*, we can compute the probability of *H* given *E* by using the simple formula T5. Suppose that *H* (into which we can incorporate pertinent background information) entails that the observable phenomenon described by *E* will occur.[49] If *H* does entail *E*, it is certain that *H* only if *E* and thus, by T4, P(*E* given *H*) = 1. Given this, P(*H* given *E*) reduces to P(*H*)/P(*E*). The equivalence of these terms tells us that, other things being equal, the more improbable the predicted *E* is, the more strongly *E* (if true) supports *H*, and that, other things being equal, the higher the antecedent probability of the hypothesis, the more strongly it is supported by the occurrence of what it predicts. This accords beautifully with two naturally acceptable (or psychologically compelling) principles of experimental inference: implausible, *ad hoc* hypotheses that accord with observable data are not (generally speaking) strongly supported by those data; and the occurrence of antecedently unlikely data strongly supports hypotheses from which it is predictable. Naturally acceptable reasoning also accords beautifully with an application of theorem T3. If *H* entails *E*, -*E* entails -*H*, which means that P(-*H* given -*E*) = 1. Thus, the non-occurrence of evidence predicted by a hypothesis *H* effectively refutes *H*, rendering its negation (conditionally) certain.

What about the problem of alternative hypotheses that I mentioned earlier? When I discussed the hypothetico-deductive method, I observed that the occurrence of predicted data cannot accord significant support to a hypothesis *by itself* because data that accord with one hypothesis always accord with other hypotheses, thus adding no support to any hypothesis in particular. Doesn't this observation undermine the usefulness of simple theorem T5? The answer is no. If, in computing the value of P(*H* given *E*), we assign a high antecedent probability to the hypothesis *H*, we single it out as a special hypothesis that (other things being equal) will receive significant support from data whose occurrence it allows us to predict. And if, on the other hand, we assign a low antecedent probability to *E*, the basis for our assignment can only be other hypotheses that we are tacitly taking account of. Given the hypothesis *H*, *E* may be highly probable – in fact, certain if *H* entails *E*. If we assign *E* a low initial probability, we are in effect assuming that it has, on the average, a low probability given the totality of hypotheses bearing upon its occurrence. This assumption would be made explicitly if we used a more complex version of Bayes' theorem, T6 or T7.

8. Inductive probability: an interpretation

The answer I gave in the last paragraph is bound to raise a more fundamental question: "How are we to ascertain the antecedent probabilities needed to apply Bayes' theorem?" Actually, I have given part of the appropriate answer. The antecedent probability of an *h* or *e* required to apply the simple theorem T5 is in large part relative to further hypotheses that are tacitly assumed. A rule of conditioning (as it is called) is, in fact, generally employed in making what appear to be absolute probability statements. When we assign a value, say *a*, to an ostensibly absolute term like 'P(*h*),'" our probability functor "P( )" represents a particular probability function, one assigning specific probability-values to statements $h_1, \ldots h_n$. Because of its specific representative function, a probability functor (the expression "P") should ideally have a subscript that distinguishes it from functors representing different functions. If we let *n* be such a subscript, the *rule of conditioning* by which the P_n value of a statement *p* is determined to be *a* might be the following:

RC: $P_n(p) = a$ iff $P_{n-1}(p \text{ given } e) = a$,

where e is the evidence on the basis of which the new probability function is formed.[50] The evidence e generated the new probability function by an application of Bayes' theorem involving the old probability function, P_{n-1}. The instance of the theorem used for this purpose might have been:

$$P_{n-1}(p \text{ given } e) = \frac{P_{n-1}(p)P_{n-1}(e \text{ given } p)}{P_{n-1}(e)}$$

171

As I noted above, this strategy gives only a partial answer to the question asked: it shows us how we can assign a probability value to a statement if other probability values have been assigned. This information is not very helpful in the present context because it does not tell us how basic probability values are determined. Without basic probability values, we cannot even employ the probability calculus. One might suppose, therefore, that the probability calculus cannot possibly help us resolve our basic philosophical problems about experimental inference.

Contrary to this supposition, I believe that the probability calculus can help us with our basic problems; but to support this belief I must deal with the question of how the probability calculus is applied and what a probability assignment is supposed to represent. An important feature of the probability calculus (understood as a formal mathematical system) is that it can be interpreted in different ways.[51] The interpretation that is appropriate, in my opinion, for the purposes of a properly reformed empiricism is a "subjectivist" one. According to this interpretation, probability assignments represent degrees of belief or confidence. One who is wholly confident that p – who regards p as utterly certain – could rightly represent or express this attitude by the absolute probability statement "$P(p) = 1$," the statement tacitly indexed, perhaps, by one's name and the time one has the attitude. By contrast, one who is equally certain that a proposition q is false could represent this contrary attitude by the statement "$P(q) = 0$" or by the equivalent "$P(-q) = 1$."

This subjectivist interpretation of probability statements accords nicely with the interpretation I gave of Hume's remarks on probability.[52] Some admirers of Hume might not worry about whether probability statements can properly be considered reasonable, but the question is certainly alive for most philosophers today. Its answer is a bit complicated, however, taking us to the deepest level of controversy about epistemic principles.

According to an influential school of statisticians whose characteristic claim was first enunciated by C. S. Peirce, the basic probabilities needed for experimental inference do not have to be well founded or accurate in some sense.[53] Experimental inference based on Bayes' theorem is self-correcting: if one begins with prior probabilities that are not extreme (close to 0 or 1) and continues to update one's probability functions by the rule of conditioning, the

effect of one's initial uninferred probabilities will become pro-
gressively smaller as one proceeds, so that two people starting out
with different basic probabilities and updating their probability
functions by successive conditioning involving the same evidential
input will eventually agree on the probabilities they ascribe to
relevant hypotheses. This claim, which can be demonstrated mathematically,[54] shows that a subjectivist can make room for "objective" probabilities. As I noted in Chapter III, Hume's skeptical
solution to his doubts about causal principles involved an idea of
this kind: people who receive the same experiences will naturally
move toward a consensus on the probability of causes. The
probabilities will be objective in the sense that informed people with
adequate experience can agree about them.

The mathematical fact that people who update their prior
probability functions by persistent conditioning on the same
evidential data will eventually agree on the probability values they
assign to resultant hypotheses does not dispose of the problem at
issue here. In any actual cases in which the resultant agreement is
approximated, there is a great deal of presupposed agreement on
the admissible evidence, on the alternative hypotheses to be considered, and on such things as the probabilistic independence of
occurrences pertinent to their calculations.[55] It is possible to seek
experimental support for what is thus presupposed; but to obtain
this support, further inferences of a probabilistic sort will have to be
made, and these inferences will require further assumptions about
prior probabilities and evidential data. To draw a conclusion we
always need a premiss; and when we are dealing with matters of fact
and existence, our premisses are never intrinsically certain and
independent of critical assessment. The support we can obtain for a
hypothesis by experimental inference is always conditional rather
than absolute: it inevitably depends on the acceptability of our
evidence and collateral assumptions, which is always subject to
further investigation.

It is important to realize that, as regards the facts of the world,
the logic of inductive inference is comparable to that of deductive
inference. The latter cannot tell us what, absolutely speaking, is true
about the world; it can merely tell us what is true *if* something else is
true.[56] As far as human behavior is concerned, the point in knowing
that Q is a deductively valid consequence of a premiss P is that we
should be inconsistent if we accept both P and $-Q$. If these

propositions concern matters of fact, the choice between them is not a logical one. If we accept *P*, we must not accept -*Q*; if we accept -*Q*, we must not accept *P*. Notice that I say "if we accept one, we *must not accept* the other." I do not say that we must *reject* one of the alternatives because logic does not tell us what positively to do. Since every premiss has infinitely many valid consequences, there are infinitely many formally distinct propositions *C* that it would be an error to accept if one accepts a premiss *P*, and the requirement actually to reject an infinite number of such propositions would be an impossible task. If we consider a valid rule of inference, we can identify what we *may do*: if we accept *P*, we may accept its disjunction with any proposition *Q*. But we make no error if we draw no conclusion from a given premiss. This point is worth emphasizing because if we were logically required to draw conclusions from premisses, we would have no logical reason to stop. The outcome would be insane: *P*, so *P or q*; so (*P or Q*) *or R*; so ((*P or Q*) *or R*) *or S*, . . . – and so on until we die or lose our minds.

According to the subjectivist interpretation, the probability calculus places consistency conditions on statements expressing degrees of belief or confidence in propositions. As Frank Ramsey put it is his pioneering essay, "the laws of probability are laws of consistency, an extension to partial beliefs of formal logic, the logic of consistency."[57] This view of the probability calculus can be illustrated by a fumbling attempt to apply Bayes' theorem.

As I mentioned earlier, the standard strategy of testing theories by using them to make predictions can be accommodated by Bayes' theorem. Since an antecedently unlikely occurrence strongly supports a hypothesis from which it is predictable, and since antecedently probable hypotheses are, other things being equal, more strongly supported by the predictions they warrant than antecedently improbable hypotheses, it might occur to a person beginning the study of probability that a favorite hypothesis H (to which he assigns a high probability of 0.8) would be very strongly supported by a testable consequence E with a low antecedent probability of 0.2. A simple computation shows, however, that this arrangement of probabilities is inconsistent. According to theorem T4, if E is deducible from H (so that "H only if E" is certain), P(E given H) = 1. Given this value of the likelihood P(E given H), it follows from T5, the simple form of Bayes' theorem, that P(H given E) = P(H)/P(E), which = 4 in this case – an impossible result, inconsistent with axiom A1. Reflection shows that if p entails q, the probability of q cannot be less than the probability of p – and this fact was not appreciated in the case I have described.

Subjectivists commonly support their view that the laws of probability are laws of consistency in "partial belief" by deploying "Dutch book" arguments. These arguments are based on assumptions about the nature of belief and the possible success of risk-taking policies.[58] As pragmatists have long insisted, beliefs are propositional attitudes on which the believer acts; and when we act on beliefs that are, for us, uncertain in some degree or other, we are in effect gambling – taking chances in an endeavor to achieve what we want and avoid what we do not want. In so far as we are rational beings, one thing we do not want is to adopt policies that will permit us to fail regardless of what takes place in the world. Failures of this kind are ensured by the unfair bets called Dutch books, and subjectivists have argued that people whose beliefs violate the conditions imposed by the probability calculus are vulnerable to them. Since it is clearly rational to avoid policies that leave one vulnerable to Dutch books, it is rational to subordinate one's belief-structure to the requirements of the probability calculus. Conforming to those requirements is a consistency condition for rational mental behavior.

The question whether Dutch book arguments really succeed in supporting Ramsey's claim that "the laws of probability are laws of consistency, the extension to partial beliefs of formal logic" is seriously debated at the present time, and I am unwilling to take a stand on it here. Doing so is not necessary for my purposes, fortunately, because the close connection between the probability calculus and consistent belief is evident from many different points of view.[59] From my point of view, the probability calculus can simply be taken as providing the framework for "experimental inference" in just the way that quantification theory provides the framework for deductive inference.

9. Prospect

The conception of induction I have outlined, Bayesian induction as it might be called, permits one to say that inductive inference conforming to the requirements of the probability calculus is valid inference, something it is reasonable to use when one's opinions are less than certain – as, for empiricists, they commonly (if not invariably) are. Since the structure of this kind of inference does not limit us to some special domain of observation, it offers a route of escape from Hume's road to solipsism. A good deal more has to be said about the premisses we are entitled to use in connection with the method and about the rational acceptability of the conclusions we may thereby obtain. But these are topics for the next chapter.

CHAPTER VII

The External World

My chief aim in this chapter is to apply the principles of my reformed empiricism to the problem of the external world and thereby solve it. To achieve this aim I must deal with a cluster of issues concerning the nature of the external world and the proper interpretation of physical theories. I must also deal with some loose ends that I did not tie down in the last chapter, one being the manner in which contingent assumptions required for the evaluation of observation reports and the application of Bayes' theorem can be rationally justified.

1. Hume's problem and its successors

The skeptical problem about the external world was explicitly posed by Hume, and its proper solution can begin with Hume's skeptical predicament. As I explained in Chapter III, Hume thought that our instinctive beliefs about the external world are rationally indefensible and that the "new system" which emerges from scientific reflections cannot be rationally defended. The difficulty with the new system is that, according to it, "the mind has never anything present to it but ... perceptions and cannot possibly reach any experience of their connection with objects."[1] Since external objects are not directly observable, their existence can be ascertained, if at all, only by inference – specifically, by experimental inference. But this sort of inference, since it is based on causal principles that are attained only from the experience of causally related instances, is clearly inapplicable in the present case. The existence of external objects cannot therefore be ascertained by any rationally acceptable form of inference. The new system is rationally unfounded.

The reasoning leading to this result is inconclusive if experimental inference is not restricted to a form of reasoning based on instantial generalization. As I explained in the last chapter, this restriction is no longer credible. We can now identify a form of reasoning, Bayesian reasoning, on the basis of which plausible hypotheses can be confirmed by reference to the successful predictions they warrant. Since hypotheses about external objects are, one would think, particularly useful in helping us specify confirmable predictions about the experiences we shall have under an extraordinarily wide range of experiential conditions, the application of Bayes' theorem to the conditions imposed by Hume's problem – that is, by the rejection of what he called our "instinctive" beliefs – provides an obvious solution to it. If a skeptical problem remains, it can be owing only to something other than the acceptability of Bayesian inference.

Considerations of this kind do suggest an initially plausible reply to Hume's skeptical argument, but problems arise that depend on matters extraneous to the acceptability of Bayesian inference. One such problem concerns the antecedent probability of the hypothesis that external objects (spatio-temporally extended particulars or aggregates of them) exist as causes of my sensory experiences. As a look at Bayes' theorem shows, this probability must be positive if anything can add credibility to that hypothesis:

$$P(h \text{ given } e) = \frac{P(h)P(e \text{ given } h)}{P(e)}$$

Thus, if $P(h) = 0$, $P(h \text{ given } e) = 0$ for any e whatever. Fortunately, this problem is easily avoided by the approach I have taken to inductive probability. According to that approach, a proposition has the probability 1 only when it is certain. Since only the negation of a certain proposition will have the probability 0, the hypothesis regarding external objects will have this probability only if its negation is certain – that is, only if it is certainly false. But it is hard to imagine a rational basis for this drastic assessment. Lacking it, we can reasonably contend that the probability of the hypothesis is positive to some degree, and this is enough to avoid the objection in point.

Another, much more serious problem arises from the ever-present possibility of alternative hypotheses. If the external physical object hypothesis h allows us to make generally successful predictions about the course of our subjective experiences, a host of alternative hypotheses will do so as well and thus be equally well confirmed by that evidence. Unless h can be shown to be rationally preferable to these alternatives (technically, to have a higher prior probability), the probability it is accorded by the available evidence (its posterior probability) will not be sufficient to render it acceptable. This can be seen from the discussion that I offered in the last chapter. The rule of conditioning, RC, allows us to assign a new posterior probability for a proposition p on the basis of its previous probability given the available evidence; but to be consistent in adopting such a probability we must keep a consequence of theorem 1 in mind, which is that $P(p)$ must always equal $1 - P(-p)$, for any probability function chosen. If, in an ideally simple case, h has just one alternative j that covers the same data equally well, we can reasonably adopt h only if we have good reason to regard it as preferable to j. The problem is, how can we possibly support one such alternative in preference to another?

An obvious answer is available for the class of alternative hypotheses that contain more information than a given hypothesis. We know that, if a hypothesis h accounts for a class of data, an additional hypothesis will also account for it because we can easily construct such an hypothesis: we can do so by adding a further, independent assumption u to h, thereby obtaining an hypothesis k that is equivalent to the conjunction of h and u. This sort of alternative to h is easily disposed of on grounds more compelling than mere simplicity, which could be seen as largely esthetic. The compelling grounds are that k is less probable than h whenever h and u are less than certain, which they are in any realistic case. This is an immediate consequence of the theorem that if p and q are independent,[2] $P(p \& q) = P(p)$ times $P(q)$: when these last probabilities are less than 1, $P(p \& q)$ must be less than either of them. Thus, all hypotheses differing from a given hypothesis merely by the addition of independent information (those less simple in this respect) are reasonably regarded as less preferable and confirmed to a lesser degree by the available evidence.

The conceivable alternatives to a given hypothesis are not always more complicated than that hypothesis, and the observation that I have just made is not helpful in dealing with them. Some of these hypotheses are the peculiar sort discovered by Russell and Goodman.[3] As I explained in the last chapter, Russell thought that such undesirable hypotheses could be avoided by an appropriate use of the probability calculus. The use he prescribed consisted in employing Bayes' theorem together with a set of postulates that were, in his view, characteristic of inferences in the physical sciences. These postulates – he identified five of them – could be used, he thought, to distinguish the desirable from the undesirable hypotheses that accord with obtainable evidence.[4] As an example, his "structural postulate" is to the effect that "when a number of structurally similar complex events are ranged about a center in regions not widely separated, it is usually the case [i.e. highly probable] that all belong to causal lines having their origin in an event of the same structure at the center."[5] It is obvious that this structural postulate provides a principle of selection by which many objectionable hypotheses can be eliminated from a set of hypotheses each of which could account for the occurrence of structurally similar events ranged about a center in regions not widely separated. In serving this sort of purpose, the postulate facilitates the application of Bayes' theorem in experimental contexts.

Even if Russell had been able to prove that the postulates he identified were sufficient to eliminate all undesirable rivals to a favored hypothesis (something he did not attempt to do), he could not have offered a non-circular justification for his belief that those postulates are true or close to it. They are assumed, he said, in scientific and even commonsensically acceptable reasoning, but that sort of reasoning cannot be justified independently of them. Wesley Salmon, a philosopher strongly influenced by Russell, has recently argued that the prior probabilities needed to apply Bayes' theorem (and, no doubt, to rank alternative hypotheses) can be supplied by analogical reasoning.[6] As he understands it, analogical reasoning reduces to (or is a form of) "induction by enumeration," which he regards as the primitive inductive rule.[7] Although the assumptions about causal structure which he uses to supply the relevant prior probabilities are intuitively very plausible, his belief that they can be supported by enumerative induction is not helpful if enumerative induction cannot be justified. Since Russell and Goodman have shown that enumerative induction is, in fact, a defective form of inference, Salmon's appeal to it is theoretically useless. If skepticism is to be avoided, some other means of defending basic probability assignments must be found.

There is another task that must also be accomplished if

skepticism is to be avoided. When we apply Bayes' theorem in an experimental context, we do not just compute the probability of a hypothesis given certain possible evidential data; we also determine whether data we predict actually occur or obtain. Normally, we determine this by making observations; yet as I explained in the last chapter, there is a fundamental problem about observation that needs to be resolved. The problem concerns the epistemic status of the background assumptions needed to assess observations (more exactly, observational beliefs or statements). These assumptions are empirical, I claimed, and yet observation statements can be accepted as correct or probable only in relation to them. How is this possible? If the acceptability of all observations depends on the acceptability of contingent background assumptions, it would appear that these assumptions cannot be justified by empirical observations. How, then, can they be justified? How can anything empirical be justified?

It is important to realize that the basic problem about observational beliefs also applies to what an eighteenth-century empiricist would have considered observation in the strict philosophical sense – namely, a person's awareness of her immediate experiences and state of mind. However this awareness is conceived of, a straightforward conception will render it formally analogous to ordinary observation, and it will therefore possess the same epistemic limitations. The formal analogy concerns the subject, object, process, and conditions of the awareness. Straightforwardly understood, the awareness will have a subject because it will be carried out or accomplished by a conscious being; it will be directed upon an impression, image, feeling, or thought; more than one species of process will evidently be possible (pains are felt, sensory expanses are "apprehended visually"); and the resulting sensory beliefs (that I am now feeling pain, for example) will be formed under subjective conditions (such as attentiveness or confusion) that affect their reliability. Such beliefs will therefore stand in the same epistemic relation to background assumptions about these subjects, objects, processes, and conditions as ordinary observational beliefs stand to background assumptions about observers, observable objects, observation processes, and conditions of observation.[8] The inevitable problem is, how can these assumptions possibly be justified without circularity?

As I noted in earlier chapters, philosophers rarely saw a problem about the reliability of psychological reports until Wittgenstein's *Philosophical Investigations* was published – and even now some claim that psychological states or properties are "self-presenting" and that the truth of propositions ascribing them to oneself are sufficiently evident to one not to require further justification.[9] I have criticized these claims in Chapter V and will not repeat them here. Although Hume was characteristically skeptical about ordinary observation, he did not recognize the problem I raised, and it is not generally recognized today – in fact, philosophers like Davidson argue (as I noted)[10] that "most" of our common-sense beliefs must be regarded as true. Two widely discussed positions in epistemology are nevertheless applicable to my problem and would resolve it if they were satisfactory. Since these positions might also, if they are satisfactory, provide a strategy for dealing with alternative hypotheses and for justifying prior probability assignments, I propose to discuss them now. They deserve my attention at this point because the solutions I accept for both problems owe their credibility partly to the fact that they provide the best available solution to these problems.

2. Chisholm's "critical commonsensism"

In the latest edition of his well-known *Theory of Knowledge* Roderick Chisholm advanced the following as basic epistemic principles:

P1 Accepting [a proposition] h tends to make h probable.
P2 If S accepts h and if h is not disconfirmed by S's total
    evidence, then h is probable for S.[11]

These principles, if acceptable, dispose of the observational problem I raised because if (to refer to a case I introduced in the last chapter) Tom's total evidence does not disconfirm his belief that he sees a yellow cat in a nearby room, then that belief is "probable for him" – meaning that he is more justified in believing that he sees the cat than in believing that he does not.[12] Since believing this h is (no doubt)[13] more justified for Tom than "withholding" it, his belief is, in Chisholm's terms, beyond reasonable doubt for him, even if he has no means of justifying the background assumptions about observers, observable objects, and so forth, that I regard as crucial for the evaluation of his observational belief.[14]

182

Two basic questions should be asked about the principles P1 and P2: "Are they acceptable?" and "How does Chisholm support them?" My answer to the first question is an emphatic no. Not only does P2 render probable and even beyond reasonable doubt (for ignorant, unreflective people) all sorts of primitive and superstitious beliefs, but if someone were pertinaciously obstinate, as Hume would say, in refusing to consider anything evidentially contrary to certain of her cherished beliefs, she would be justified in holding them as the result of this irrational obstinacy. I will concede that most people are not obstinate in this way and that most of their everyday, mundane beliefs are, in fact, fairly well founded; but my basis for this concession is strictly empirical, involving contingent assumptions about observers and observable objects. Except on matters of such things as politics, morals, and religious faith, where significant disagreement is often allowed or expected, people in our culture are commonly criticized for making false statements – whether those statements be lies or simple errors. As a result, their casual beliefs on ordinary and undisputed matters are, I should say, significantly more than 50 per cent reliable (at least as measured by the opinions of their informed, unbiased, and reliable fellows). My opinion here is, I repeat, empirical, and to justify it in a philosophically satisfactory way I must resolve my problem about observation statements, not tacitly assume that it does not arise.

How did Chisholm defend the principles P1 and P2? He said that they can be justified by an *a priori* truth and a general presupposition that epistemologists make when they ask Socratic questions about evidence and justification. He expressed the general presupposition this way:

> I am justified in believing that I can improve and correct my system of beliefs. Of those that are about matters of interest and concern to me, I can eliminate the ones that are unjustified and add others that are justified; and I can replace less justified beliefs about those topics by beliefs that are more justified.[15]

The *a priori* truth to be used for the justification of a basic epistemic principle is a conditional statement whose antecedent is the conjunction of the propositions expressed in Chisholm's statement of the presupposition and whose consequent is the principle to be justified. If "GP" expresses the general presupposition as a single complex statement, then "If GP then P2" expresses one of the requisite conditional statements that can, according to Chisholm, be known *a priori* to be true.

If the conditional statement "If GP then P2" is indeed true *a priori*, then if GP is true, the principle P2 is also true. Is GP true? As far as I can tell, Chisholm does not give us the slightest reason to believe that it is. Since he accepts it and also accepts "If GP then P2," *he* would be inconsistent (according to the probability calculus) in believing that P2 is false or less probable than GP. But this fact does *nothing* to render P2 credible. Of course, if P2 is true, Chisholm's belief that he is justified in believing he can improve and correct his system of beliefs (and so forth) is, for him, probable (given his presumed lack of evidence to the contrary) and perhaps even beyond reasonable doubt. The hypothesis here is precisely what is in question, however. If we have no reason to accept it, the fact that we do accept it or have what Chisholm calls "that faith in oneself with which the epistemologist sets out" does *nothing* to show that P2 is in the slightest degree credible.

But is the conditional statement "If GP then P2" really an *a priori* truth? Chisholm thinks yes, but he offers no reason for this opinion. It is unfortunate that he does not attempt to do so because anyone who accepts his position on *a priori* truth should find his claim or "suggestion" that the conditional is true *a priori* highly dubious. When he raised the question of how P1 and P2 might be justified, Chisholm said that it would not be plausible to say that they are *a priori* because "many philosophers have understood them without thereby seeing that they are true."[16] By this test, it would not be plausible to say that "If GP then P2" is *a priori* either. The presupposition is easy enough to understand, but its connection with P2 should be very hard for anyone to make out. Why should the belief that one is justified in believing one has the stated epistemic abilities lead one to suppose that accepting any h tends to make h probable or that any h one accepts that is not disconfirmed by one's total evidence is thereby probable for one? The conceptual gap between antecedent and consequent here is really enormous, and if the claim that the conditional is actually true *a priori* is to be taken seriously, we should be given some indication how it can be proved *a priori* – that is, how it can be derived from *a priori* axioms.

3. Justification by "coherence"

The other epistemic strategy, which, if sound, would solve my problem about observation statements, is a "coherence" theory of epistemic justification. Such a theory has, in fact, been proposed by Laurence BonJour as a means of solving a problem very similar to mine.[17] I shall say just enough about BonJour's theory to show its application to my problem and to indicate why I cannot accept it.

As I described it, the problem about observation statements is that the assumptions necessary for their evaluation are empirical (not *a priori* truths) and require evaluation themselves – something that can be accomplished, for a good empiricist, only by reference to empirical observation. If the evaluation or justification appropriate here is, as BonJour puts it, *linear*, then a vicious circularity threatens. My problem is to show how the relevant background assumptions can be satisfactorily justified without objectionable circularity.

BonJour, whose problem is focused specifically on the justification of empirical beliefs, attempts to avoid both an endless regress of justifications and an objectionable circularity among justifications by arguing that epistemic justification is only *apparently* linear. As he understands it, epistemic justification is actually "systematic and holistic." Beliefs are justified by their inferential relations to other beliefs, but there is no ultimate relation of epistemic priority among the totality of these beliefs: they are collectively justified by their mutual coherence.[18] Epistemic justification appears linear because the partial justifications of beliefs offered in everyday life (BonJour calls them "local justifications") support a given belief by inferring it from other beliefs that are regarded as acceptable. These latter beliefs are not beyond reasonable doubt, however; they are merely "contextually basic." If their acceptability is challenged, the semblance of a linear justification is soon lost, and supporting considerations become "global": justification is (or can be) then given only by reference to the "coherence" of the entire system of beliefs. If the system is appropriately coherent, its members will be epistemically justifiable because their approximate truth provides the best explanation of their mutual stability and agreement.

BonJour does not offer a precise, detailed account of what he means by the "coherence" of a set of beliefs, but he says enough about it to indicate why he thinks coherence is a "truth-conducive" property. Apart from the mutual consistency, inferability, and explanatory unification of the beliefs, an important feature of their coherence is their collective, "relatively long-term" stability under persistent observational input.[19] A system possessing this last feature satisfies what BonJour calls "the observational requirement" for a coherence theory of epistemic justification, the "underlying idea" being that any belief not justifiable *a priori* "should in principle be capable of being observationally checked, either directly or indirectly, and thereby confirmed or refuted."[20] As an addendum to this requirement, he adds that "a user of the system must make a reasonable effort to seek out relevant, possibly conflicting observations, if his beliefs are to be justified."[21] The confirmation and refutation resulting from the satisfaction of this requirement is, of course, local and conditional, presupposing general beliefs about observers, observable objects, and the like. The relatively long-term stability of the system under the impact of beliefs constantly *evoked* by observational efforts is what helps overcome this "local" limitation.

As I explained in Chapter V, an acceptable inference to the best explanation can be reconstructed as an application of Bayes' theorem. BonJour seems to accept this view because, when he presents his "meta-justificatory argument" for the claim that a system of empirical beliefs justified according to the standards of a coherence theory probably corresponds to reality, he explicitly relies on that theorem.[22] To apply it to his problem, he must defend two crucial premisses: one, that he (or someone offering the meta-justification) has an approximately accurate overall grasp of the coherent system of beliefs, and two, that the antecedent probability of the correspondence hypothesis (the one he accepts) is greater than that of any other hypothesis on which the evidence (the coherent system of beliefs) is equally likely. Although the first premiss records a matter of fact requiring (for a good empiricist) experimental support, BonJour accepts it as "doxastic presumption" – something presupposed by the very raising of the issue of justification.[23] He argues that the second premiss is an *a priori* truth, that the alternative hypotheses in question are *a priori* less likely to be true than the correspondence hypothesis.

If the problem I raised about observation is contemplated in its most general form, BonJour's doxastic presumption will be seen as question-begging. We may justifiably presume that we have a relatively specific system of beliefs when we raise the question of how those beliefs can be justified, but if we consider the wider question of how our propositional attitudes can be rationally assessed, a doxastic presumption puts the cart before the horse. To be sure, philosophers have historically expressed little doubt about our ability to monitor our thoughts and beliefs, but this estimate should appear excessively optimistic to a reader of Freud or Dostoyevsky. As these writers emphasize, self-deception is ubiquitous in everyday life, and people who are deceived about their personality and character are commonly deceived about many of their beliefs.[24]

A narrower problem about external observation does not equally preclude BonJour's doxastic presumption, and I will concede that the presumption is reasonably made if one is concerned only (or mainly) about observation so understood. But what about BonJour's other premiss, his assertion that the correspondence hypothesis is antecedently more probable (on *a priori* grounds) than alternative hypotheses? He defended this premiss by an argument in which he considered two sorts of alternative hypotheses, "normal" and "skeptical."[25] A good empiricist would not allow that factual hypotheses can reasonably be assessed on *a priori* grounds, and this is what Bonjour attempted to do – in my view, unsuccessfully. I shall not review the case BonJour made against the alternative hypotheses he considered because there is something more fundamental that he failed to do – namely, to consider all conceivable alternative hypotheses.

BonJour's failure to consider all conceivable alternatives to his hypotheses is particularly significant for my purposes in this book. When I turned to the epistemic positions of Chisholm and BonJour, my aim was to find solutions to two basic problems that arise in connection with Bayes' theorem, one concerning observation statements and the other concerning alternative hypotheses. Although BonJour constructed his coherence theory to resolve the first problem, it seemed reasonable to suppose that it might help with the second one as well. It now turns out that, far from helping with this latter problem, his theory presupposes that it has a non-coherentist solution. The solution BonJour accepted was not only *a priori* (something objectionable to a good empiricist) but it did not even implicitly survey all possible alternative hypotheses: as I said above, BonJour considered only "normal" and "skeptical" ones.

The need to consider alternatives that do not plausibly fit into the categories of normal or skeptical stands out when one recalls the inductive hypotheses discovered by Russell and Goodman, which are logically troublesome but not, at least officially, skeptical. Their peculiarity is that their implications for unobserved cases diverge in odd or surprising ways from their implications for observed ones. People who apply Bayes' theorem in real life generally proceed, as BonJour did, with a fairly small set of alternative hypotheses in mind – those they regard as realistic, plausible, or worth the trouble of considering. Strictly speaking, this practice requires justification. If it cannot be given, the general formula T7 cannot justifiably be applied and a value for P(e) in T5 (see Chapter VI, p. 169) cannot reasonably be assigned. BonJour did not even suggest a way of coping with the problem as it applies to his attempted meta-justification; and for that reason alone, his argument did not succeed. It also (for that reason) cannot help me with my general problem about alternative hypotheses.

4. Standards, ends, and justification

If inductive reasoning is carried out by means of the probability calculus, it can be logically valid, just like standard deductive reasoning. When reasoning of any sort is valid, we are logically entitled to draw a certain conclusion from given premisses, but we are not thereby assured that those premisses are true. One consequence of what I have been arguing is that antecedent certainty about empirical premisses is never possible. Not only are there no intrinsically certain empirical premisses, but it is illusory to suppose that premisses can obtain a derivative certainty from their mere coherence with others. This raises a serious problem for a reformed empiricist: How can we justifiably hold opinions on empirical matters if our premisses are neither intrinsically certain nor acceptable by virtue of their coherence with other things? In my view the only satisfactory way of resolving this problem is to acknowledge that under certain circumstances, at least, we can justifiably accept premisses *that we know to be uncertain.*

To see how we can be justified in accepting such premisses, we must explore the notion of justifiable behavior. Exploring this notion is necessary here because accepting a premiss is, broadly speaking, an action or doing, and those who do what they are entitled to do, or may do, are justified in doing it. Since doing what one may do is doing what is permissible, the justification appropriate to the acceptance of uncertain empirical premises will ultimately concern the permissibility – specifically, the epistemic permissibility – of accepting them. Since doing A is permissible, generally speaking, just when doing A is not forbidden, the task of showing that one is epistemically justified in accepting uncertain premises under such-and-such conditions is tantamount to showing that accepting them under those conditions is not epistemically forbidden.

If one is entitled to do something A, doing A must accord with some appropriate standards. Since the sort of permissibility that I am concerned with here is epistemic, the appropriate standards must be epistemic as well. How are such standards identified and defended? The answer must be "By reference to appropriate ends or purposes." Since the standards are epistemic, the ends or purposes must be epistemic as well. The question is, "What are these ends or purposes, and why should our epistemic behavior be assessed by reference to them?"[26]

BonJour says that there is just one fundamental end that is relevant here: "We want our beliefs to correctly and accurately depict the world."[27] In his view:

> It is only if we have some reason for thinking that epistemic justification constitutes a path to truth that we as cognitive beings have any motive for preferring epistemically justified beliefs to epistemically unjustified ones.[28]

As I see it, this view is too strong and too simple. It is too strong because, owing to inductive uncertainty if nothing else, we cannot actually know that the experimental methods we use will bring us to the truth in the short run that is the life of our species; and it is too simple because truth is not, and does not deserve to be, our sole epistemic value.

Philosophers who say that our principal epistemic end is that of discovering "the truth" mistakenly suppose that there is such a thing as *the* truth. Plato's Socrates seemed to suppose such a thing when he spoke of the philosopher or dialectician aiming to carve reality "at the joints,"[29] and it is implicit in the medieval view that God created natural things in accordance with His Divine Ideas, thus bringing about a system with a right because divinely intended

189

structure. Venerable as it is,[30] I think this supposition is false. As I view matters, it is up to us – human beings – to create kinds or sorts (to specify nature's joints) by our classificatory practices. The world may or may not contain instances of these kinds; I have noted that it contains no instances of the kind *lunatic*. When it does contain instances of a specified kind, parts of the world satisfy *our* kind-criteria. In satisfying these criteria the appropriate parts of the world render some propositions true, but their truth is relative to the criteria. Such criteria are always associated with a classificatory system (a conceptual scheme) to which there are alternatives, possible and sometimes even actual. Since some of these alternative systems are, in my view, equivalent rather than incompatible,[31] we cannot suppose that there is a unique system of truths that every rational being is attempting to discover.

If a rational being had a single alethic purpose, it would be to discover what is true, or approximately true, about the world relative to a conceptual scheme of some special kind. I speak vaguely of a "special kind" of conceptual scheme here because even partly rational beings have a number of distinct epistemic values, and different rational beings actually rank such values in different ways. Some, like Descartes, are primarily interested in certainty and impatient with mere probabilities; others, like me, have almost the opposite attitude. And then some are interested in the big picture while others are obsessed with details. Even among philosophers there are, as Gustav Bergmann once remarked, both blue-print theorists and sketch theorists.[32] An ideally rational being with ideal epistemic interests (supposing we can make sense of such a thing) would no doubt possess a scheme that is more catholic than those of even the wisest actual people, but it would embody several distinct epistemic values.

The values I am thinking of here are reminiscent of a coherence theory. One is *simplicity of conceptual apparatus* – meaning, roughly, minimal redundancy of concepts and explanatory principles. Another value is *comprehensiveness*: the whole world should be covered by the scheme, extensively and intensively. These first two values are united in a third, which might be called "*systematic unity*." The ideal, somewhat vaguely expressed, is to achieve a conceptual picture of the world that is maximally comprehensive and yet unified by a minimal set of explanatory principles (ideally, the smallest set compatible with the desired intensive and extensive comprehensiveness). A final value is *fidelity*. This is not simply truthful representation but something more qualified – perhaps minimal error compatible with the realization of other epistemic values.[33] A highly comprehensive, well-systematized view of the world that is only approximately true is no doubt preferable (at least for many thinkers) to a less comprehensive, less well-organized view whose truth is less approximate.

Supposing that an appropriate epistemic end can be identified on the basis of such epistemic values, the next question to face is: "How, in relation to such an end, can standards for epistemic behavior be identified?" Since our human condition is, as Quine put it, a Humean condition,[34] we cannot expect to identify standards that, if conscientiously adhered to, will ensure the attainment of such an end. We must allow that the relation between standards and end will be weaker than this. I suggest that, if the end is to obtain a maximally comprehensive yet maximally simple conceptual scheme that can reasonably be hoped to be minimally erroneous, two sorts of epistemic standards are appropriate. The first prescribes policies that actively promote the end. To obtain the intended comprehensiveness in one's conceptual scheme, for example, one should seek "causes" or explanations for observed phenomena; and to obtain the intended simplicity and systematic connection in the scheme, one should minimize redundancy, attempt to subsume disparate phenomena under common principles, eliminate nomological danglers, and so forth. Conceptual activity will be epistemically permissible only when it accords with such policies. Standards of the second sort promote the end indirectly – by prohibiting things that will frustrate it. The key policy here is consistency, both deductive and inductive. As I have explained, the basis for the latter is the probability calculus.

5. Uninferred premisses and intellectual bootstrapping

It is time to relate these remarks to the subject that prompted them, the basis on which we can justifiably accept uninferred, uncertain premisses. The point to fix upon is that we are epistemically entitled to accept such premisses if doing so is consistent with reasonable epistemic standards. Is accepting an observational belief (one that simply comes to mind when one has certain sensory experiences) consistent with such standards? Not necessarily: one may have evidence against that belief. But suppose one lacks such evidence. Chisholm would say that the belief is then "probable for one" and even "beyond reasonable doubt for one." I have rejected this view, claiming that it would add objectionable epistemic weight to baseless beliefs that fanatics protect from contrary evidence. Yet if an uninferred belief is held in a properly tentative spirit by one who has the *will* to consider what can be said against it and to revise or even reject it if contrary evidence becomes available, it will then be held critically and I can allow that the believer will be epistemically justified in accepting it *for the time being*.

As I argued earlier, an observational belief is normally assessed by reference to background assumptions concerning four things – the observer, the ostensibly observed object, the observational process, and the conditions under which observation took place. In ordinary life these background assumptions are for the most part contextually acceptable, as BonJour would say, and their epistemic authority is not questioned. If we seek support for them, we shall probably consider the success we have in using them; but to determine this success, we must make some further assumptions that we regard as reliable: at the very least, that certain other observations or memories of such are accurate. Since these latter assumptions are as fallible as the former ones, they too are subject to testing – but further assumptions will be needed to accomplish it. Clark Glymour has called the process of using an assumption to check other assumptions intellectual "bootstrapping."[35] It is rational, obviously, only if it is pursued critically, with no assumption protected against refutation. To avoid outright circularity in this bootstrapping, one should, of course, avoid using an assumption A_1 in obtaining support for A_2 if one's support for A_1 involves A_2 in a significant way. Doing this successfully is not easy, but it is about the only thing we can do at the fundamental level. We can test one assumption by reference to others, but we cannot test all our assumptions simultaneously.

To apply Bayes' theorem we need more than justifiable observation statements, of course; we also need prior probabilities, "likelihoods," and premisses identifying pertinent alternative hypotheses. Premisses of these kinds can often be inferred from other premisses, but some prior probabilities or other and some disjunctions of alternative hypotheses must eventually be accepted without inference. As far as ultimate priors are concerned, these have a status comparable to that of observation statements: they are justifiable as initial premisses if (a) they are consistent (according to the probability calculus) with other beliefs reasonably regarded as justifiable and (b) they are clearly recognized as provisional attitudes, subject to revision or even rejection by further investigation. I explained in Chapter VI that the effect of moderate priors (not close to 0 or 1) is minimized by persistent conditioning, but the convergence of rational opinion emphasized by radical Bayesians is not assured merely by probabilistic consistency involving the same or similar evidential input: it also depends on the identity of the alternative hypotheses recognized and the probabilities accorded them.[36]

As I have observed, there is (abstractly speaking) no limit to the number of possible alternatives to a given hypothesis, but only a small number are considered in any actual case. This practice requires justification, I said; I now say the general justification can only be that, in considering the alternatives one does consider, one is doing one's epistemic best. If the hypotheses one considers are the only plausible ones that come to mind, one can reasonably draw conclusions on the basis of them, but in doing so one must recognize that one's set of alternatives is provisional, that new alternatives must be attended to, and that new alternatives may upset one's current apple cart.

The sort of perverse or "bent" hypotheses discovered by Russell and Goodman raise special problems, and it is important to say something about them. As I mentioned earlier, their peculiarity is that they diverge in strange ways from "normal" hypotheses in respect to unexamined instances.[37] This is nicely illustrated by Goodman's famous hypothesis, "All emeralds are grue." If a grue object is, by definition, something that is green before a distantly future time t or blue after that time, then all examined emeralds accord equally well with Goodman's hypothesis or, for us, the more natural hypothesis that all emeralds are green. Since the two hypotheses have incompatible implications for emeralds existing after t, we ought to have some basis for choosing between them. The problem is, what can this basis be?

Since the time t is arbitrarily far in the future, we shall never be able to examine an emerald after that time. Thus, we cannot hope that our subsequent experience will eventually turn up a case that will refute one of the hypotheses. A Bayesian might insist that the bent hypothesis should be accorded a lower prior probability than the normal one and that this difference would render the bent one less strongly confirmed than the other by the emeralds we have examined. But what basis could we have for accepting this difference in prior probability? We cannot reply, as some Bayesians have, that the probability of the grue hypothesis should be lower than the other because we have good inductive evidence that the color of a whole class (a large, scattered class) of objects will never abruptly change all at once at some tick of a clock. We cannot offer this reply (and expect it to be accepted) because the character of our evidence about color changes is one of the things put in question by Goodman's hypothesis. Until we have resolved the matter of grue emeralds, we cannot confidently make more general assertions that will rule it out.

If we have no evidential basis for according one hypothesis a higher prior probability than another, we can reasonably proceed with both of them in mind if we think there is a decent chance that we shall obtain evidence that will confirm one but disconfirm the other. We cannot do this with the alternative hypotheses Goodman has identified because he designed them to be insulated from cases that could support one at the expense of the other. Though patently contrived, his hypotheses do not create a pseudo-problem, for there are infinitely many alternatives like them that have to be dealt with. Goodman's solution was squarely in the tradition of Hume: it amounted to giving rules that permit us to identify a preferred hypothesis from a set of Goodmanian alternatives by reference to the predicates used.[38] The hypothesis that emeralds are green is preferable to the hypothesis that emeralds are grue not because we have some rational assurance that it is more likely to be true; it is preferable because it accords better with a descriptive policy that we now employ. This policy is not necessarily better than any alternative. It simply has the virtue of being in effect and of providing an inductively consistent means of confirming hypotheses, one that does not result in irresolvable conflicts regarding untestable cases. It seems to me that this basic strategy is the right one to take.[39]

A little perspective may be helpful at this point. As Hume rightly emphasized, the reasoning we employ in "experimental" contexts cannot guarantee that the conclusions we draw are true or even close to it. If it is logically impeccable, it conforms to principles of deductive and inductive validity, but these principles merely ensure that our conclusions accord with our premises – that our reasoning is consistent. Goodman's strategy imposes consistency conditions of a further kind – conditions associated with our descriptive vocabulary rather than the formal structure of our inferences. Since reasoning that is consistent in these ways cannot guarantee certain conclusions, one might wonder why it deserves to be commended. The answer is that consistent reasoning is extremely valuable – far more so than the alternative, which is inconsistent reasoning or no reasoning at all. Inconsistent reasoning produces conclusions at odds with our premises – reasoning that guarantees falsity or error. No-reasoning lacks this defect, but it yields no view of the world at all: its upshot is random groping (as Kant called it), unrelated to a coherent purpose. If we reason consistently, we can create a view that might well be correct, at least in part. For even this limited reason, it is worthy of commendation. It it also required by the epistemic aim I described earlier – an aim that we actually have (most of us, tacitly) and that is, certainly, rationally permissible.[40]

6. Inferring the existence of the external world

If Bayes' theorem provides a valid form for experimental inference and if, in addition, we may justifiably accept (under the conditions I mentioned) observational premises, prior probability assignments, and delimited sets of alternative hypotheses, the way is then open for solving the traditional problem about our knowledge of the external world. I introduced a basic strategy for doing this in section 1 of this chapter, but I was deterred from pursuing important details by the need to deal with problems about alternative hypotheses and observational beliefs. Having dealt with these problems to the best of my ability, I can now attend to the pertinent details.

Although I naturally think of the colored expanses I see, the sounds I hear, and the odors I smell as belonging to mind-independent, external objects, the considerations adduced by Locke, Berkeley, and Hume have convinced me that the occurrent qualitative items I immediately apprehend in these cases are really subjective phenomena belonging to a unified bundle, which Hume considered a mind or self. My conviction on this matter does not require me to draw Hume's skeptical conclusions, however. Armed with more powerful inferential methods than Hume possessed, I can provide experimental support for my belief that I am not identical with the bundle of apprehended objects but a psycho-physical being (a sentient, rational animal) that apprehends them.

The experimental support that I can provide for my beliefs about my self and, indeed, the world around me does not relate those beliefs to presumed "hard" sensory data. On the contrary, the hardness of any data is, absolutely speaking, an illusion – as I have in effect been arguing. The data do not have to be considered "subjectless" either, or properly describable only in a Wittgenstei-nian "private language." I can consistently regard my "objective" beliefs as rationally supported by data that always have involved a reference to my self. This is possible because my current beliefs about my self and its relation to a wider world have had a dynamic history; the versions I now wish to defend by reference to my sensory data as I now conceive those data are, in fact, much more sophisticated than the versions I started with. Before reading Locke, Berkeley, and Hume, I thought of myself as a living thing whose skin is puffy, soft, and occurrently pink; but I now think of myself as a gappy aggregate of smaller units – cells at one level, and exotic particles at another. By attending to what I believe to be the experiences of such an aggregate, I hope to confirm my belief that that aggregate and others more or less like it actually exist.

The reasoning by which specific scientific beliefs about one's self and the world can be rationally supported is interesting to contemp-late, but the application of Bayes' theorem to humdrum beliefs about one's self and one's situation in the world raises important philosophical issues that deserve to be handled first. A modest belief (or hypothesis) to begin with is the commonsensical one that I am now at my desk in my study at home looking into the monitor of my word-processor. How can I confirm this by specifically Bayesian reasoning?

Here is an illustrative strategy. On the basis of my current assumptions about myself, my ability to move, the character of my study, and the absence of objects in my environment that might interfere with my vision, I make the predication that, if my humdrum hypothesis (about myself in my study) is true and I will to raise my eyes from the monitor, I shall almost certainly be visually aware of a window looking out upon my neighbor's house. (I deduce this prediction from the assumptions I have mentioned.)

The probability of e (that I will have the indicated object of awareness) given that h and k (h being the hypothesis and k the assumption that I will to raise my eyes) is thus very high. Yet the antecedent probability that I will be visually aware of such a window if I merely will to raise my eyes is very low, for there is no presumption that willing to raise my eyes will always or even usually be succeeded by this specific visual experience. I do will to raise my eyes and I have the visual experience specified by "e." Since the antecedent probability of h given k is clearly positive (there is nothing impossible about it), Bayes' theorem shows h to be positively supported by the truth of k and e.[41] This support can be significantly augmented by the success of numerous other predictions that I can make on the basis of this humdrum hypothesis.

Although I have not specifically mentioned the fact thus far, the truth of an evidence statement e will provide confirming evidence for an hypothesis h under the following equivalent conditions: one, when e raises h's probability – that is, when the probability of h given e is greater than the antecedent probability of h; and two, when the probability of e given h is greater than the antecedent probability of e.[42] I relied on this last condition to show that the antecedently unlikely experience of "seeing" a certain window when I willed to raise my head positively supported the hypothesis that I am sitting at my desk in my study. A look at Bayes' theorem shows that if P(e given h) is high, the degree to which e confirms h is inversely proportional to the antecedent probability of e: the lower this last probability, the higher e supports h. This is a highly intuitive result: hypotheses are highly confirmed by the occurrence of antecedently unlikely phenomena predictable on the basis of them.

The argument I have given for the hypothesis about my study might strike some readers as too good to be true. "Surely," they will say, "the results predictable by your hypothesis are equally predictable by hypotheses you would not want to accept – for example, by the hypothesis that you are a brain in a vat being fed the experiences you associate with your study and a window looking out on your neighbor's yard. Unless you can offer some rational means of ruling out this and countless other hypotheses, the reasoning you offered will not add significant weight to your 'hypothesis' about the external world. More formally put, the point is that if both h_1 and h_2 warrant the prediction e, the truth of e will support h_1-or-h_2. Since $P(h_1) = 1-P(h_2)$ if h_1 and h_2 are mutually exclusive alternatives, the probability of h_1 given e may or may not be greater than the probability of h_2 given e."

This objection is worth discussing because its limitations, when properly spelled out, increase the credibility of the reasoning I have identified. A point to keep in mind in approaching the objection is that, although countless alternative hypotheses could, in principle, yield the predictions obtained from the hypothesis I mentioned, a reasonable person can be expected to deal only with those hypotheses that actually come to mind and are sufficiently plausible (or antecedently likely) to deserve consideration. As I argued in the last section, one can be rightly criticized for neglecting a hypothesis when doing so shows dogmatism, narrowmindedness, culpable ignorance, or intellectual laziness; but these intellectual sins are not committed if one merely neglects a hypothesis that no one seriously advances. The mere fact that I did not mention the brain-in-a-vat hypothesis exposes no defect, therefore, in the reasoning I gave. On the other hand, since that hypothesis has now been brought to mind, I must be willing to consider it. (The critical attitude I insisted upon requires me to do so.) The question to ask is, "Is the hypothesis sufficiently plausible to cast doubt on the alternative I adopted?"

The plausibility of a hypothesis is its prior probability – something that is, in effect, normally determined by a rule of "conditioning": the antecedent probability of p at a time t is the posterior probability of p given the pertinent evidence available at this time.[43] At the present time I have, I believe, a great deal of evidence about the means by which my perceptual experiences are brought about, and this evidence renders the brain-in-a-vat hypothesis extremely unlikely. The capability of the supposed computer, its interface with a living brain, and the required programming know-how all vastly exceed anything we know to be possible. Unfortunately, this sort of evidence is inappropriate in the present discussion, where I am concerned to defend humdrum beliefs about myself and my position in the world. (I am treating myself as a representative "external" object!) To accomplish the task at hand, I must therefore assess the antecedent probability of the vat hypothesis in a way that does not presuppose what I am attempting to defend. The problem is: how can I possibly do this if I cannot use what I take to be available evidence?

Since there is nothing inherently incredible about the vat hypothesis,[44] its antecedent credibility or prior probability is not reasonably assessed as zero. Assuming the same is true of the realist hypothesis that I defended, about the only thing I can do without using the proscribed data is to treat the two hypotheses as rivals and subject them to some kind of experimental test. If one "works" better than another in experimental contexts, it can be regarded as rationally preferable to the other, even if the two hypotheses cannot be assigned determinate prior probabilities. (I will assume, for the reason I gave, that they both have non-zero probabilities.)

When one attempts to compare the vat hypothesis with its realist alternative, one is faced with an important fact: the vat hypothesis, at least as I have stated it thus far, is fundamentally untestable: it is too sketchy, too indeterminate as it stands, to warrant any specific predictions. It conveys a picture, one that I take to represent a bare possibility, but it is insufficiently spelled out to warrant any predictions – even about what I shall be visually aware of after I think to myself "One, two, three."

I can imagine the reader mentally objecting, "It is easy to make such a prediction. If you are visually aware of the window-expanse you spoke of a moment ago, then if you will to retain that awareness and count to yourself 'One, two, three,' you will, *I* predict, be aware of the same or a very similar window-expanse. Try the experiment and see! If you want to make further predictions, the strategy is to consider the predictions you would make on the basis of your current experience and your realist hypothesis. According to the vat hypothesis I propose, your brain is wired up to a machine that mimics what you would consider real-life experiences. The experience you would have, according to this hypothesis, if you had such and such experiences, is just the experience that you would expect on the basis of the realist theory you normally use. As I propose the vat hypothesis, it warrants, for you, exactly the same predictions as your realist hypothesis: the two theories are, for you, observationally equivalent. By attending to your experience, you cannot tell which theory is correct; in fact, you cannot tell whether one of these or a particular instance of countless additional alternatives is correct. Yet these alternatives do warrant predictions – the same predictions that are warranted by the alternative that you accept."

To appreciate the weakness in this objection it is vital to see that the predictions warranted by the vat hypothesis are properly identifiable only by reference to another hypothesis, the realist alternative. The objector speaks of the predictions I would make on the basis of my realist hypothesis, but if the vat hypothesis is to be, as he claims, observationally equivalent to my realist hypothesis, this description of those predictions is strictly incorrect: the predictions I would make on the basis of hypothesis h cannot be identified with the predictions warranted by h because (for one thing) I might occasionally make unwarranted predictions. Thus, the vat hypothesis, call it v, must be understood as asserting that I (at least) am a brain in a vat and so connected to a machine that the experience I will have on any subjectively ascertainable occasion is what I would have then if h (my realist hypothesis) were true. For convenience, I shall represent this last component of v, the component specifying the experience e I would have if h were true and I had experiences $e*$, by the formula "$h(e*) = e$."

Although "$h(e*) = e$" is compatible with both h and v, it does not merely relate experiences that, according to h, are associated with external objects to other such experiences; it also identifies experiences that, according to h, are associated with the physical processes by which experiences are produced in me. These processes concern the propagation of light, the transmission of sound waves, the diffusion of odors, and the neurological means by which these processes indirectly affect my consciousness. If we attempt to confirm h (so understood) by showing that predicted experiences actually occur, we are attempting to confirm a theory (a constantly growing one, actually) about our place in the world and the detailed manner in which we interact with it. The hypothesis v provides no genuine alternative to this. In asserting merely that I am a brain in a vat whose experiences are produced by a mechanism that mimics the experiential effects predictable by the hypothesis h (and auxiliary assumptions about my state of mind), the vat hypothesis provides no real account of what produces my experiences and how it does so; it merely alludes to such an account. To be a serious rival to h, it must do more than allude to an explanatory account; it must actually present one. I concede that v alludes to a possibility (a very bare one) which could conceivably be actual. But until appropriate details are provided, v does not specify an alternative to h that significantly diminishes the probability of h, given the evidence I cited.

7. *On scientific realism*

The detailed view of myself and the world around me that results from the confirmatory process I have described will remind some readers of the sort of view defended by scientific realists. Philosophers meeting this description contend that the aim of science is to secure, by the development and confirmation of theories, a literally true account of what the world is like; and in accordance with this contention, they hold that accepting a scientific theory involves believing that it is true.[45] Although I have not actually committed myself to this view of science, some of the remarks I have been making certainly suggest it. Since scientific realism has recently come under serious attack by accomplished philosophers of science, I want to round out my response to external-world skepticism by saying something about it and the criticism recently brought against it.

The principal objection to scientific realism goes back to Descartes: it is that the doctrine presumes more than we can possibly verify. Scientific claims about the world are verified by the observations we can make; yet as Descartes had to acknowledge in his *Principles of Philosophy*, there is an infinity of different ways in which the things we observe could have been formed "by the great Artificer" or, as we might put it less piously today, "could have arisen from unobservable causes."[46] In view of this, the most that can reasonably be required of a scientific theory is that it be what Bas van Fraassen calls "observationally adequate": it must be correct in what it says about observable phenomena.[47] Descartes disclosed essentially the same opinion when he said that he will have done all that is required of him (as a scientist) if the causes he assigns are such that they correspond to all the phenomena of nature: it is not necessary to inquire whether it is really by means of these causes or others that the phenomena are produced.[48]

Although I would not insist that every acceptable scientific theory should be understood as purporting to provide a literally true picture of the world (or part of it), I can see nothing in legitimate scientific method that justifies the metaphysically favored status Descartes and van Fraassen place on observable phenomena. We do indeed confirm hypotheses about unobservables by observational beliefs, but the latter are rationally acceptable, I argued, only by virtue of their relation to general beliefs (that is, acceptable hypotheses) about observers, observation, observable objects, and conditions of observation – beliefs that involve ideas as high-level and "theoretical" as any others. van Fraassen has asserted that what is observable is a theory-independent question,[49] but this opinion seems clearly false. A question is theory-independent if a rationally acceptable answer can be found that does not presuppose theoretical assumptions or principles. I contend that a rationally acceptable answer to a question about what is obscrvable (in some way, by some kind of observer, under such and such conditions) must at least tacitly allude to principles (beliefs or well-founded assumptions) that deserve to be considered theoretical.

What is an observation? In respect to human beings, at least, the generic answer is "an interpretive act or process – something a person does." One may observe a thing (a bird, a tree, a sunset), and one may observe *that* something is such and such. Both sorts of observing are interpretive, I should say, because both involve some conception of what one is attending to. I can observe Mr Jones buying a newspaper without knowing that the man I observe is Mr Jones, but I could not observe him buying a newspaper if I did not mentally single him out in some way from the scene before me – an accomplishment requiring some conception of my mental target. In the case of observing *that* something, S, is P, I both attend to (or observe) some thing and also come to believe something. I might, for example, observe that Tom is not in his chair; in doing this, I no doubt observe his chair and form the belief that Tom is not in it. When I observe anything by my senses, I have appropriate sensory experiences. These experiences play a causal role in the formation of my belief and in the focusing of my attention, but I do not generally attend to them in any conscious way. Essentially, they are sensory triggers to which the formation of specific beliefs is an automatic response. I have been calling beliefs thus formed "observational beliefs."

As one might conclude from the fact that an observer does not generally attend to the sensory experiences prompting an observational belief, the contents or objects of such a belief may be conceptually unrelated to any experience the observer may have. The content of an observational belief may, in fact, involve patently high-level, "theoretical" concepts: *That's NaCl* would be an instance of this. The fact that such beliefs are generated by sensory experience does not render them minimally erroneous or maximally informative about the nature of reality. Both features will be heavily dependent on the context. Under certain circumstances (in an ordinary kitchen, for instance) the observational belief *That's NaCl* may be highly reliable, although in other circumstances (a chemistry laboratory containing a wide variety of similar salts) it may be extremely questionable. The belief's informativeness will also be context-dependent; it will be particularly dependent on what is otherwise known or regarded as probable. Since the acceptability of an observational belief is not intrinsic to it but must be assessed by higher-order general beliefs that are not themselves observational, the security that Descartes and, apparently, van Fraassen find in observation is pure illusion. Our theories are rationally acceptable, not because they accommodate (or are true to) certain "phenomena" but because accepting them accords with reasonable epistemic ends and a maximally critical procedure.

Do the remarks I have just made commit me to scientific realism? The answer is, "Not if scientific realism is understood as I characterized it above." According to that conception, a scientific realist accepts a scientific theory (presumably, any theory) only when he believes that the theory is true. This is a stronger statement than I would be willing to make. As I see it, one can reasonably "accept" a scientific theory for all sorts of reasons. If one lacks a theory one believes (fairly strongly) to be true in a certain domain, one may "accept" as indispensable for dealing with that domain a theory one regards as false: the conclusions it allows one to draw, or the predictions it allows one to make, may be acceptably close to the truth for important purposes. This last possibility is associated with the fact that one may be very confident about certain aspects of a theory while very doubtful about others. Thus, one may be extremely confident that electrons are negatively charged entities but doubtful about their nature or character as individuals. Are they "waves" or what? When one uses a theory, or accepts it for legitimate scientific purposes, one does not necessarily accept all its implications. A reason why this is sometimes allowable is that theories are not, in practice, neatly individuated: we draw conclusions from a body of considerations, some only tacitly at work in our thinking, and (as Quine, following Duhem, has repeatedly emphasized)[50] an objectionable consequence cannot always be firmly assigned to one particular theory. The "acceptance" of a theory is thus in practice an untidy affair, and it does not correlate with belief (and degrees thereof) in any simple, uniform way.

These critical observations about scientific realism apply only to one part of it, the part concerned with belief. The other part, the part concerning the aim of science, is also oversimplified, but I am sympathetic with its basic thrust. Since it is only intelligent beings that have aims, I cannot seriously attribute this aim to the abstraction, science. Yet one can certainly identify what I have called ideal aims; and one can, as I did, associate such aims with a certain idealized activity or group of interests. The ideal epistemic aim I identified – that of obtaining a maximally comprehensive yet maximally simple conceptual scheme that one can reasonably hope to be minimally erroneous – is no doubt similar to some actual aims of some actual people, and people who acknowledge this aim (or something tantamount to it) have one means of justifying a broadly empiricist approach to matters of fact and existence. In view of the vitality of empiricist strategies in science, I am convinced that many experimental scientists do, in fact, share something like that ideal aim. But some scientists are no doubt less speculative and more "instrumentally minded." I cannot say that the aim I identified is the correct one, but I can say that it is reasonable. And that's enough for me.

Another point needs to be made, however. Even if one agrees that ascertaining the actual nature of the world is a legitimate scientific aim and that a given theory is not just a useful predictive device but a fairly accurate theoretical representation of some part or aspect of the world, one may still be uncertain about the theory's "ontological commitments" – that is, about what entities must exist if the theory is true. Contemporary philosophers generally follow what they take to be Quine's strategy for ascertaining a theory's ontological commitments: they look to the existentially quantified formulas involved in the theory (or in a regimented version of it) and identify the values of the variables involved. Quine's actual strategy is more complicated than this, however, and also more reasonable; but it is difficult to apply. His strategy prescribes the identification of entities that *must* be counted as values of quantified variables if the theory is true (or the assertions making up the theory are true). This strategy is preferable to the one customarily adopted because some quantified statements (for example, "Some zoological species are cross-fertile") can be eliminated from a theory by paraphrase and thus be regarded as convenient notation that is not necessary to the theory's content.[51] The strategy is difficult to apply because there is no generally agreed upon means of deciding what is or is not necessary to a theory's content.

For reasons related to this last matter, Quine has in fact now abandoned the strategy: he no longer is willing even to speak of "the" ontological commitments of a theory. As he sees it now, theories are "referentially indeterminate," and it does not even make sense to say "what, absolutely speaking, the objects of a theory are"; one can merely say "how one theory of objects is interpretable or reinterpretable in another."[52] I do not propose to discuss Quine's new doctrine here, important as it is;[53] I shall merely explain how, in my opinion, we can reasonably proceed to clarify what we take a theory to say about the world without even tacitly interpreting it in terms of another theory.

Clarifying a theory's ontological commitments is closely related to clarifying one's meaning in using language of this or that kind. It is obvious that most people do not intend to refer to existing things when they use certain familiar locutions. An historically important example of such a locution is "the average plumber." Near the turn of the century, Bertrand Russell focused a good deal of attention on such expressions, calling them "incomplete symbols."[54] A distinctive feature of incomplete symbols as Russell described them is that they contribute to the meaning or referential import of a sentence without standing for something themselves. His favorite example of an incomplete symbol was a definite description, "the present king of France." Like "the average plumber," this complex noun does not refer to anything; but the contribution it makes to a sentence differs greatly from that of "the average plumber," which does not even purport to be a definite description. When we use these terms, we know we are not referring to anything real; but to discover what we are using them to do, we may have to do some careful thinking. The thinking is analytical, but it does not consist in relating an "incomplete symbol" to a counterpart in another language. I think that, in part at least, it involves "fixing one's meaning" in the Peircean way I described in the last chapter – that is, deciding what immediate conclusions one is willing to have drawn from assertions in which it occurs and also, perhaps, indicating the sort of assertions from which the latter may immediately be inferred.

Cartesian has clearly identified what this property is. The second objection is that propositions claimed to be self-evident by cautious, earnest thinkers have sometimes been refuted or shown to be highly improbable by subsequent investigation. One proposition of this kind is the axiom of abstraction, which Bertrand Russell refuted in a famous letter to Gottlob Frege;[47] another is the traditional principle that every event must have a cause, which has been refuted by the development of quantum mechanics. The axiom of abstraction was widely regarded as obvious before Russell proved that it led to contradiction; and the causal principle was held to be self-evident not only by Descartes but by responsible twentieth-century philosophers such as Sir David Ross.[48]

Claims that, like the two I have mentioned, cannot be accepted on account of their presumed obviousness or self-evidence may yet be acceptable on other grounds. Can such grounds be offered for Chisholm's Cartesian claims? The answer, I believe, is no: with their ingredient adverb "necessarily," they are too strong for principles true of the natural world. If the world consists of continuants (persisting things) having attributes, this can be known only by some kind of empirical investigation – and it is not a necessary fact about the way things are. Also, the ability of human beings to identify their feelings, emotions, beliefs and so on in a reliable way is also not something that can be known *a priori* – or, in this case, not even known *simpliciter*, for some people are positively unreliable in identifying some of their "mental" states or attitudes. The claims I am making here cannot be defended by the principles of classical empiricists: a new, improved empiricist epistemology is required. I shall expound and defend such an epistemology in the next chapter; I shall do so by making appropriate changes in classical empiricism.

Obviously, it is not just the significance of terms like "the average plumber" or "the present king of France" that stimulate ontological reflections in fastidious thinkers. Terms such as "space," "time," and 'field" (as in "gravitational field") have also raised ontological anxieties. As a result, philosophers and philosophically-minded scientists have asked themselves whether legitimate theoretical purposes require them to assume that there really is such a thing as space, time, or the electromagnetic field. With specific theories in mind, some have said yes and others have said no. Instead of acknowledging that there is such a thing as time, a continuous manifold containing instants, Russell argued that it is only necessary to postulate a domain of temporally overlapping events: the "manifold" can be understood as a mere logical construction.[55] And instead of acknowledging that there is such a thing as a magnetic field in a certain region, others have claimed that it is sufficient to assume that true existents in that region will behave in such and such ways, depending on their kind, their spatio-temporal relations to one another, and so forth.[56] A contrasting ontological claim was made by Russell when he insisted that the special theory of relativity requires us to think of the world as ultimately composed of "events" arranged (as it were) in a four-dimensional manifold.[57] Although we ordinarily speak of objects – chairs, for example – as persisting in time, we must now regard such "objects" as mere constructions, Russell thought: the genuine reality corresponding to our everyday object-word "chair" is not a persisting thing but a spatio-temporally extended series of chair-events or chair-stages, each such event or stage being a complex reality consisting (at one level of analysis) of the micro-stages appropriate to micro-objects.[58]

It seems to me that the scientific realism involved in Russell's interpretation of physics is substantially correct. Not only did he not claim that every physical theory should be understood as providing a literally true account of what the world is really like; he did not claim that the theoretical terms (as we should say today) of our most confidently used theories should all be interpreted as referring to something real. The right realist attitude is difficult to pin down in precise terms, but it is clearly a cautious attitude. Ideally, our well-confirmed theories should contribute to our understanding (to the fallible picture we possess) of what our world is like and how it is put together. But the ontological import of a given theory should be ascertained or estimated by an analytical process in which entities are not multiplied beyond necessity and in which that theory is related to other theories – the ones we have, and the ones we are beginning to have. As scientific realists, we want what Plato called a "synoptic view" of ourselves and the world;[59] and to develop it, we must consider our various theories (and their relative acceptability) together. There is, at least in principle, more than one way of picturing the world (more than one possible way of sorting its objects), but a fully satisfactory picture must be true to the word: if it is depicted as containing Russellian events, such events must actually exist in it, not just be imagined as being there.

Appendix

The following example illustrates my claim that the convergence of rational opinion resulting from persistent applications of Bayes' theorem to the same evidential input is not assured merely by probabilistic consistency.[1]

An unscrupulous gambler has two coins, one fair and the other biased towards heads. Having thrown the latter many times, he believes that the probability of its turning up heads is 0.6. Looking for a game, he takes one of the coins from his pocket; but before he has a chance to see which coin it is, another player snatches it from his hand and announces that the gambler's coin is almost certainly biased: the chances are 8 to 2, he says, that the coin is unfair. The gambler thinks the chances are about equal that the player has the biased coin, though he agrees with the player that the probability of getting heads on a toss of the biased coin is 0.6. (Both believe the probability of getting heads on a fair coin is 0.5.) The following reasoning shows that, if (a) the gambler and the player are willing to correct their opinions about the fairness of the coin (that is, update their "priors") by applying Bayes' theorem to the results of seeing it thrown, and (b) the results of ten successive throws are H,H,T,H,H,H,H,H,T,H, then their opinions will converge in a striking way.

The key probabilities for the example are displayed in the tables below. To indicate the progressive manner in which the gambler's and the player's opinions are changed by the results of seeing the coin thrown, I give the updated probabilities obtained from the first five flips and then the probabilities obtained from the second five. A *likelihood*, remember, is the probability of an outcome given a certain hypothesis, and *posterior* is the probability of a hypothesis given certain experimental data. Since there are two alternative hypotheses about the coin (one that it is fair and one that it is biased), the instance of Bayes' theorem approporiate to the example takes the form of:

$$P(h_1 \text{ given } e) = \frac{P(h_1)P(e \text{ given } h_1)}{P(h_1)P(e \text{ given } h_1) + P(h_2)P(e \text{ given } h_2)}.$$

Here are the gambler's probabilities for the first five flips, which are, again, H,H,T,H,H:

Hypotheses	Priors	Likelihoods	Priors times Likelihoods	Posteriors
Fair	0.5	$(0.5)^5$	0.015625	0.38
Biased	0.5	$(0.6)^4 (0.4)$	0.02592	0.62
			Sum = 0.041545	

Plugged into the instance of Bayes' theorem I have given above, these probabilities assume the pattern:

$$\text{Posterior} = \frac{\text{Prior times Liklihood}}{\text{Sum}}$$

For readers new to the subject, the first likelihood listed in the table above is the value of a term that can be denoted by "P(HHTHH/ fair)"; this value is set at $(0.5)^5$ because the probability of each outcome on a fair coin is 0.5, and there are five such outcomes, each independent of the others. The second likelihood is the value of a term that can be denoted by "P(HHTHH/biased)"; this value is set at $(0.6)^4 (0.4)$ because the sequence of outcomes contains four heads, each with a probability of 0.6 on the hypothesis the coin is biased, and one tail, which has a probability of 0.4 on that hypothesis.

Here are the player's probabilities for the first five flips:

Hypotheses	Priors	Likelihoods	Priors times Likelihoods	Posteriors
Fair	0.2	$(0.5)^5$	0.00625	0.13
Biased	0.5	$(0.6)^4 (0.4)$	0.041472	0.87
			Sum = 0.047722	

The extent of the initial disagreement about the coin was 0.3, the gambler thinking the probability that it is biased equal to 0.5, and the player thinking it equal to 0.8. The first five flips changed this disagreement, for the gambler now thinks the probability that it is biased equal to 0.62 and the player thinks it equal to 0.87, a difference of 0.25.

The gambler's probabilities for the next five outcomes (H,H,H,T,H) with his revised priors and new posteriors are:

Hypotheses	Priors	Likelihoods	Priors times Likelihoods	Posteriors
Fair	0.38	$(0.5)^5$	0.011875	0.27
Biased	0.62	$(0.6)^4 (0.4)$	0.032141	0.73
		Sum = 0.044016		

The player's revised probabilities for the next five flips are:

Hypotheses	Priors	Likelihoods	Priors times Likelihoods	Posteriors
Fair	0.13	$(0.5)^5$	0.004062	0.08
Biased	0.87	$(0.6)^4 (0.4)$	0.045101	0.92
		Sum = 0.049163		

Here, after ten flips, the disagreement about the probability of the coin being biased amounts to 0.19, or 0.92−0.73. If further data were collected, further revision of the priors would bring the gambler's and the player's opinions even closer. The standard Bayesian claim is that if enough data were considered, the opinions of the two people would eventually become indistinguishable.[2]

It should be obvious that the convergence of opinion that I have shown here depends on contingent assumptions whose acceptability is not dictated by the evidence of the throws or probability theory. One such assumption – a particularly salient one – is that the coin in question is either fair or biased 6 to 4 in favor of heads. This assumption is needed to obtain the instance of Bayes' theorem that I used from the simpler instance having "P(e)" as a denominator. To obtain the more complex instance one must regard the disjunction "The coin is fair or the coin is biased" as equivalent to "The coin is fair or - (the coin is fair)." (See my remarks in Chapter VI on the derivation of theorem T7: p. 169.) If "biased" meant simply "not fair," the equivalence of the two disjunctions would be acceptable on logical grounds; but since "biased" is here understood as meaning "biased 6 to 4 in favor of heads," the equivalence is acceptable only on a contingent basis not included in the reasoning I have given. That reasoning, which is representative of the reasoning showing the convergence of priors by persistent conditioning, is therefore not unqualifiedly acceptable. To employ it, we must make assumptions that are not warranted merely by observable evidence and probability theory.

The limitations of a purely *a priori* argument for the eventual convergence of priors are similar to the limitations of Pascal's Wager.[3] Pascal wanted to show that, although we cannot actually know whether God exists, we are rationally justified in believing that He exists because the consequences of believing that He exists are demonstrably preferable to the consequences of believing that He does not exist. Since believing that God exists is tantamount to accepting a certain theory postulating a divine being with specified characteristics (the will to reward faith, for example), Pascal must show that accepting that theory, call it h_1, is preferable to accepting some alternative theory, h_2.

Although there is (one may concede) no problem in estimating the relative value of accepting and rejecting h_1 given that it is true, there is a problem about h_2. The problem arises in two ways. First, if the hypothesis h_2 amounts to no more than $-h_1$, there is no basis for assigning a value either to accepting or to rejecting this alternative:

	h_1 is true	h_2 is true
Value of accepting h_1	Big plus	?
Value of rejecting h_1	Big minus	?

The mere assertion that one theological theory, h_1, is false does not rule out the truth of infinitely many other theories assigning an infinite variety of utilities to accepting and rejecting $-h_1$. As a result, the information Pascal supplies does not justify us in assigning any particular utility to this alternative. Since we cannot do this, we cannot conclude that accepting h_1 is preferable to accepting this h_2: half the matrix cannot be filled in.

If, second, h_2 is a particular theory providing a rational basis for assessing the relative utility of accepting h_1 and h_2 when h_1 is false, then we must have reason to believe that h_1 and h_2 are the only alternatives pertinent to assessing the desirability of "believing in God." But not only does Pascal not offer such a reason, his acknowledged skepticism about what we can know in divine matters precludes him from offering it. This undermines his argument. If we really lack all knowledge in theological matters, we have no rational basis for deciding what is true if h_1 is false. This lack of knowledge also prevents us from filling in half of the matrix. The reason this time is not that we cannot assign a value to accepting and rejecting h_1 when a certain alternative to h_1 is true; it is that we cannot identify the alternative (or alternatives) that we ought to consider.

The analogy with the "convergence of priors" argument is that if we make no assumptions about the world (which we must support empirically), we shall have no basis for concluding that persistent conditioning will result in the convergence of alternative priors. In the case I described, we would have no basis for computing the crucial likelihoods, $P(\text{HHTHH}/\text{biased})$ and $P(\text{HHHTH}/\text{biased})$. If we attempted to avoid computing these likelihoods by employing simpler instances of Bayes' theorem (i.e. using the version T5) containing only the hypothesis "The coin is fair," we could show the convergence of the gambler's and the player's probability assignments to it by assuming that these men agree on the prior probability of the experimental outcomes. Showing this amounts to showing that the convergence of certain probability values can be inferred from the agreement on certain others. If we want an absolute assurance that some probability assignment or other is acceptable, we shall get no help from a Bayesian convergence argument."

Notes

I Descartes

1 *Meditations on First Philosophy*, in John Cottingham *et al.* (editors and translators), *The Philosophical Writings of Descartes*, vol. II, Cambridge, Cambridge University Press, 1984, p. 12. In what follows I shall refer to both volumes of these writings as "PWD."

2 ibid., pp. 12ff.

3 ibid.

4 See *Principles of Philosophy*, Principle 5, in *PWD*, vol. I, p. 194.

5 ibid.

6 ibid.

7 ibid., p. 17.

8 See PWD, vol. I, p. 194.

9 Descartes, "Reply to Second Objections," in *PWD*, vol. II, p. 100.

10 He includes *cogito* arguments in his *Discourse on Method*, in his *Meditations on First Philosophy*, in his *Principles of Philosophy*, in his *Replies to Objections*, and in his dialogue, *The Search After Truth*.

11 *PWD*, vol. I, p. 196.

12 ibid.

13 *Second Meditation*, in *PWD*, vol. II, p. 18.

14 ibid., p. 19.

15 *PWD*, vol. II, p. 113.

16 Bertrand Russell, *A History of Western Philosophy*, London, Allen & Unwin, 1945, p. 567.

17 *Second Meditation*, *PWD*, vol. II, p. 17.

18 Principle 11, *PWD*, vol. I, p. 196.

19 See *Meditation II*, *PWD*, vol. II, p. 21.

20 See Bertrand Russell, *Human Knowledge: Its Scope and Limits*, London, Allen & Unwin, 1948, Part IV.

21 See Principle 49, in *PWD*, vol. I, p. 209.

22 In Descartes' system, as in Aristotle's, thoughts are not primary things or substances; they are "modes" or "accidents" – and thus semi-things, as we might say. The point is worth making because, if thoughts do not count as genuine things, Descartes' *cogito* will *not* (as he said) depend on the knowledge of any thing.

23 *Second Set of Replies*, in *PWD*, vol. II, p. 115.
24 *PWD*, vol. II, p. 14.
25 See the perceptive discussion in Anthony Kenny, *Descartes: A Study of his Philosophy*, New York, Random House, 1968, ch. 8. The adjective "Cartesian" is derived from the form Descartes' name assumed in Latin writings, "Renatus Cartesius."
26 See the discussion in Kenny, *Descartes*, p. 189.
27 *PWD*, vol. II, p. 103.
28 *Meditation III*, in *PWD*, vol. II, p. 24.
29 In his *Principles*, Descartes actually said – in his gloss on Principle 43, which states that "we cannot go wrong when we assent only to what we clearly and distinctly perceive" – that since God is not a deceiver, "the faculty of perception which he has given us cannot incline us to falsehood." He added, however, perhaps to avoid the charge of circular reasoning, that "even if there were no way of proving this, the minds of all of us have been so moulded by nature that whenever we perceive something clearly, we spontaneously give our assent to it and are quite unable to doubt its truth." See *PWD*, vol. I, p. 207.
30 Principle 45, in *PWD*, vol. I, pp. 208–9.
31 See *Rules for the Direction of the Mind* (written about 1628), in *PWD*, vol. I, p. 14.
32 He sometimes called it "induction" as well: see *PWD*, vol. I, p. 14 (see note of translator, who misses the point I am making here). At the time Descartes wrote, "induction" was commonly applied to the process Aristotelians called "intuitive induction." In this latter process a connection between universals became apparent to a mind (or "intuited") after the latter had obtained sufficient experience of instances. Descartes may have thought that the intuitive elements in both intuitive induction and deduction (as he understood it) are the same. He suggests this when he says that the "evidence and certitude . . . which belongs to intuition is required . . . in discursive reasoning of whatever sort." ibid.
33 ibid., p. 15.
34 ibid.
35 ibid.
36 *PWD*, vol. II, p. 54.
37 ibid., p. 55.
38 See *Principles of Philosophy*, Part II, 23, in *PWD*, vol. I, p. 232.
39 See *PWD*, vol. II, pp. 56–7.
40 ibid., p. 56.
41 Descartes sometimes writes as if the certainty of his existence is intuitive, sometimes as if it is a "necessary inference" from intuitions. See above, section 3.
42 The inference I question here appears less dubious in John Cottingham's new translation of the *Meditations*, which appears in *PWD*. Instead of having Descartes say that he does *not remark* that anything necessarily belongs to his nature except that he is a thinking thing (as Descartes is represented as saying in the older Haldane and Ross

translation), Cottingham has him say that he *sees* that "absolutely nothing else" belongs to his nature except that he is a thinking thing. But not only is Descartes not entitled to this stronger claim by the meager data available in the *cogito*, Cottingham's rendering transforms a dubious inference into an unsupported redundancy. From the premiss I have cited Cottingham renders the conclusion "I can correctly infer that my essence consists solely in the fact that I am a thinking thing." The crucial passage occurs on page 54 of Cottingham's translation.

43 *PWD*, vol. I, p. 247.

44 These are his first, second, and third laws of nature as expressed in Part II of the Principles; see ibid., pp. 240–2.

45 Principle 201 of Part IV, ibid., pp. 286–7. Although Descartes did not believe in empty space and explicitly attacked Democritus' doctrine of atoms and the void, he did think that there must be bodies smaller than those that can be perceived by the senses. His objection to Democritus' view was directed to the idea of empty space and to the claim that atoms are indivisible. As he saw it, the physical world is an infinitely divisible, three-dimensional plenum in which bodies can be distinguished within bodies without theoretical limit. This is not incompatible with the view, which Descartes may or may not have held, that the parts of some micro-particles always remain together, so that the world can be said to be composed, on one level of analysis, of atomic, insensible bodies of certain definite kinds.

46 I discuss this form of inference in Chapter VI, section 5.

47 *PWD*, vol. I, p. 286.

48 ibid., p. 288.

49 ibid., p. 289.

50 See Bas C. van Fraassen, *The Scientific Image*, Oxford, Clarendon Press, 1980, p. 57. I discuss van Fraassen's view in Chapter VII, section 9.

51 ibid., p. 290.

52 ibid.

53 ibid.

II Locke and Berkeley

1 *Essay Concerning Human Understanding*, ed. and abr. by A. S. Pringle-Pattison, Oxford, Clarendon Press, 1924, Bk. IV, Ch. I, section 2, p. 255. "Actual" knowledge is the present view the mind has of the relations between its ideas; the knowledge one might have after actual knowledge has been achieved (e.g. the knowledge one has that white is not black) Locke terms "habitual." See ibid., pp. 258f.

2 See *Essay*, Bk. IV, Ch. 6, section 9; P-P, p. 294.

3 See Bk. II, Ch. 23, section 15; P-P, p. 164.

4 See Bk. IV, Ch. 10.

5 The inconsistency might indicate, rather, that my idea of my self or God is defective in some way. Here is an analogy. Suppose my idea of Zed

is the idea of the natural number preceding zero. (I simply form this idea.) Given the identity "Zed = the number preceding 0," I may conclude by standard description theory that 0 has a predecessor, a proposition inconsistent in number theory. The conclusion to draw is not that the axioms of number theory are false; it is that *Zed* is a defective, illegitimate idea. The same could be true of a certain idea of one's self or God.

6 *Essay*, IV, 2, 14; P-P, p. 265.
7 J. L. Austin, *Sense and Sensibilia*, reconstructed from manuscript lecture notes by G. J. Warnock, Oxford, Clarendon Press, 1962, p. 48.
8 Locke's reply to the skeptic occurs in Chapter 2 of Book IV; his four reasons are given in Chapter 10 of that book.
9 *Essay*, IV, 11, 3; P-P, p. 322.
10 *Essay*, IV, 11, 4; P-P, p. 322.
11 *Essay*, IV, 11, 5; ibid.
12 *Essay*, IV, 11, 6; ibid.
13 *Essay*, IV, 11, 7; P-P, p. 324.
14 *Essay*, IV, 11, 2; P-P, p. 321.
15 Locke was prepared to speak of memory knowledge as well as sensitive knowledge, but he restricted the latter to the assurance that "heretofore things that affected our senses have existed." See ibid.
16 *Essay*, IV, 11, 10, p. 327.
17 *Essay*, IV, 14, section 1; p. 333.
18 See Ian Hacking, *The Emergence of Probability*, Cambridge, Cambridge University Press, 1975, Ch. 1.
19 *Essay*, IV, 15, 3; p. 335.
20 For the various meanings of "likelihood" in the seventeenth century, see the *OED*. Hacking, *The Emergence of Probability*, pp. 28f., emphasizes the importance of the renaissance notion of a sign (as in "a sign of fever") in the development of the modern notion of probability (which Locke had not yet attained).
21 See ibid., pp. 22f.
22 For a useful discussion of Boyle's and Newton's remarks on scientific inference, see Maurice Mandelbaum, *Philosophy, Science, and Sense-perception*, Baltimore, Johns Hopkins, 1964, Ch. 2.
23 *Essay*, IV, 16, 6; p. 338.
24 ibid.
25 *Essay*, IV, 15, 4; p. 336.
26 ibid.
27 *Essay*, IV, 16, 12; pp. 340ff.
28 Newton's third rule of reasoning in philosophy is a principle of analogy: "The qualities of bodies which admit neither intensification nor remission of degrees and which are found to belong to all bodies within the reach of our experiments are to be esteemed universal qualities of all bodies whatsoever." Quoted in Mandelbaum, *Philosophy, Science, and Sense-perception*, pp. 82f.
29 Hume did not distinguish it from what is now called "enumerative induction," saying, "All our reasonings concerning matters of fact are

founded on a species of Analogy, which leads us to expect from any cause the same events, which we have observed to result from similar causes." See David Hume, *Enquiry Concerning the Human Understanding*, in L. A. Selby-Bigge, (ed.), *Hume's Enquiries*, Oxford, Clarendon Press, 1902, p. 104.

30 See Bertrand Russell, *Human Knowledge: Its Scope and Limits*, London, Allen & Unwin, 1948, where the principle is formulated this way: "Given two classes of events A and B, and given that, whenever both A and B can be observed, there is reason to believe that A causes B, then if, in a given case, A is observed, but there is no way of observing whether B occurs or not, it is probable that B occurs; and similarly if B is observed, but the presence or absence of A cannot be observed" (pp. 511f.).

31 See note 12.

32 *Essay*, IV, 3, 27; p. 284.

33 See note 14.

34 See Descartes, *Principles of Philosophy*, Principle CCI; in *PWD*, p. 286.

35 *Essay*, II, 23, 9–10; pp. 159f.

36 *Essay*, II, 23, 1–3; pp. 154–8.

37 See *Phaedrus*, 265E.

38 III, 3, 20; p. 237.

39 *Essay*, II, 8, 15; p. 69.

40 These quotations come from a single sentence in the *Essay*, I, 1, 8; pp. 15f.

41 *Essay* II, 8, 12; p. 68.

42 *Essay*, II, 23, 11; pp. 160f.

43 *Essay*, II, 23, 9; p. 159.

44 George Berkeley, *Three Dialogues Between Hylas and Philonous*, ed. David M. Armstrong, *Berkeley's Philosophical Writings*, New York, Macmillan, 1965, pp. 146–7.

45 A contextual definition specifies the meaning of a symbol in the context of a formula; it does so by providing a rule according to which a formula containing a given symbol can be replaced by an equivalent formula not containing that symbol. Simple examples of such definitions can be found in elementary mathematics. To define subtraction in terms of addition, we equate an open formula (equation) containing the minus sign with a different formula containing the symbol for addition. The definition is:

$$(a - b) = c \text{ iff } a = (b + c).$$

46 See *Three Dialogues*, pp. 151–5.

47 ibid., p. 33.

48 According to contemporary estimates, these gaps are enormous, relatively speaking. See Jeremy Cherfas, *In Search of Schrödinger's Cat: Quantum Physics and Reality*, New York, Bantam Books, 1984, p. 31.

49 *Three Dialogues*, p. 150.

50 I say "ultimately" because a geometrical feature can often be dis-

tinguished in a primary way by reference to another such feature – for instance, by saying, "the parallelogram is the figure next to the circle." Ultimately, some feature will have to be distinguished by a colored line, a color expanse, or some other content feature.

51 As Berkeley pointed out, *extension* is the basic primary quality. Philonous observes that "if *extension* be once acknowledged to have no existence without the mind, the same must necessarily be granted of motion, solidity, and gravity – since they all evidently presuppose extension." See ibid., p. 155.
52 ibid., p. 169.
53 Berkeley pointed this out in his *Principles of Human Knowledge*, section 73. See *Berkeley's Philosophical Writings*, p. 91.
54 Bertrand Russell, *A History of Western Philosophy*, New York, Simon & Schuster, 1945, p. 654.
55 See ibid., pp. 201f.
56 See my discussion in *Metaphysics: the Elements*, Minneapolis, University of Minnesota Press, 1985, pp. 46–51.
57 *Principles*, section 95.
58 ibid., section 49.
59 See note 45
60 ibid., p. 156.
61 See *Principles*, "Introduction."
62 *Principles*, section 7.
63 ibid., section 124.
64 *Principles*, section 48.
65 *Principles*, section 3; in *Berkeley's Philosophical Writings*, p. 62.
66 ibid., section 58.
67 *Three Dialogues*, p. 175.
68 *Philosophical Commentaries*, entry 580; in *Berkeley's Philosophical Writings*, p. 367.
69 *Dialogues*, p. 194.
70 *Dialogues*, p. 175.
71 See ibid., pp. 201–2.

III Hume and Solipsism

1 *Enquiry Concerning Human Understanding*, in L. A. Selby-Bigge, (ed.), *Hume's Enquiries*, Oxford, 1902, section IV, Part 1, p. 25.
2 Locke, *Essay*, Bk IV, Ch. 1.
3 I discuss Kant's distinction in the next chapter, the distinction of recent empiricists in Chapter VI.
4 *Enquiry*, p. 25.
5 *Treatise of Human Nature*, ed. L. A. Selby-Bigge, Oxford, 1888, Part III, section I, pp. 69f.
6 I discuss this conception of analytic truth in Chapter VI.
7 *S* is explicitly contradictory iff S has the form of "*P & -P*."
8 *Treatise*, I, III, p. 79. See also p. 70.

9 See Chapter II above, pp. 28–9.
10 See *Enquiry*, section VI, p. 56, fn.; a similar qualification appears in the *Treatise*, Part III, section XI, p. 124.
11 *Enquiry*, IX, p. 104. I have altered Hume's punctuation in this passage.
12 *Enquiry*, section II, p. 19.
13 ibid. I shall discuss some possible exceptions a little later.
14 *Enquiry*, section II, p. 22.
15 The image comes from T. S. Eliot's "Morning at the Window," *Collected Poems*, London, 1952, p. 16.
16 *Enquiry*, section XII, Part II, p. 165.
17 ibid., p. 26.
18 ibid., p. 27.
19 ibid., pp. 105f., where Hume speaks of an animal *inferring* "some fact beyond what immediately strikes his senses."
20 In view of what he eventually says, his use of "knowledge" here should no doubt be understood as "loose and popular."
21 *Enquiry*, section IV, Part I, p. 30.
22 ibid., p. 32.
23 ibid., p. 35f.
24 Q can be obtained from P and If P then Q by the sequence: If P then Q; $-(P \& -Q)$; $-P v - - Q$; P; $- - P$; $- - Q$; Q.
25 I shall discuss this conception of probability in chapters VI and VII.
26 *Enquiry*, section XII, Part I, p. 151.
27 ibid.
28 In the *Treatise* Hume complained that the popular system rests on a gross illusion – namely, that "our resembling perceptions are numerically the same": see Book I, Part IV, section II, p. 217.
29 ibid.
30 ibid., p. 153.
31 ibid., p. 222.
32 ibid.
33 *Treatise*, I, IV, VII; pp. 268f.
34 *Enquiry*, XII, Part I, p. 151.
35 ibid., p. 153.
36 Descartes also offered a purely "ontological" version of the argument in *Meditation* V.
37 "Solipsism" comes from the Latin *solus* (= alone) and *ipse* (= self).
38 *Treatise*, p. 252.
39 Norman Malcolm has argued that one makes a "profoundly false" assumption in saying that when someone occurrently remembers something, something takes place then that is her remembering. His argument, in brief, is that none of the events occurring when someone remembers something can be *identical* with her remembering because those events "could have occurred" when the person was not remembering the relevant thing. Malcolm's argument is fallacious, however, as the following analogy shows: An event (an act of stabbing) occurring in circumstances C can be truly described as an act of killing (and thus be such an act) even though the act (the stabbing) "could have occurred"

without anyone dying. For an event to count as a memory event, certain events must have obtained that need not have obtained – one being that the ostensibly remembered event actually took place. See Norman Malcolm, *Memory and Mind*, Ithaca, N.Y., Cornell University Press, 1977, pp. 48, 75.

40 Bertrand Russell, *An Outline of Philosophy*, London, Allen & Unwin, 1927, p. 7.

41 I myself have pushed the skeptical line further on behalf of strict empiricist principles in "The Paradox of Empiricism," *Metaphilosophy*, I (1970), 128–38. The key consideration is that observation (or perception) can provide well-founded knowledge only if there is reason to believe that observational (or perceptual) beliefs are true at least more often than not. Such a reason cannot be given if we are restricted to the strictest empiricist principles. On such principles there is no way of supporting a correlation between a perceptual belief and the entities that would make it true.

42 Our idea of a necessary connection between events seems to be the idea of something in the objective world, but it is really quite different since it is generated from the mind's customary imaginative transition from the idea of one event to the idea of the event constantly conjoined with it: the transition is felt by the mind and an idea results. See *Enquiry*, section VII.

43 *Treatise*, I, Part II, section VI, p. 67.

44 *Treatise*, pp. 217, 215, 218.

45 ibid.

46 ibid., p. 271.

47 ibid., p. 271.

48 ibid., p. 272.

49 *Treatise*, pp. 225f

IV Kant and Phenomenalism

1 See *Prolegomena to Any Future Metaphysics*, trans. James Ellington, Indianapolis, Hackett Publishing Company, 1977, p. 5. The corresponding page in the Prussian Academy edition of Kant's works, vol. 4, is 260.

2 See below, p. 94 and also notes 15 and 16.

3 *Critique of Pure Reason*, second edition, trans. N. K. Smith, London, Macmillan, 1961, Bxvii–xviii. Here and in what follows I follow the standard practice of referring to pages of his first and second editions by A or B plus the relevant number. These pages numbers are given in the margins of Kemp Smith's translation.

4 Cf. the review article by Karl Ameriks, "Recent Work on Kant's Theoretical Philosophy," *American Philosophical Quarterly*, 19 (1982), 1–14.

5 ibid., A7, B11.

6 ibid., A8, B12.

7 See *Prolegomena*, p. 12; Academy edition p. 267.

8 See *Critique of Pure Reason*, B141, and also Kant's *Logic*, trans. Robert B. Hartman and Wolfgang Schwarz, Indianapolis, Bobbs-Merrill, 1974, p. 111. The obvious way of reducing a hypothetical judgment to a categorical one is to say that "If P then Q" amounts to "All P-situations are Q-situations"; and the obvious reduction of a disjunctive judgment to a categorical one is to say that "P or Q" amounts to "All -P-situations are Q-situations." Less mechanical translations can be obtained by verbal juggling. In the days when undergraduates were routinely taught Aristotelian logic (I can still remember them) every logic teacher was skilled in reducing quite complicated molecular sentences to those of standard categorical form.

9 The logical form of "Some bachelors are married" is *Some S is P* or (in a different notation) *sIp* – obviously, not a contradictory form of judgment.

10 *Critique of Pure Reason*, B2.

11 ibid., B4.

12 Etymologically, "synthesis" and "construction" are very similar, "synthesis" from Greek words meaning "a placing together" and "construction" from a Latin counterpart meaning "to pile together."

13 ibid., Bxviii.

14 Although arithmetical propositions are synthetic in Kant's view, he argued that the relation of their subjects to their predicates can be ascertained *a priori* by reference to time, which provides an *a priori* medium in which calculations can be carried out. Synthetic propositions about space can be proved *a priori* by formal, spatial constructions.

15 Kant spoke of metaphysics "in its first part" in this connection; see Bxviii.

16 See my *Metaphysics: the Elements*, Minneapolis, University of Minnesota Press, 1985, Ch. 1.

17 For what it is worth, the crucial sentence by which Kant relates forms of judgments to the abstract concepts he calls "categories" is this: "The same understanding, through the same operations by which in concepts, by means of analytical unity, it produced the logical form of a judgment, also introduces a transcendental content into its representations, by means of the synthetic unity of the manifold in general." ibid., A79, B105.

18 My reconstruction is based largely on the version in the second edition, though I begin with some of the material that Kant included in his first edition version. For a very illuminating discussion of Kant's deduction and very useful remarks on recent Kant scholarship, see Paul Guyer, *Kant and the Claims of Knowledge*, Cambridge, Cambridge University Press, 1987.

19 *See Enquiry Concerning Human Understanding*, section VII.

20 ibid., A91, B124.

21 ibid., A91–2, B124.

22 ibid., B159.

23 Kant recognized that my consciousness of my representations as mine may be merely potential: if a given representation is mine, I must be capable of recognizing it as such. See ibid., B133.

24 ibid., B134.

25 Compare ibid., B159, where he says, "I exist as an intelligence which is conscious solely of its powers of combination." His other reasons for thinking of transcendental selves as minds include those summed up in his description of the threefold synthesis that he emphasizes in his first edition deduction: the synthesis involves the recognition of apprehended and reproduced (recollected) items "in a concept." (The four notes I mentioned earlier may thus be recognized as belonging to the opening measure of Beethoven's Fifth Symphony.)

26 ibid., B143.

27 The germ of truth is captured by Kant's transcendental idealism, which I discuss in section 6 below.

28 ibid., A104.

29 Here I paraphrase the last clause of Kant's last sentence of A106.

30 One of my students recently showed me a device that produced a three-dimensional illusion of a ceramic frog hovering over a hole in the device's surface. The illusion was so good that when my finger moved "through" the illusion I repeatedly experienced a strange feeling of surprise – even though, knowing that I was dealing with an illusion, I did not expect my fingers to encounter resistance.

31 Kant explicitly criticized Locke in his 1874–5 lectures: "Locke in his essay on human understanding says: We represent substance to ourselves as the *portitor* [bearer] of accidents. . . . But the accidents are not particular things that exist, rather only particular ways of considering existence; they do not therefore need to be borne, but rather signify only the manifold determination of one and the same thing." This quotation is translated by Paul Guyer and is cited in his book, *Kant and the Claims of Knowledge*, Cambridge, Cambridge University Press, 1987, pp. 212f. In his *Critique*, A187, B230, Kant also emphasized that what are called "accidents" are nothing but special ways in which a substance exists.

32 ibid., A216, B263.

33 At B72 Kant says, "This mode of intuiting in space and time need not be limited to human sensibility. It may be that all finite, thinking beings necessarily agree with man in this respect, although we are not in a position to judge whether this is actually so."

34 ibid., B158.

35 In his preface to the second edition of the *Critique*, Kant says that, "though we cannot *know* these objects as things in themselves, we must yet be in a position to *think* them as things in themselves; otherwise we should be landed in the absurd conclusion that there can be appearance without anything that appears." See Bxxvii.

36 See A191, B236.

37 B275.

38 ibid.

39 See A24, B39.

40 Kant held that space is infinite in a potential sense: its representation never terminates in any direction; representations of spatial regions can be endlessly augmented in any direction. See Kant's solution to his First Antinomy, A518–23, B546–51.

41 The doctrine that "everything intuited in space and time, and therefore all objects of any experience possible to us, are nothing but appearances, that is, mere representations, which, in the manner in which they are represented, as extended beings, or as series of alterations, have no independent existence outside our thoughts. . . . I entitle *transcendental idealism.*" A491, B519.

42 According to his "Postulates of Empirical Thought," an object is *actual* in the world of experience just in case it is "bound up with the material conditions of experience, that is, with sensation." See A219, B266.

43 See Guyer, *Kant and the Claims of Knowledge*, p. 414.

44 See Bxx.

45 The only one of Kant's antinomies that is still alive in contemporary discussion is the one about freedom and determinism. An incompatibility is recognized by a minority of English-speaking philosophers, but Kant's means of dealing with it excites little if any enthusiasm. I discuss the subject briefly in my book *Kant's Theory of Morals*, Princeton, N.J., Princeton University Press, 1979, pp. 90–103.

46 Bxxvii.

47 Russell wrote this book in 1914 and produced a revised edition in 1929.

48 This was published in Berlin in 1928.

49 John Stuart Mill, *Examination of Sir William Hamilton's Philosophy*, Ch. 11, quoted in A. J. Ayer and Raymond Winch (eds), *British Empirical Philosophers*, London, Routledge & Kegan Paul, 1962, pp. 547f. The italics in the quoted passage are mine.

50 ibid.

51 ibid., Ch. 12; Ayer and Winch, *British Empirical Philosophers*, pp. 555f.

52 ibid.

53 For an admirably clear, dispassionate assessment of what I call linguistic phenomenalism, see A. J. Ayer's essay, "Phenomenalism," in A. J. Ayer, *Philosophical Essays*, London, Macmillan, 1954, pp. 125–66.

54 This is nicely brought out by Ayer; see ibid.

V A New Start

1 Bertrand Russell, *Human Knowledge: Its Scope and Limits*, London, Allen & Unwin, 1948, p. 527. A pertinent text by Rudolf Carnap is his essay "Testability and Meaning," *Philosophy of Science*, vols 3 & 4 (1936–7).

2 Ludwig Witttgenstein, *Philosophical Investigations*, trans. G. E. M. Anscombe, Oxford, Basil Blackwell, 1959.

3 Representative recent publications are Saul Kripke's *Wittgenstein on Rules and Private Language*, Cambridge, Mass., Harvard, 1982; and David Pears, *The False Prison*, vol. 2, Oxford, Clarendon Press, 1988.

4 Wittgenstein introduced the notion of a private language, one that "cannot" be understood by another person, in §243 of *Philosophical Investigations*; Norman Malcolm, in his influential "Review of Wittgenstein's *Philosophical Investigations*," said, "The idea of a private language is presupposed by every program of inferring or constructing the 'external world' and 'other minds.' It is contained in the philosophy of Descartes and in the theory of ideas of classical British empiricism, as well as in recent and contemporary phenomenalism and sense-datum theory." *Phil. Rev.*, vol. 63 (1954), p. 531.

5 David Hume, *Treatise of Human Nature*, L. A. Selby-Bigge, (ed.), Oxford, Clarendon Press, 1888, p. 3.

6 Wittgenstein, §243.

7 *PI.*, §256.

8 ibid., §258.

9 In the context of his "private language" argument Wittgenstein did not distinguish "same sensation" from "sensation of the same kind." The latter is arguably appropriate in the case of our actual language, but this case is not under investigation in his argument.

10 ibid., §265.

11 See H. N. Castaneda, "The Private Language Argument," in C. D. Rollins (ed.), *Knowledge and Experience*, Pittsburgh, University of Pittsburgh Press, 1963, pp. 88–105.

12 Kripke, *Wittgenstein on Rules and Private Language*.

13 ibid., p. 20.

14 Wittgenstein, §244.

15 These subjects were the center of concern in my first book, written in the early 1960s: *Knowledge, Mind, and Nature*, New York, Random House, 1967 (reprinted by Ridgeview Publishing Company). But see my discussion of what I called "the new empiricism" in Bruce Aune, *Rationalism, Empiricism, and Pragmatism*, New York, Random House, 1970, pp. 86–99.

16 See Chapter I, section 7.

17 Aristotle's principal form of certainty-preserving inference was encoded in the syllogism, but he also allowed "intuitive induction." See *Posterior Analytics*, 99^b 17–100^b17.

18 See Chapter II, section 1.

19 See David Hume, *Enquiry Concerning Human Understanding*, section X, Part I; in *Enquiries*, ed. L. A. Selby-Bigge, Oxford, Clarendon Press, 1902, p. 112.

20 ibid., p. 46.

21 ibid., p. 25.

22 This point became apparent in my discussion of Descartes' method of doubt. The doubting appropriate to that method could not be rational

doubting, if the method is to yield basic knowledge, because rational doubting must have a rational basis, and none is available until the method finds it. Since non-rational doubting is no more significant, epistemically, than the doubting of a madman, Descartes' method of doubt, however interpreted, can accord no rational credibility to the principles it selects. See Chapter I, section 4.

23 See my discussion of these paradoxical implications in Chapter II, pp. 39–42.

24 Their lack of a determinate spatio-temporal position is a consequence of the indeterminacy equations of quantum mechanics. For stimulating, non-technical discussions of this matter, see Jeremy Cherfas, *In Search of Schrödinger's Cat: Quantum Physics and Reality*, New York, Bantam Books, 1984; and Nick Herbert, *Quantum Physics*, Garden City, New York, Anchor Books, 1987.

25 R. M. Chisholm, *Person and Object*, London, Allen & Unwin, 1976, Ch. 1.

26 ibid., p. 24.

27 ibid.

28 He regards propositions as "subspecies" of states of affairs. See ibid., p. 189.

29 ibid.

30 It thus appears that, for Chisholm, the theory of implication or entailment is a branch of *a priori* psychology!

31 Chisholm has recently changed his view of the primary object of intentional attitudes. He used to think they are propositions; now he thinks they are direct attributions of properties. This change of opinion affects his conception of psychological certainty. Instead of thinking that "I am wise" expresses the proposition that I am wise, he now thinks that this sentence expresses "my direct attribution of wisdom to myself." Since he takes the locution "x directly attributes to y the property of being F" as undefined in his recent work, it is unclear how he thinks the relevant sort of attribution of mental properties to oneself is accomplished. Can this be done without mentally representing oneself (denoting it) in some way? However this may be, the change in Chisholm's view does not undermine the criticism I make in the text, for a feeling of depression (or any other feeling) contrasts with the direct attribution of a property in just the way that I say such a feeling contrasts with a first-person proposition. Incidentally, Chisholm still holds that propositions are what is certain. In the case of self-presenting states, the proposition now said to be certain is the proposition that someone has the relevant self-attributed property. See R. M. Chisholm, "A Version of Foundationalism", in P. French *et al.* (eds), *Midwest Studies in Philosophy*, vol. 5, Minneapolis, University of Minnesota Press, 1980, pp. 543–64.

32 Chisholm, *Person and Object*, p. 25

33 According to Chisholm's new view, the proposition that is certain for people is the proposition that someone has this feeling. See note 31.

34 Or without any properties being self-attributed to a self: see note 33.

35 Hume explicitly speaks of necessities rather than impossibilities, but the latter are obviously definable in terms of the former: it is impossible that p iff it is necessary that not p.

36 David Hume, *Treatise*, Bk I, Part IV, section VI, p. 251.

37 ibid., p. 632.

38 Chisholm, *Person and Object*, p. 39.

39 I discuss this principle in Chapter III, section 3: see pp. 74–5.

40 ibid., p. 25.

41 P. F. Strawson, *Individuals*, London, Methuen, 1959, p. 109.

42 Donald Davidson, "On the Very Idea of a Conceptual Scheme," in Davidson, *Inquiries into Truth and Interpretation*, Oxford, Clarendon Press, 1974, p. 197.

43 Another defect is that the interpretation of others' speech does not require the assumption that most of their beliefs are actually true; it is sufficient to assume that they are reasonable or plausible in the circumstances, and given a certain point of view. I support this claim in Bruce Aune, "Action and Ontology," *Philosophical Studies*, 54 (1988), pp. 209f.

44 W. V. O. Quine, *Word and Object*, Cambridge, Mass., Wiley, 1960, pp. 270–6.

45 See above, pp. 130f.

46 See Chapter I, p. 121.

47 The principle is that there is a class corresponding to every concept or property-specification; more exactly, $(\exists c)(x)(x \; \varepsilon \; c \equiv \Phi x)$. For a discussion of Russell's refutation, see Patrick Suppes, *Axiomatic Set Theory*, Princeton, N.J., Van Nostrand, 1960, pp. 5–8.

48 See W. D. Ross, *Foundations of Ethics*, Oxford, Clarendon Press, 1939, p. 223.

VI Reforming Empiricism

1 Some of the most serious criticism was launched nearly forty years ago, for Quine's "Two Dogmas of Empiricism" was first published in January of 1951. I speak of thirty years in the text because Quine's critical attitude was slow to catch on.

2 Reprinted in W. V. O. Quine, *From a Logical Point of View*, Cambridge, Mass., Harvard University Press, 1953, pp. 20–46.

3 ibid., p. 7.

4 ibid., pp. 42, 41.

5 See George Bealer, "The Philosophical Limits of Scientific Essentialism," in James Tomberlin (ed.), *Philosophical Perspectives*, vol. 1, Atascadero, Calif., Ridgeview Publishing Company, 1987, pp. 289–366.

6 See Chapter V, section 7.

7 See Gottlob Frege, *The Foundations of Arithmetic*, second edition, trans. J. L. Austin, Oxford, Basil Blackwell, 1950, p. 4.

Notes

8 Lewis Carroll (C. L. Dodgson), "What the Tortoise said to Achilles," *Mind*, 4 (1895), 278–80.

9 Note that this formula is equivalent to one that corresponds to Kant's conception in the *Prolegomena*: "S is analytically true iff an explicit contradiction is formally deducible from a set of formulas consisting of nothing but -S, general logical laws, and definitions."

10 For my purposes here, an appropriate context for substitution of synonymous expressions can be understood as an extensional context.

11 Quine claims that in reasonable explication certain favored verbal contexts which include the antecedent usage of the explicatum (or definiendum) should be synonymous with corresponding contexts that include the antecedent usage of the explicans (or definiens). See ibid., p. 25.

12 Quine's more appreciative attitude is expressed in an unpublished letter to Carnap, an excerpt of which is quoted in Richard Creath's essay, "Every Dogma Has Its Day," in *Erkenntnis* (forthcoming).

13 As he put it in "How to Make Our Ideas Clear," see *Collected Papers of Charles Sanders Peirce*, Charles Hartshorne and Paul Weiss (eds), Cambridge, Mass., Harvard University Press, 1935, vol. 5, para. 393.

14 See ibid., vol. 5, para. 447.

15 When we identify pertinent implications of our words, we fix our meaning only in a relative sense. If a given implication (or consequence) of a formula is not understood, then the meaning of that consequence (that formula) must be fixed by reference to further formulas. Since no formulas are intrinsically understandable (or understandable without reference to other formulas) the process of meaning-fixing within a language or conceptual system can take one in a high-level circle. This fact does not disclose a fatal flaw with Peirce's approach to meaning fixing because understanding the expressions of one's own idiolect (knowing their conceptual meaning) can be identified with understanding their interrelations – their grammar and mutual implications – and being able to use them appropriately in observation reports and (roughly) imperatival constructions. Understanding this sort of meaning is often identified with "knowing truth-conditions"; but if knowing the latter differs from knowing how the given expression is properly translated into the language of some truth-theory, it can amount only to having an ability to make appropriate responses of some kind. If the responses are observational, they are covered by the last clause of my statement.

16 See vol. 5, para. 165.

17 See Donald Davidson, "The Logical Form of Action Sentences," in Davidson, *Essays on Actions and Events*, Oxford, Clarendon Press, 1982, pp. 105–21.

18 This is clearly implied by Rudolf Carnap in Appendix B ("Meaning Postulates") of his *Meaning and Necessity*, Chicago, University of Chicago Press, 1956. The importance of the claim in Carnap's dispute with Quine on analyticity is brought out vividly by Richard Creath in "Every Dogma Has Its Day," section IV.

19 Donald Davidson, "A Coherence Theory of Truth and Knowledge," in Ernest LePore (ed.), *Truth and Interpretation*, Oxford, Basil Blackwell, 1986, p. 313.

20 I discuss Davidson's view and compare it with my own in my book, *Metaphysics: The Elements*, Minneapolis, University of Minnesota Press, 1985, pp. 143–55.

21 An *OED* entry from 1600 is "If the moon be euill placed, either it maketh men extatical, lunatick, or subject to the king's euill."

22 This is reprinted in W. V. O. Quine, *The Ways of Paradox*, New York, Random House, 1966, pp. 70–99.

23 See the discussion in William and Martha Kneale, *The Development of Logic*, Oxford, Clarendon Press, 1962, pp. 538–52.

24 David Lewis, *Convention*, Cambridge, Mass., Harvard University Press, 1969.

25 In "Two dogmas . . .," p. 43, Quine says, "Revision even of the logical law of the excluded middle has been proposed as a means of simplifying quantum mechanics; and what difference is there in principle between such a shift and the shift whereby Kepler superseded Ptolemy, or Einstein Newton, or Darwin Aristotle?" Additional motives for revising standard logic could be drawn from the need to deal with various sources of self-reference. If, for example, "This statement is false" is allowed as a substituend in the schema, -(S & -S), the law of contradiction might have to be revised.

26 In a seminar at UCLA many years ago Carnap said that epsilon "looked like a logical symbol" to him.

27 See Carnap, "Meaning Postulates."

28 See Carnap, *Philosophical Foundations of Physics*, New York, Basic Books, 1966, Ch. 27.

29 Carnap spoke indifferently of rules or postulates in this connection because he was convinced that a formula identified as a postulate or axiom could be taken as a rule authorizing the inference of that formula from any premiss whatever. See Kneale and Kneale, *The Development of Logic*, p. 534.

30 David Hume, *Enquiry Concerning the Human Understanding*, section XII, Part I, in *Enquiries*, ed. L. H. Selby-Bigge, Oxford, Clarendon Press, 1902, p. 151.

31 See Chapter II, p. 34.

32 See above, p. 33.

33 For some experimental evidence supporting this possibility, see Milton H. Erickson, "Experimental Demonstrations of the Psychopathology of Everyday Life," in S. S. Tompkins and H. A. Murray (eds), *Contemporary Psychopathology*, Cambridge, Mass., Harvard University. Press, 1944, pp. 524–5.

34 Hume, *Enquiry*, p. 152.

35 *Tractatus Logico-Philosophicus*, trans. C. K. Ogden, London, Routledge & Kegan Paul, 1922, p. 189. Ogden translates this as "Whereof one cannot speak, thereof one must be silent."

36 See Chapter III, section 2 above.

37 Bertrand Russell, in *Human Knowledge: Its Scope and Limits*, London, Allen & Unwin, 1948, p. 419, stated the principle of what he called "induction by simple enumeration" probabilistically, as follows: "Given a number n of α's which have been found to be βs, and no α which has been found to be not a β, then the two statements: (a) 'the next α will be β,' (b) 'all α's are β's,' both have a probability which increases as n increases, and approaches certainty as a limit as n approaches infinity."

38 Analogical inferences have been said to be reducible to inductive generalization. The idea is this: to conclude that unexamined E's will, like examined ones, have the property P, we first infer that all E's have P and then deduce the desired conclusion. If our observations warrant only a statistical conclusion, we can obtain the desired conclusion only by introducing an appropriate quantitative notion of probability.

39 *Enquiry*, section XII, Part I, p. 153.

40 See Russell, *Human Knowledge: Its Scope and Limits*, p. 432 and, for further discussion, pp. 418–38 and 451–5; and also Nelson Goodman, "The New Riddle of Induction," in *Fact, Fiction, and Forecast*, second edition, Indianapolis, Indiana, Bobbs-Merrill, 1965, pp. 59–83.

41 Russell used this last property to illustrate the "shaky" character of induction by simple enumeration in his essay "John Stuart Mill," in *Portraits from Memory*, London, Allen & Unwin, 1956, p. 126.

42 See Gilbert Harmon, "Inference to the Best Explanation," *Philosophical Review*, 74 (1965): 88–95.

43 See my discussion in *Rationalism, Empiricism, and Pragmatism*, New York, Random House, 1970, pp. 167–75.

44 If this remark is confusing to anyone, he or she may need reminding that a general principle is invalid if it has a single exception; an invalid principle may, therefore, have instances that are acceptable or true.

45 Russell, *Human Knowledge*, p. 451.

46 This version of the probability calculus is given in Michael D. Resnik, *Choices: An Introduction to Decision Theory*, Minneapolis, University of Minnesota Press, 1987, Ch. 3. If the notion of conditional probability is defined (rather than taken as primitive) by the formula I call T2, only three axioms are necessary: what I call axiom A4 is then provable as a theorem.

47 The term "equivalent" in T3 is often interpreted in such a way that "p is equivalent to q" just when "$p \equiv q$" is a tautology or logical truth. I do not understand it this way here. In accordance with the interpretation of the Probability Calculus I shall adopt here, I understand "p is equivalent to q" as meaning that "$p \equiv q$" is certain – in the sense of "certain" appropriate to axiom A2. This sense of "certain" amounts to "maximally credible"; I attempt to clarify it in the text below.

48 See note 47.

49 If we keep the background information normally needed to infer a specific prediction (or observation statement) from a hypothesis separate from that hypothesis, we must employ a slightly more complicated form of Bayes' theorem – namely, "P(H given A & E) =

P(H given A)P(E given H & A)/P(E given A)." This form of the
theorem is easily derived from the axioms I have given, but it makes the
points I am introducing at this point in the text a little more difficult to
see.

50 It is important to realize that, although a value for "P(h given e)" can be
computed by reference to the antecedent probability (rather than the
truth) of e, one can use the rule RC to update one's probability function
by "conditioning on e" only when one is convinced that e is in fact true.
In merely using Bayes' theorem to determine "the probability conferred
on h by the truth of a predicted e" (i.e. by the occurrence of the
phenomenon thus described) one should make one's computation by
considering the antecedent probability of e even though, at the time one
makes the computation, one has verified this prediction and become
convinced that e is actually true.

51 For a lucid survey of standard interpretations of the probability
calculus, see Wesley Salmon, *The Foundations of Scientific Inference*,
Pittsburgh, University of Pittsburgh Press, 1979, section V.

52 See Chapter III, pp. 68–70.

53 Peirce's claim was that "properly conducted inductive research corrects
its own premisses"; see Charles Peirce, *Collected Papers*, vol. 5, para.
576. The school of statisticians I advert to are called Bayesians; an
excellent textbook written from the Bayesian point of view is Lawrence
Phillips, *Bayesian Statistics for Social Scientists*, London, Nelson,
1973.

54 I illustrate the phenomenon in the Appendix, in the course of making
critical remarks about the significance of a "convergence argument."
For further discussion, see Phillips, *Bayesian Statistics for Social
Scientists*, Ch. 4.

55 See the Appendix to this volume.

56 I am assuming here that a tautology does not tell us what is true about
the world.

57 F. P. Ramsey, "Truth and Probability," in *The Foundations of
Mathematics and Other Logical Essays*, London, Routledge & Kegan
Paul, 1931, p. 182.

58 Dutch book arguments are helpfully expounded by Brian Skyrms,
Choice and Chance, second edition, Encino, Calif., Dickenson, 1975,
pp. 175–89, by Resnik, *Choices*, Ch. 4, and by Roger Rosenkrantz,
Foundations and Applications of Inductive Probability, Atascadero,
Calif., Ridgview, 1981, Ch. 2, section 1.

59 For a very perceptive, thorough discussion of this matter, see Colin
Howson and Peter Urbach, *Scientific Reasoning: The Bayesian
Approach*, La Salle, Illinois, Open Court, 1989, pp. 71-6.

VII The External World

1 *Enquiry Concerning the Human Understanding*, in L. A. Selby-Bigge

(ed.), *Hume's Enquiries*, Oxford, Clarendon Press, 1902, p. 151.

2 Since p and q are probabilistically independent just when P(q) = P(q given p), the consequence in question follows immediately from axiom 4 of the last chapter.

3 Some philosophers would disagree with me here, claiming that Goodman's grue hypothesis is more complicated than the more natural green hypothesis because "All emeralds are grue" is equivalent to the compound assertion "All emeralds existing before time t are green and all emeralds existing after time t are blue." The claim fails because the complexity of a given hypothesis is not determined by the structure of some equivalent hypothesis. If the complexity of a hypothesis could be determined this way, then, as Goodman pointed out, a grue speaker could argue that the green hypothesis is more complex than his grue one because the former would be equivalent to "All emeralds existing before time t are grue and all emeralds existing after time t are bleen."

4 See Bertrand Russell, *Human Knowledge: Its Scope and Limits*, London, Allen & Unwin, 1948, Part VI, and also *My Philosophical Development*, London, Allen & Unwin, 1959, pp. 190–207. A penetrating discussion of Russell's views on non-demonstrative inference, which are still not generally appreciated, is James Hawthorne, "Giving Up Judgment Empiricism: The Bayesian Epistemology of Bertrand Russell and Grover Maxwell," in C. Wade Savage and C. Anthony Anderson (eds), *Rereading Russell: Minnesota Studies in the Philosophy of Science*, vol. XII, Minneapolis, University of Minnesota Press, 1989, pp. 234–48.

5 Russell, *Human Knowledge*, p. 511.

6 See Wesley Salmon, *The Foundations of Scientific Inference*, Pittsburgh, University of Pittsburgh Press, 1967, Ch. 7; and *Scientific Explanation and the Causal Structure of the World*, Princeton, N.J., Princeton University Press, 1984, pp. 229–38 and *passim*.

7 See Salmon, *Scientific Explanation and the Causal Structure of the World*, p. 234.

8 See my discussion in Chapter VI, pp. 156–61.

9 See Chapter V, pp. 130f.

10 See Chapter V, pp. 138f.

11 R. M. Chisholm, *Theory of Knowledge*, third edition, Englewood Cliffs, N.J., Prentice Hall, 1989, p. 72.

12 ibid., p. 10.

13 According to Chisholm, to be justified in withholding h one must be justified in not believing h and not believing -h. Since Tom does believe that he sees a yellow cat and has (we may assume) no actual evidence that he is not seeing such a thing, Tom will hardly be more justified in withholding this h than believing it. See ibid., p. 11.

14 ibid.

15 ibid., p. 73.

16 ibid., p. 72.

17 See Laurence BonJour, *The Structure of Empirical Knowledge*, Cambridge, Mass., Harvard University Press, 1985. BonJour

formulates the basic problem to which his theory is a solution on pp. 30–3.

18 ibid., p. 90.
19 ibid., p. 153. Here BonJour emphasizes: "It is only such long-term coherence which provides any compelling reason for thinking that the beliefs of the system are likely to be true."
20 ibid., p. 141.
21 ibid., p. 142.
22 ibid., p. 181.
23 ibid., p. 128.
24 See my essay, "Other Minds After Twenty Years," *Midwest Studies in Philosophy*, X (1986), 559–74.
25 BonJour, *The Structure of Empirical Knowledge*, p. 173.
26 The following five paragraphs are indebted to my essay, "Epistemically Justified Opinion," in John W. Bender (ed.), *The Current State of the Coherence Theory*, Dordrecht, Kluwer, 1989, pp. 220–3.
27 BonJour, *The Structure of Empirical Knowledge*, p. 7.
28 ibid., p. 8.
29 Plato, *Phaedrus*, 265E.
30 The view is not defunct, either; it is implicit, I believe, in the currently fashionable Putnam–Kripke interpretation of natural-kind expressions. I have criticized this view in "Determinate Meaning and Analytic Truth," forthcoming the *Proceedings of the C. S. Peirce Sesquicentennial International Congress*.
31 See Bruce Aune, *Metaphysics: The Elements*, Minneapolis, University of Minnesota Press, 1985, pp. 125f.
32 See Gustav Bergmann, *The Metaphysics of Logical Positivism*, New York, Longmans, Green, & Co., 1954, p. 89.
33 Some interesting conflicts between fidelity and other epistemic ends are perceptively discussed by Catherine Elgin, "The Epistemic Efficacy of Stupidity," in Nelson Goodman and Catherine Elgin, *Reconceptions in Philosophy*, Indianapolis, Hackett, 1988, pp. 135–52.
34 The *mot* occurs in "Epistemology Naturalized," in W. V. O. Quine, *Ontological Relativity and Other Essays*, New York, Columbia University Press, 1969, p. 72.
35 See Clark Glymour, *Theory and Evidence*, Princeton, N.J., Princeton University Press, 1980, Ch. V.
36 See Appendix.
37 See above, Chapter VI, pp. 163–5.
38 See Nelson Goodman, "The New Riddle of Induction," in Goodman, *Fact, Fiction, and Forecast*, second edition, Indianapolis, Bobbs-Merrill, 1965, Chapter 2.
39 In his classic article, "Does the Philosophy of Induction Rest on a Mistake?," *Journal of Philosophy*, 79 (1982), pp. 86–92, Roger Rosenkrantz rejected Goodman's solution on the ground that hypotheses involving novel, grue-like predicates have often marked the breakthroughs that we are wont to label "scientific revolutions." In developing his objection Rosenkrantz overlooked one crucial fact, however:

Goodman's solution requires us to reject hypotheses containing novel predicates only when corresponding hypotheses containing familiar predicates are (roughly speaking) supported by the same data. This is not true of hypotheses introduced in scientific revolutions: they are accepted only because they are, in their way, better supported by available evidence. They can account for facts that pre-revolutionary hypotheses cannot account for. See Goodman, *Fact, Fiction and Forecast*, pp. 94f.

40 The reader might recall that Hume adopted essentially the same line in defending the "permanent, irresistible, and universal" epistemic principles he favored against the rival principles of "ignorant and stupid barbarians who are ready to swallow even the grossest delusion." See above, Chapter III, section 4.

41 I am here relying on the following form of Bayes' theorem: P(h given e & k) = P(h given k)P(e given h & k)/P(e given k). This form of the theorem is readily deducible from the definition of conditional probability.

42 The equivalence of the two confirming conditions is evident from the fact that P(h given e)/P(h) = P(e given h)/P(e), which is an immediate consequence of Bayes' theorem.

43 A well-known alternative to the rule of conditioning that I mentioned in Chapter VI is the rule of Jeffrey conditioning, so called after Richard C. Jeffrey who invented it: see Jeffrey, *The Logic of Decision*, second edition, Chicago, University of Chicago Press, 1983, Chapter 11. According to the simple version of this rule where -p is treated as the sole alternative to p, if evidential input at a time t changes our estimate of the probability of p from $P_{old}(p)$ to $P_{new}(p)$, then for any statement q, the new probability $P_{new}(q)$ should be computed as $P_{new}(p)P_{old}(q$ given $p)$ + $P_{new}(-p)P_{old}(q$ given $-p)$. For a useful comparison of Jeffrey's rule with the standard rule, see Colin Howison and Peter Urbach, *Scientific Reasoning: the Bayesian Approach*, LaSalle, Ill., Open Court, 1989, pp. 284–8.

44 Hilary Putnam, in *Reason, Truth, and History*, Cambridge, Cambridge University Press, 1981, Chapter 1, argued that the hypothesis is "necessarily false," but his reasoning is faulty and based on a false premiss. The false premiss (see p. 14) is that the word "vat" could refer to a real vat only if tokens of it were causally connected to real vats; this is far too strong to be accepted even by a verificationist. The reasoning is faulty because even if Putnam's premisses are accepted, the most he can validly conclude is that either the sentence "We are brains in a vat" is false or our utterance of it does not have the meaning the reader (or someone) supposes it has.

45 My description of scientific realism is substantially the one given by Bas C. van Fraassen in *The Scientific Image*, Oxford, Clarendon Press, 1980, p. 8.

46 See Chapter 1, note 38.

47 See van Fraassen, *The Scientific Image*, p. 57.

48 See Chapter 1, p. 25.

49 van Fraassen, *The Scientific Image*, p. 57.

50 See Quine, "Two Dogmas of Empiricism," in W. V. O. Quine, *From a Logical Point of View*, Cambridge, Mass., Harvard University Press, 1953, p. 41.
51 See Quine, "On What There Is," in ibid., p. 13. The existentially quantified statement about zoological species can be paraphrased by a statement quantifying over animals species-classifiable in different ways.
52 See Quine, "Ontological Relativity," in W. V. O. Quine, *Ontological Relativity and Other Essays*, p. 50.
53 I have discussed central aspects of Quine's new approach in my essay "Conceptual Relativism," in James Tomberlin (ed.), *Philosophical Perspectives*, vol. I, Atascadero, Calif., Ridgview Publishing Company, 1987, pp. 269–88.
54 See Bertrand Russell, *Introduction to Mathematical Philosophy*, London, Allen & Unwin, 1919, p. 182.
55 See Bertrand Russell, *Analysis of Matter*, London, Allen & Unwin, 1927, Chapters 28 and 29.
56 See ibid., p. 328.
57 See Bertrand Russell, *Human Knowledge: Its Scope and Limits*, London, Allen & Unwin, 1948, pp. 305–9.
58 See ibid., pp. 238–48.
59 *The Republic*, 537d.

Appendix

1 My example is adapted from an example Lawrence Phillips used to illustrate the convergence of priors under Bayesian conditioning. See Philips, *Bayesian Statistics for Social Scientists*, London, Nelson, 1973, pp. 77.
2 This claim is made by Phillips, ibid.
3 See Blaise Pascal, *Pensées*, trans. G. B. Rawlings, Mt Vernon, New York, Peter Pauper Press, n.d., pp. 9–12.

Bibliography

Karl Ameriks, "Recent Work on Kant's Theoretical Philosophy," *American Philosophical Quarterly*, 19 (1982), 1–14.

Aristotle. *The Basic Works of Aristotle*, ed. Richard McKeon, New York: Random House, 1941.

Aune, Bruce, *Knowledge, Mind, and Nature*, New York: Random House, 1967.

—— "The Paradox of Empiricism," *Metaphilosophy*, I (1970), 128–38.

—— *Rationalism, Empiricism, and Pragmatism*, New York, Random House, 1970.

—— *Kant's Theory of Morals*, Princeton, N.J., Princeton University Press, 1979.

—— *Metaphysics: the Elements*, Minneapolis, University of Minnesota Press, 1985.

—— "Other Minds After Twenty Years," *Midwest Studies in Philosophy*, X (1986), 559–74.

—— "Conceptual Relativism," in James Tomberlin (ed.), *Philosophical Perspectives*, vol. I, Atascadero, Calif., Ridgeview Publishing Company, 1987.

—— "Action and Ontology," *Philosophical Studies*, 54 (1988), 195–213.

—— "Epistemically Justified Opinion," in John W. Bender (ed.), *The Current State of the Coherence Theory*. Dordrecht, Kluwer, 1989.

—— "Determinate Meaning and Analytic Truth," *Proceedings of the C.S. Peirce Sesquicentennial International Congress*, forthcoming.

Austin, J. L., *Sense and Sensibilia*, reconstructed from manuscript lecture notes by G. J. Warnock, Oxford, Clarendon Press, 1962.

Ayer, A. J. Phenomenalism', in Ayer, *Philosophical Essays*, London, Macmillan, 1954.

Bealer, George, "The Philosophical Limits of Scientific Essentialism," in James Tomberlin (ed.), *Philosophical Perspectives*, vol. 1, Atascadero, Calif., Ridgeview Publishing Company, 1987.

Bergmann, Gustav, *The Metaphysics of Logical Positivism*, New York, Longmans, Green, & Co., 1954.

Berkeley, George. *Three Dialogues Between Hylas and Philonous*, in

David M. Armstrong (ed.), *Berkeley's Philosophical Writings*, New York: Macmillan, 1965.

BonJour, Laurence, *The Structure of Empirical Knowledge*, Cambridge, Mass: Harvard University Press, 1985.

Carnap, Rudolf, *Der Logische Aufbau der Welt*, Berlin, Weltkreis-Verlag, 1928.

———— "Testability and Meaning," *Philosophy of Science*, 3 (1936), 420–68 and 4 (1937), 1–40.

———— "Meaning Postulates," in Carnap, *Meaning and Necessity*, Chicago: University of Chicago Press, 1956.

———— *Philosophical Foundations of Physics*, New York: Basic Books, 1966.

Carroll, Lewis (C. L. Dodgson), "What the Tortoise Said to Achilles," *Mind*, 4 (1895), 278–80.

Castaneda, H. N., The Private Language Argument', in C. D. Rollins (ed.), *Knowledge and Experience*, Pittsburgh, University of Pittsburgh Press, 1963.

Cherfas, Jeremy. *In Search of Schrödinger's Cat: Quantum Physics and Reality*, New York, Bantam Books, 1984.

Chisholm, R. M., *Person and Object*, London, Allen & Unwin, 1976.

———— "A Version of Foundationalism," in P. French *et al.* (eds), *Midwest Studies in Philosophy*, vol. 5, Minneapolis, University of Minnesota Press, 1980.

———— *Theory of Knowledge*, third edition, Englewood Cliffs, N.J., Prentice Hall, 1989.

Creath, Richard. "Every Dogma Has Its Day" in *Erkenntnis* (forthcoming).

Davidson, Donald. "On the Very Idea of a Conceptual Scheme," in Davidson, *Inquiries into Truth and Interpretation*, Oxford, Clarendon Press, 1974.

———— "The Logical Form of Action Sentences," in Davidson, *Essays on Actions and Events*, Oxford, Clarendon Press, 1982.

———— "A Coherence Theory of Truth and Knowledge," in Ernest LePore (ed.), *Truth and Interpretation*, Oxford, Basil Blackwell, 1986.

Descartes, René, *The Philosophical Writings of Descartes*, edited and translated by John Cottingham, Robert Stoothoff, and Dugald Murdoch, 2 vols, Cambridge, Cambridge University Press, 1984.

Elgin, Catherine. "The Epistemic Efficacy of Stupidity," in Nelson Goodman and Catherine Elgin, *Reconceptions in Philosophy*. Indianapolis, Hackett, 1988.

Erickson, Milton H., "Experimental Demonstrations of the Psychopathology of Everyday Life," in S. S. Tompkins and H. A. Murray, (eds), *Contemporary Psychopathology*, Cambridge, Mass., Harvard University Press, 1944.

Frege, Gottlob, *The Foundations of Arithmetic*, second edition, trans. J. L. Austin, Oxford, Basil Blackwell, 1950.

Glymour, Clark, *Theory and Evidence*, Princeton, N.J., Princeton University Press, 1980.

Bibliography

Goodman, Nelson. "The New Riddle of Induction," in Goodman, *Fact, Fiction, and Forecast*, 2nd edition Indianapolis, Bobbs-Merrill, 1965.

Guyer, Paul, *Kant and the Claims of Knowledge*, Cambridge, Cambridge University Press, 1987.

Hacking, Ian, *The Emergence of Probability*, Cambridge, Cambridge University Press, 1975.

Harmon, Gilbert, "Inference to the Best Explanation," *Philosophical Review*, 74 (1965), 88–95.

Hawthorne, James. "Giving Up Judgment Empiricism: The Bayesian Epistemology of Bertrand Russell and Grover Maxwell," in C. Wade Savage and C. Anthony Anderson (eds), *Rereading Russell: Minnesota Studies in the Philosophy of Science*, vol. 12, Minneapolis, University of Minnesota Press, 1989.

Herbert, Nick, *Quantum Physics*, Garden City, N.Y., Anchor Books, 1987.

Howson, Colin and Peter Urbach, *Scientific Reasoning: The Basyesian Approach*, Indianapolis, Bobbs-Merrill, 1989.

Hume, David. *Enquiry Concerning the Human Understanding*, in L. A. Selby-Bigge (ed.), *Hume's Enquiries*, Oxford, Clarendon Press, 1902.

––––– *Treatise of Human Nature*, ed. L. A. Selby-Bigge, Oxford, Clarendon Press, 1888.

Jeffrey, Richard C., *The Logic of Decision*, second edition, Chicago, University of Chicago Press, 1983.

Kant, Immanuel, *Critique of Pure Reason*, 2nd edition, trans. N. K. Smith, London, Macmillan, 1961.

––––– *Prolegomena to Any Future Metaphysics*, trans. James Ellington, Indianapolis, Hackett Publishing Company, 1977.

––––– *Logic*, trans. Robert B. Hartman and Wolfgang Schwarz, Indianapolis, Bobbs-Merrill, 1974.

Kenny, Anthony, *Descartes: A Study of his Philosophy*, New York, Random House, 1968.

Kneale, William and Martha Kneale, *The Development of Logic*, Oxford, Clarendon Press, 1962.

Kripke, Saul, *Wittgenstein on Rules and Private Language*, Cambridge, Mass., Harvard University Press, 1982.

Lewis, David, *Convention*, Cambridge, Mass., Harvard University Press, 1969.

Locke, John, *Essay Concerning Human Understanding*, ed. A.C. Fraser, 2 vols, Oxford, Clarendon Press, 1894.

Malcolm, Norman, "Review of Wittgenstein's *Philosophical Investigations*," *Philosophical Review*, 63 (1954), 530–59.

––––– *Memory and Mind*, Ithaca, N.Y., Cornell University Press, 1977.

Mandelbaum, Maurice, *Philosophy, Science, and Sense-perception*, Baltimore, MD, Johns Hopkins University, 1964.

Mill, John Stuart, *Examination of Sir William Hamilton's Philosophy*, Ch. 11, quoted in A. J. Ayer and Raymond Winch (eds), *British Empirical Philosophers*. London, Routledge & Kegan Paul, 1962.

Pascal, Blaise, *Pensées*, trans. Gertrude B. Rawlings. Mt Vernon, N.Y., Peter Pauper Press, n.d.

Pears, David. *The False Prison*, vol. 2, Oxford, Clarendon Press, 1988.

Peirce, Charles Sanders, *Collected Papers of Charles Sanders Peirce*, ed. Charles Hartshorne and Paul Weiss, vol. 5, Cambridge, Mass., Harvard University Press, 1935.

Phillips, Lawrence, *Bayesian Statistics for Social Scientists*, London, Nelson, 1973.

Plato, *The Collected Dialogues of Plato*, ed. Edith Hamilton and Huntington Cairns, New York, Pantheon Books, 1961.

Putnam, Hilary, *Reason, Truth, and History*, Cambridge, Cambridge University Press, 1981.

Quine, W. V. O. "Two Dogmas of Empiricism," in Quine, *From a Logical Point of View*, Cambridge, Mass., Harvard University Press, 1953.

—— "Ontological Relativity," in Quine, *Ontological Relativity and Other Essays*, New York, Columbia University Press, 1969.

—— "Epistemology Naturalized," in Quine, *Ontological Relativity and Other Essays*, New York, Columbia University Press, 1969.

—— *Word and Object*, Cambridge, Mass., Wiley, 1960.

—— *The Ways of Paradox*, New York, Random House, 1966.

Ramsey, F. P., "Truth and Probability," in Ramsey, *The Foundations of Mathematics and Other Logical Essays*. London, Routledge & Kegan Paul, 1931.

Resnik, Michael D., *Choices: An Introduction to Decision Theory*, Minneapolis, University of Minnesota Press, 1987.

Rosenkrantz, Roger, *Foundations and Applications of Inductive Probability*, Atascadero, Calif., Ridgeview, 1981.

Ross, W. D., *Foundations of Ethics*, Oxford, Clarendon Press, 1939.

Russell, Bertrand. *Our Knowledge of the External World*, Chicago and London, Open Court, 1914; second edition, London, Allen & Unwin, 1919.

—— *Introduction to Mathematical Philosophy*, London, Allen & Unwin, 1919.

—— *Analysis of Matter*, London, Allen & Unwin, 1927.

—— *An Outline of Philosophy*, London, Allen & Unwin, 1927.

—— *A History of Western Philosophy*, London, Allen and Unwin, 1945.

—— *Human Knowledge: Its Scope and Limits*, London, Allen & Unwin, 1948.

—— "John Stuart Mill," in Russell, *Portraits from Memory*, London, Allen & Unwin, 1956.

—— *My Philosophical Development*, London, Allen & Unwin, 1959.

Salmon, Wesley. *The Foundations of Scientific Inference*, Pittsburgh, University of Pittsburgh Press, 1979.

—— *Scientific Explanation and the Causal Structure of the World*, Princeton, NJ., Princeton University Press, 1984.

Skyrms, Brian, *Choice and Chance*, second edition, Encino, Calif., Dickenson, 1975.

Strawson, P. F., *Individuals*, London, Methuen, 1959.

Suppes, Patrick, *Axiomatic Set Theory*, Princeton, N.J., Van Nostrand, 1960.

Bibliography

van Fraassen, Bas C., *The Scientific Image*, Oxford, Clarendon Press, 1980.

Witttgenstein, Lugwig, *Tractatus Logico-Philosophicus*, trans. C. K. Ogden, London, Routledge & Kegan Paul, 1922.

—— *Philosophical Investigations*, trans. G. E. M. Anscombe, Oxford, Basil Blackwell, 1959.

Index

acquaintance, direct 130ff.
appearances, world of 101–8
a priori knowledge 88f., 143;
  synthetic *a priori* 90, 92, 94,
  126, 144–56; *versus a posteriori*
  knowledge, 58f.
analogy, principle of 34ff., 216;
  and induction, 229
analytic-synthetic distinction 57,
  86–90, 144–56
Aristotle 11, 125, 126
Austin, J. L. 29
axiomatic method 1–7; *see also*
  Descartes

Bayes' theorem 167, 169–77,
  192–200
Bender, J. xiv
Bergmann, G. 190
Berkeley, G. 27, 41–56, 116, 117,
  127, 128, 129, 141, 145, 195;
  criticism of Locke 41–56; on
  primary qualities 44–51; on
  secondary qualities 41–4; and
  subjective idealism 51–6
BonJour, L. 185–9, 192
bootstrapping 191f.
Boyle, R. 32, 37
brain-in-a-vat hypothesis 198ff.,
  233

Carnap, R. 108, 115, 147f., 155f.
Carroll, L. 146

Chisholm, R. M. 146; critical
  commonsensism 182ff., 192;
  object of intentional attitudes
  225; on the self, 130–7
categories: *see* Kant
coherence 185ff.
conditioning, rule of 171ff., 179;
  Jeffrey's rule 233
consistency: value of 195
convention, truth by 153f.
convergence argument 208–11

Davidson, D. 138f., 150ff., 182
deduction: and intuition 17f.;
  transcendental 97–100; *see also*
  Descartes
definition: contextual 41, 217;
  reportive 147
Descartes, R. 27, 32, 56, 76f., 117,
  125f., 140ff., 201, 203; approach
  to external world 18–22;
  argument for God's existence
  19f.; Cartesian circle 15f.; on
  certainty, moral and
  metaphysical 26; and *cogito* 7–
  11; criticism of system 22–6; on
  distinction between soul and
  body 22f.; and divine guarantee
  13; development of system 16ff.;
  on explanatory hypotheses 25f.;
  fundamental principles of 11–16;
  on insensible parts of bodies
  24f.; intuition and deduction

Index

17f., 125f.; on laws of nature 24; method of doubt 1–7; on self-evident truths 13

Doubt: method of 1–7, 224–5; rational and irrational 3f., 6ff.

dream argument 4, 29f.

Duhem, P. 202

Dutch book arguments 175

Dostoyevsky, Feyodor 187

empiricism: reformed 144–76; traditional: *see* Locke, Berkeley, Hume

epistemic standards and ends 188–91

essences, real and nominal 37f.

explication 147, 156

external world: inferring existence of 195–200

form: of experience 93; *versus* content 47ff.; judgmental 94–7, 118

foundation of knowledge 3, 126f.

Frege, G. 143, 146, 149

Genzen, G. 154

Glymour, C. 192

Goodman, N. 163ff., 179f., 188, 193ff.

Hume, D. 27f., 34, 85, 98, 116ff., 119, 126–30, 132–41, 144, 148f., 156–63, 176ff., 182f., 191, 194f.; on *a priori* knowledge 57ff.; attitude to skepticism 81–4; epistemic principles 57–63; on experimental inference 63–71; principle of significance 60–3, 80f.; and road to solipsism 71–81

hypothetico-deductive method 164ff.

idealism: and Berkeley, 51–6, 105f.; transcendental 103–8

ideas: Berkeley on 48f., 55f.;

Locke on 27f., 38; and notions 55f.

incomplete symbols 205

indeterminancy: of meaning 149–52; referential 205; of translation 205

induction 32; intuitive 214; principle of 217; problem about 161–7; *see also* inference

inference: Bayesian 167–76, 178–82; to best explanation 16f.; experimental: *see* induction; point of 173f.

intuition: Cartesian 148; and alleged obviousness of 142; *see also* Descartes

judgments: needed for knowledge 117; table of 94–7

justification: linear and global 185ff.

Kant, I. 86–90, 114, 116, 118, 133, 146, 163, 195; and analytic-synthetic distinction 57; and categories 94–7; and Copernican revolution 85, 90ff., 99; epistemology of, 106–8; on forms of judgment 94–7; on objects of experience 93–7; and phenomenalism 108, 112f.; transcendental deduction 97–100

knowledge: concept of 1; and certainty 1–9; *see also* Descartes, Locke

Kripke, S. 122ff.

LePore, E. xiv

Locke, J. 57, 73, 97, 116f., 126–9, 141, 145f., 148, 158, 195; and Berkeley 41–56; justification for beliefs about external objects 30f.; on knowledge, 27–31; limits to demonstration 31; on nature of external objects 36–41; on probability 31–6

logical truth 153ff.

241

memory: and Hume 79
metaphysics, general and special 94
method: axiomatic 1; of doubt 1–9
Mill, J. S. 108–12, 116, 126, 163
mind: Berkeley on 55f.; Descartes on 7–11, 22f.; Hume's bundle theory of 78

Newton, I. 32, 34

objects of experience 90–4
observation: nature of 202f.; problems about 156–61, 181
ontological commitment 204ff.

Pascal's wager 211f.
Peirce, C. S. 148f., 172–5
phenomenalism 108–15, 125; and Kant 108, 112f.; metaphysical and analytical 108
Plato 189, 207
primary qualities 41–55, 129
probability: calculus of 167–70; and Hume 63–71; inductive 171–5; and Locke 31–6; prior 193, 198f.

qualities, primary and secondary 36, 41–55, 128f.; Locke on 36–41; Berkeley on 41–51
Quine, W. V. O. 139, 144–9, 151–6, 203ff.

radical translation 151
Ramsey, F. P. 175
rationalism, epistemological 142, 148; *see* Descartes
realism, scientific 201–7
relativity-of-perception arguments 45f.
Rosenkrantz, R. xiv, 232f.
Ross, Sir D. 143
Russell, B. xii, 10f., 34, 44, 52f.,

79f., 108, 115, 143, 163, 167, 179f., 188, 191, 193, 205f.

Salmon, W. xiv, 180
science, aim of 204
secondary qualities 36–44, 128; *see also* Descartes, Berkeley self: Chisholm on 130–40; and *cogito* 7–11; empirical and transcendental 99f.; Hume on 78; problems about 130–40
self-evidence: objections to 142f.; appeal to: *see* Descartes
self-presenting, the 130ff., 141
sense data 113
simplicity of hypotheses 166, 179, 190
Socrates 189
solipsism 27, 57, 71–81, 114, 125, 127, 161
space: Berkeley and Kant on 105f.
Strawson P. F. 137ff.
substances: material 36; world of and Kant 101ff.
substrata: Berkeley on 51ff.; Hume on 74; Kant on 96ff.; Locke on 37
synonymy 147f.
synthesis: and Kant 91, 93

testimony, assessment of: Locke on 33f., Hume on 157, problem of 158f.; and bootstrapping 191f.
transcendental argument 103
transcendental deduction 97–100
transcendental idealism 103–6

van Fraassen, B. C. 201ff.
Voss, S. xiv

Wetzel, L. xiv
Whitehead, A. N. 49
Wittgenstein, L. 115, 137, 161, 182, 196; and private language argument 115–25, 127f., 130